# Prestwick's Pioneer

## A Portrait of David F. McIntyre

### DOUGAL McINTYRE

*Dougal McIntyre*

Woodfield

*This book is dedicated to*

*the memory of*

*Marjorie F. McIntyre*

# PRESTWICK'S PIONEER

First edition, published in 2004 by

WOODFIELD PUBLISHING
Bognor Regis, West Sussex PO21 5EL
United Kingdom
www.woodfieldpublishing.com

© Dougal McIntyre, 2004

ISBN 1-903953-59-6

# CONTENTS

# ABOUT THE AUTHOR

Dougal McIntyre is the oldest of David McIntyre's three children. Aviation featured constantly during his childhood as a result of his Father's aviation interests and who by example encouraged him into an active participation in the building of model aircraft.

After starting a design engineering apprenticeship at Scottish Aviation's factory in Prestwick, he entered a four-year sandwich course in Aeronautical Engineering at Glasgow University. His final year work experience was conducted at the De Havilland Aircraft factory at Hatfield where he was involved in the advanced Projects design group working on the DH 125 jet executive design studies. It was here that he was first introduced to the business computer, a Ferranti Pegasus valve machine used by the Projects Group for aerodynamic calculations.

Following a year's post graduate business management course at the Glasgow Royal College of Science & Technology (now Strathclyde University) he joined the Singer Manufacturing Company at Clydebank, becoming involved in their business system redesign and learning to program their early mainframe computer during a period of intensive modernization. This led to a 30-year career designing business systems culminating with the development of the systems for the Caledonian Airways engine overhaul base at Prestwick Airport.

More recently he has been researching the history of aviation in Scotland for a project, which involved sourcing and digitising some 1800 images on the subject. In addition many thousand words were written to describe the images, which have been included in a national database of Scotland's history on the Internet. He was also involved in a similar project on the life of Robert Burns, now completed.

Dougal is married with two grown up sons and as keeper of the family archives his aim in writing this book is to present David McIntyre's life and achievements in a definitive manuscript. Only recently has the family collection of personal papers and letters been thoroughly investigated and these documents reveal much of the motivation and thoughts behind his achievements as well as detail of his activities. These have been woven into the aviation history encompassed by the events of his career from 1926 to 1957.

# ACKNOWLEDGEMENTS

Personal conversations with David McIntyre's Scottish Aviation contemporaries, the late Dick Ellison, David McConnell, the late John Blair, and Hugh McLaren have enabled me to add anecdotal information which has proved most useful and I am indebted to them for their assistance.

Of the many images in this account some 30 or so have been obtained from other sources where there was no appropriate image in the family collection to illustrate a significant part of the story. Those tagged:

- (MOF) are courtesy of the Trustees of the National Museums of Scotland - Museum of Flight at East Fortune,
- (SLB) courtesy of the Bruce/Leslie collection,
- (IWM) courtesy of the Imperial War Museum, London,
- (602 M) courtesy of the 602 Squadron Association Museum,
- (DC) courtesy of the Dugald Cameron collection,
- (LEN) courtesy of the Hamilton family collection at Lennoxlove.
- (BHG) courtesy of the Brough Heritage Group,
- (WW) courtesy of the Wilf White collection.

To all of whom I am indebted for the permission to use their images.

All other photographs are from the David McIntyre collection or are the property and copyright of BAE SYSTEMS

I am much indebted to BAE SYSTEMS for their permission to use the Scottish Aviation material residing in the family collection and for vetting the content. In this regard I also have to thank Lord James Douglas-Hamilton and Alan Robertson for giving the early draft the once over and for their helpful comments.

Acknowledgements are due to the present Duke of Hamilton, Roddy Capper and the late John Blair, for giving me access to their or their respective father's log books which helped correlate events and made up in a small way for the loss of my Father's log books over a significant period of his flying career.

In particular I must thank Alan Robertson for permitting me to extract from his excellent history of Scottish Aviation, "Lion Rampant and Winged", also to Hector MacLean for some of his recollections of David McIntyre in "Fighters in Defence", and similarly for extracts from Sandy Johnstone's book "Where no Angels Dwell", and Douglas McRoberts book on 602 Squadron "Lions Rampant". Also my thanks to many other authors who in a major or minor way have helped to add to my base of knowledge which has made this account possible.

I would like to thank my friend and colleague Andrew Freeland for his helpful design advice and support during the long period of gestation of this account and finally my thanks for the encouragement and advice from my wife and family without whose forbearance this account would not have come to fruition.

# INTRODUCTION

This book details the life of an exceptional aviator who transformed his passion for flying into a flourishing business bringing hope and prosperity to the West of Scotland. David McIntyre's formative years marched alongside the early years of the developing aviation industry in Scotland. He joined the fledgling City of Glasgow Auxiliary Air Force bomber squadron no 602 in 1927.

By 1933, with his piloting prowess and maturity established, he was the second of two Scots selected to embark on one of the last great natural earthbound challenges of aviation — to fly over the world's highest mountain. The Houston Mount Everest Flight and its ultimate success catapulted David McIntyre into the public limelight and cemented his vision for Scotland's aviation industry.

Ironically it was military conflict which provided the opportunity for his civilising dream to be realised when the flying training school of Scottish Aviation was formed at Prestwick in 1935. His geographically strategic choice of Prestwick as an airfield and his characteristic determination while Station Commander was to see the airfield develop during the war into a major international passenger hub. At the same time Scottish Aviation, led by David McIntyre, established an extensive Spitfire repair and aircraft modification factory on the airfield at Prestwick. They built a reputation working on American bomber and transport aircraft which evolved into a post war aircraft manufacturing business.

Life for David McIntyre in the post war period was a continual struggle to turn his vision into a practical reality against the nationalising forces of the then Labour government. The book draws from his personal letters a telling picture of this struggle and his difficulty in establishing a major Airline business for Scotland in those austerity days. Aircraft manufacture was the third string to David McIntyre's visionary bow from which stemmed the design and manufacture at Prestwick of the Pioneer series of aircraft along with a wide variety of aircraft engineering activities. This story reveals, with the assistance of 300 or so images, the spectrum of professional and family life of this charismatic and inspirational Scotsman.

Some 160 letters written by David Fowler McIntyre to Marjorie Florence Potts (his fiancée and later his wife) have been preserved. These were mostly written over a period from August 1933 to July 1935 and provide a unique record of his life during these two years, which were to prove so important in his future career. They give an extraordinary insight into the depth of their relationship and I have attempted to distil the relevant material from these hundreds of pages, to amplify the basic history of this period covering his courtship, engagement and marriage. All the extracts from David McIntyre's personal writings have been quoted in italics. It is true to say that without Marjorie McIntyre's devotion to her husband and the interest she took in his business to squirrel away many photographs and documents for safe keeping and in her later years to marshal and assemble these into meaningful collections, this account would not have been possible.

**Dougal McIntyre**
March 2004

# 1. The McIntyre Family

The McIntyre line is believed to have migrated from Glenorchy to become farmers on the island of Bute about the beginning of the eighteenth century. In 1805 David McIntyre's great great Grandfather James McIntyre moved to Greenock to work as a shipwright at the Scott's shipyard. His third son John McIntyre was father to 10 children, and the eighth of these Robert became a shipwright and was also father to 10 children. His third child John was David McIntyre's father.

John McIntyre served his shipbuilding apprenticeship at (his Uncle Hugh's yard) the H. McIntyre & Co shipyard at Paisley and while a journeyman he played half back in the St Mirren Football Club for two seasons 1878/9. At this time his parents lived in Glasgow's Kelvinhaugh Street and he lived in lodgings in Paisley. Later his parents moved to a house in Dalmuir. He then worked as a draughtsman with the Napier, Shanks and Bell shipyard at Yoker for a while and with the shipbuilding firm Williamson's in Workington as chief draughtsman at the yard, which built four-masted sailing ships. This lasted for a year

Robert McIntyre at home in Crookston, Glasgow. David McIntyre's grandfather who died in Glasgow in 1915 at the age of 82

or two then he returned to Glasgow in March 1884 to work for A & L Main in Possil Park, a bridge & roof engineering company, where he started as a calculator and rose to be chief

John McIntyre—after his return from Canada

draughtsman. He was married in 1886 at West End Park Street, Glasgow on 29th June. Again due to the depression the engineering job did not last long and he went to work at his father's business, the Clyde Forge in Renfrew but this closed later in 1886.

On the advice of friends, and with some of his Mother's relatives having already settled in Canada, he emigrated in July 1887. His wife and eldest daughter Bunt, then 4 months old, followed him to Montreal on the steamer "Silurian" arriving on 30th September 1887.

Canada, however, did not turn out to be the land of opportunity he had been promised. He settled in Montreal and found design work in various shipbuilding and engineering outfits over a period of about six years latterly living in the nearby village of Côte St Paul. During this period his wife gave birth to two sons Robert and Hugh but he was unable to establish a secure position. Reluctantly, he decided it would be best to send the family back to Scotland, so his wife and three children set sail from Quebec in the summer of 1893 bound for Glasgow. He stayed on to give himself a last chance to get established, hoping to send for his family later, but wrote in his diary that he did not wish to be separated from them for any great length of time. Devastated by the news of the deaths of his sons Hugh and Robert who died from diphtheria within a week of each other in Dec 1893, he immediately sailed back to Glasgow himself over the Xmas and New Year period.

On his arrival he stayed with his wife and daughter at his parent's home in Glasgow and, after finding work for a short spell with the

The John McIntyre family c 1919 - David McIntyre seated on left—back row l-r James, John, Bunt, Annie

Abercorn Shipbuilding Co in Paisley, he moved to Alloa to join his Uncle Hugh. Hugh McIntyre had by then established himself in a yard at Alloa on the river Forth building trawlers and passenger steamers for the western isles service. It was while in Alloa that his fourth child, daughter Annie was born in 1894. This job only lasted a short while and he returned to Glasgow where, by early 1895, he obtained the post of assistant manager at the London & Glasgow Co in Govan and remained for some years with this shipyard as Chief Draughtsman where he established a good reputation.

During this period he lived in Ibrox, where his three sons, John, James and David were born. In 1908 he was offered the position of General Manager of the Ailsa Shipbuilding Co based at Troon. Here he remained until August 1910 having by then become their Managing Director. His leaving present from this firm was a grandfather clock made in the

shipyard at Troon which is still in the family collection. On leaving the Ailsa Shipbuilding Co, he returned to Glasgow where he joined the Govan shipbuilding firm of Mackie & Thompson Ltd as their Managing Director. This firm later moved their premises to Irvine and at the same time changed their name to the Ayrshire Dockyard Co. Their first ship built in Irvine was launched in 1914 and the yard went on to build many ships for the Clan Line and other steamship companies. It was here that he finished his working life in about 1924. Having moved home to The Durdans in Monument road in 1918, his retirement years in Ayr were taken up with civic administration, becoming a town councillor from 1926 and

David McIntyre on the right during his mud student days

Dean of Guild until 1931.

He was a Director of the Ayr County hospital for a number of years and when he died it was reported in the local paper that, "Flags in the town on Wednesday were at half mast as a token of respect for a worthy citizen".

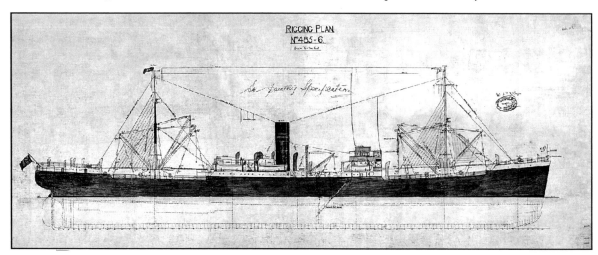

One of the ships designed at the Ayrshire Dockyard Co 1923 under the supervision of John McIntyre. Drafting of this vessel was conducted by his son John

# 2. The Early Days of David McIntyre

David McIntyre was born on 24th January 1905 at ten past four in the afternoon in the Glasgow parish of Govan at 2 Tantallon Terrace, Ibrox. He was the youngest of seven children born to his parents of which only five survived into adulthood. His oldest sister Bunt, being eighteen years his senior, was by all accounts responsible for a good deal of his early upbringing.

It is not clear what event in David McIntyre's formative years kindled his ambition to become an aviator, but he grew up in a period when aviation was blossoming. At the time of his Govan birth in 1905 Scotland's aviation history had hardly begun and it would not be long before the success of the Wright brothers at Kittyhawk in North

Lapel badge collected by DFM depicting the Wright Memorial at Kittyhawk North Carolina

Carolina in 1903 inspired Scots engineers. The Barnwell brothers in Stirling, the Gibsons in Edinburgh and Preston Watson in Dundee were all to achieve powered flight by 1910. In this year, when David McIntyre was a 5 year old, the Scottish Aeronautical Society organised the famous week long Aviation Meeting at Lanark racecourse where the American flier J. Armstrong Drexel set a new World height record of 6,750 feet, Englishman James Radley established the British flying mile speed record at 75.94 mph, and Scotsman Bertram Dickson won the cross country event covering 67 miles in a Farman biplane.

By 1911 the first Scottish Aviation Company (not to be confused with the later

Barnwell Brothers biplane at Stirling 1910 (MOF)

James Radley in his Bleriot at the Lanark Aviation event in 1910 (MOF)

"Scottish Aviation" company at Prestwick) opened a flight training school at Barrhead aerodrome and began designing its first aeroplane, a Bleriot style monoplane named the "Dart". This would have been while David McIntyre's schooling was being conducted at Bellahouston Academy, where he received a prize dated June 1912 awarded to him for 'General Excellence', and a "very good" attendance certificate for the year 1913. In June

The 1911 factory of the Scottish Aviation Co at Barrhead with their Dart monoplane (SLB)

1914 a week-long Aviation meeting was held at Scotstoun where the Scottish height record was raised to 7,100 ft and an aeroplane was reported to have performed the first loop in Scotland, at which time David McIntyre was midway through his 9th year. Little did he know that in less than 20 years he would be flying at 35,000 feet in one of the most hostile environments in the world over the summit of Mount Everest.

The Glasgow shipyards and engineering companies such as Beardmore and Weirs at Cathcart, were to become heavily involved in aeroplane construction during the 1914 - 1918 war with the Moorpark (Renfrew) aerodrome becoming established as the Royal Flying Corps aircraft acceptance park for the newly constructed military machines. Aircraft would be flown from the Carmunnock field of Weirs for testing at Renfrew and onward deployment to the forces. These would probably have been overflying the outskirts of Glasgow close to David McIntyre's early Govan home.

During this time David McIntyre's father moved the family to the Ayrshire coast from Glasgow to an address at 47 Bellvue Crescent in Ayr, some time after becoming General Manager of the Ayrshire Dockyard Co in Irvine in 1914. Ayr racecourse had become a centre of aviation activity in the area during WWI when No1 School of aerial fighting formed there in early 1917. It was perhaps at Ayr racecourse that David McIntyre was first introduced to the intrigue of flight.

No1 Fighting Unit transferred from Ayr to Turnberry in 1917 (SLB)

His schooling continued at Ayr Academy until 1919 when he was sent to Merchiston Castle public school in Edinburgh. By all accounts he did not like this much and after only two terms is said to have escaped. The remaining two years of his school days were spent at Glasgow Academy but the record of his academic achievement in his later years or what if any sports he played has not been recorded.

After leaving school he moved outdoors to become a "mud student", which is akin to being a farmer's apprentice, in a hill sheep farm near Sanquhar on the Ayrshire/Dumfriesshire border. He must have spent a year at least in this activity around 1922/3. What he did between then and 1926 when his flying days begin is not entirely certain. John McIntyre recorded in his notes

that two of his sons, John (who emigrated to New Zealand in 1923) and James, had become the fifth generation of shipwrights in the family while they worked at the Ayrshire Dockyard Co. However due to the 'great slump' of 1923 they both left the shipyard to embark on other occupations. James, after a spell operating his own coaster, the "Star o' Doon", had taken up with the Clutha stevedoring company at Princes dock in Glasgow, where David McIntyre joined him in this venture presumably about 1924. Later on they became partners in their own stevedoring business with the Clutha Company becoming one of their competitors.

## 1926 — Taking to the air

His father John McIntyre was aware of the hazardous nature of flying and because of this, discouraged his youngest son's aspirations to become an aviator until he reached the age of 21. To learn to fly in 1926 as it does today is a costly business, which David McIntyre could not afford to pay for himself and it needed the support of his Father to fund the initial lessons at the Beardmore Flying School at the Moorpark Aerodrome, Renfrew. The Royal Auxiliary Air Force (City of Glasgow) bomber Squadron No 602 had been formed at Renfrew in 1925, the first of the British Auxiliary squadrons to be commissioned. Their part time Pilot Officers

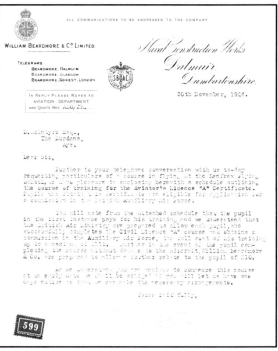
Letter to DFM from Wm Beardmore arranging his flying lessons in 1926

Beardmore's Avro 504K in which David McIntyre started his flying training (MOF)

could join only if they were already qualified pilots and if accepted, the Air Ministry would refund £115 towards the cost of the 13 hours of flying lessons, (not a lot less than the £130 cost of a new Austin 7 car at the time, and about £4,500 in year 2001 money). Beardmore also generously undertook to refund £10 of the cost of the lessons if the training was completed "without damage to the aircraft". David McIntyre made his initial contact with the Beardmore Flying School on 30th November 1926 and by the 14th of December he was having his first flying lesson instructed by, the later to become famous display flier, Captain Kingwill of Beardmore's. The correspondence from Beardmore's is preserved and one page specifies the aerial and ground based tasks which the trainee pilot had to achieve in order

Beardmore's fleet of training aircraft at Renfrew Aerodrome c 1927

to obtain the pilots 'A' licence. These seem very rudimentary by today's standards but reflect the limited capability of the aircraft of the time.

## 1927 — David McIntyre gets his Wings and joins 602 Squadron

David McIntyre's log book shows 13 dual instruction flights on 12 separate days for a little over 10 hrs before making his first solo

flight on 18th February 1927. Two of the flights he recorded in that period were with the 602 Squadron Adjutant Flt Lt Dan Martyn in one of the Squadron Avro 504N (Lynx)'s. The aircraft he mostly flew were the rotary Le Rhone engined Avro 504K biplanes, G-EAHY and G-EBIS. Three more solo flights saw him pass his test on 7th March, being signed off with his Aviators Licence "A" Certificate, and he was accepted into 602 Squadron as a Pilot Officer on 29th March. He was the 4th Pilot Officer to join the squadron whose CO at the time was regular RAF officer, Squadron Leader

Aerial view of Renfrew Aerodrome in 1928 - 602 Sqn and Beardmore Flying School aircraft in view. (DC)

J.D. Latta. It was reported that when the formation of the Glasgow Squadron was announced in 1925 there were over 200 applications to join the unit mostly as ground crew, aircraft fitters, maintenance engineers and the like.

The next pilot to join in May was to become his close friend Douglas (Douglo) Douglas-Hamilton, then the Marquis of Douglas and Clydesdale, who had learned to fly and obtained his 'A' licence at the De Havilland Aircraft flying school at Stag Lane near Edgeware in London.

It is difficult to get an appreciation of the life which the Auxiliary Squadron pilots led with a full time job through the day and sporadic mid week and weekends only flying. David McIntyre through this period worked with his brother James in their stevedoring business on the Clyde and his correspondence shows that he lived in the Officers Mess in Renfrew for the early period.

His first Squadron flight commenced on 6th May 1927 and on 8 days during the rest of the month his flying continued with basic dual

The Avro 504 two seat biplane was used extensively during the 1914-1918 war. It became the standard ab-initio trainer for the RAF squadrons in the inter war years. The early Rotary engined 'K' types were re-developed with the Lynx radial engine, designated 'N' and fitted with an improved undercarriage, as flown by David McIntyre in his early days in 602 Squadron

Avro 504N of 602 Squadron c 1932 (602M)

instruction for 7 hours and a little under 3 hours solo which included his first cross country flight, landing at Turnhouse and back. In the month of June his dual instruction flights reduce to only 1.5 hrs with 13 hrs of solo flights recorded. One of his solo flights was to a height of 17,100 feet to determine the height ceiling of the Avro 504N trainer aircraft.

The month of July was traditionally when the 602 Squadron Annual camp was arranged during the two weeks of the Glasgow "Fair" holiday and for the years to 1930 these were held at RAF Leuchars in Fife near St Andrews. Until the 1927 Leuchars camp David McIntyre's flying had been exclusively in the Avro

The De Havilland DH9A day bomber was first used by the RAF in 1918. It was the standard issue to the newly formed Auxiliary Squadrons in 1925. With a 450 hp Napier Lion engine it had a max speed of 123 mph at 10,000 ft David McIntyre had only one flight in this aircraft.

DH9A day bomber of 602 Squadron at 1927 camp at Leuchars

504 trainer biplanes but during the July camp he was introduced to the De Havilland DH9A bomber, which was the Squadron's, fighting aircraft on which he was given an hour's dual instruction. During the 23 hours solo flying in July, his log book recorded such activities as practised forced landings, stunting, low flying on the sands, formation flying, camera work, reconnaissance, and participation in a stunt flying competition.

By the time of the Squadron camp at Leuchars in 1927, the Pilot Officer compli-ment of 602 Squadron had reached 7 with the addition of Robert Faulds and Douglas Farqu-har. And so it remained through 1928 with only one addition until 1929 when the strength doubled. McIntyre, Clydesdale and Farquhar were all later to become Commanding Offi-cers of the Squadron.

During August and September he recorded only two short flights in the Avro, which were

1927 Leuchars Camp. David McIntyre - centre rear, On his left is Clydes-dale. DH9A in the background. (The total compliment of 5 Pilot Officers+ CO Fullerton centre, Doc Allen on his left and Adjutant Dan Martyn on his right)

purely practising landings and aerobatics, but activity picked up in October with the arrival of the new (to 602 Squadron) Fairey Fawn II aircraft to replace their old DH9A's. In the Fawn that month he recorded some 11 hours solo flying after an hour's dual instruction. Two of these flights were height tests to 15,000ft. It is at this point that he graduated to the role of an operational pilot rather than a trainee. In November he logged another 12hrs in the Fawn including a 1 hr 30 min flight to 19,000ft to establish the operational height ceiling of the aircraft, presumably without oxygen. A

David McIntyre to the right of CO Fullerton in centre and Doc Allen on his right with 602 Squadron contingent at Leuchars camp in 1927 (LEN)

single day's flying in December 1927 concluded his first year as a pilot, during which he clocked up 68 hrs solo and 24 hrs dual.

## 1928 — Experiences the hazards of flight

This proved to be an eventful year, which started quietly, his first flight on Feb 18th being a dual instruction flight after 2 months absence, brushing up his skills with the Adjutant Flt Lt Martyn. By April things got somewhat more active with quite a bit of test flying in both the Fawn and the Avro 504's including a number headed 'wireless test'. In May the first mention of gunnery activity appears in his log book and an interesting item in the family collection is a gunnery training manual titled 'Turnberry 1918' issued to David McIntyre while in 602 Squadron. In it are described a

The Fairey Fawn replaced the DH9A in only 5 of the RAF squadrons, it being the first new design to go into service after the 1918 armistice. Only 100 were built, powered by a 470hp Napier Lion engine, giving it a slower max speed of 114 mph at 10,000ft but carried a larger bomb load than the DH9A. An inferior design as a result of short sighted post war officialdom.

David McIntyre flying in a Fairey Fawn at Leuchars camp in 1929

number of different gun types as installed in Sopwith Camels and other 1914–18 war aircraft, detailing the methods for adjusting, maintaining and operating them. It is surprising to see that by 1928 the RAF did not appear to have moved to any more advanced forms of armament training than that which existed during the First World War. Also in May, David McIntyre recorded his first solo flight out of Scotland with an overnight stay at Sealand near Chester (home of No 5 Flying Training School) while ferrying a new (to 602) Fawn J7190 from RAF Henlow via Castle Bromwich to Renfrew. Although not an entry in David McIntyre's Log Book, the Squadron suffered its first pilot fatality on May 28th when Pilot Officer no 1, J.P Drew crashed during an aerobatic manoeuvre.

David McIntyre's Fawn J7188 being dismantled after crash landing at Renfrew Aerodrome 16 June 1928

On June 16th the entry 'crashed' appeared in David McIntyre's log book for the first time on arrival back from a cross-country formation flight in Fawn J7188 to Turnhouse. The folklore to this event suggested that David McIntyre, having observed how larger birds were able to approach downwind and execute an abrupt 180 degree turn before alighting, attempted a similar manoeuvre only to find that the aerodynamic abilities of the Fawn were unable to match those of their feathered counterparts. There is one report, which commiserated with 602 as having been the only Auxiliary Squadron to be inflicted with these 'cumbersome' ex RAF machines. Following this incident on the same day, his log book recorded a 'dual landing' flight with the Adjutant, another 'Landings' session on his own, followed the next day with a 15 min entry, which says 'Test'. It would suggest that his superiors took a dim view of his experiment. No further record of this aircraft appears in his log book and it may have been a write-off although David McIntyre was unhurt.

On the 29th of June there is an entry, described 'RAF Display' and recorded him piloting Fawn J7219 from Renfrew to Turnhouse, Catterick, Thorne, Waddington and North Weald accompanied by LAC Cunliffe. It is not known for sure what the Display occasion was, but the RAF's No 29 Squadron had in April just moved to North Weald in their new Armstrong Whitworth Siskins and this might have been an opening ceremony of some sort. David McIntyre's return journey from North Weald on 2nd July came to an abrupt halt at Catterick where his engine failed with a burnt valve. It is not clear if this was an in-flight failure or one detected on the ground after landing. He was rescued the next day by his friend Denis McNab who flew down in one of the Squadron's Avro 504's to collect him.

The Leuchars camp in July 1928 provided David McIntyre with 24 flying hours for the month which included a forced landing at Lenzie in one of the Avro 504's due to engine failure and competitions for landings in the Fawn and aerobatics (stunting) in the Avro. A record of his prowess in these events has not been uncovered. In one of the group photos of the Squadron at the camp, a propeller is shown resting across the knees of the seated front row officers, which seems to be a trophy but it has so far not been possible to trace its origin to explain what the event might have

602 Squadron Pilots and regulars at 1928 Leuchars camp. Propeller Trophy on the knees of CO Fullerton with DFM on his right and Farquhar on his left.

been. On the last day of the Camp there was a photo session with David McIntyre flying the Fawn J7190 with LAC Poole as gunner during which a number of air-to-air photos of this aircraft were taken. The last 5 months of his year included 3 or 4 days flying each month amounting to about 18 hours in total, the only

David McIntyre flying in Fairey Fawn J7190 over the hills south of the Tay estuary from Leuchars camp in 1928

entry of note being one which shows formation loops with his contemporary Douglas Farquhar which must have been fun as well as challenging having no radio communication at the time. This brought his solo flying hours up to 161 by the end of the year.

## 1929 — David McIntyre gets a new set of wings & joins the Caterpillar Club

In his first two years, the 602 log books of David McIntyre were signed off by their resident RAF Adjutant, Dan Martyn and his assistant Flt Lt Finney, but by 1929 these names are replaced by those of Flying Officer P.R Barwell and Flight Lieutenant John Whitford the Squadron's new Adjutant. Whitford was to become a lifelong friend of David McIntyre and the names Barwell and Martyn appear in the annals of the Everest flight and it is likely that they are the same Officers. 1929 was notable for the introduction of the Westland Wapiti to 602 Squadron in place of the obsolete Fawns, and for the winning of the Auxiliary Air Force Squadron's Esher Trophy by 602 Sqn and finally for David McIntyre's first parachute descent, more of which later.

Unlike the previous year, David McIntyre's log book in January is more active recording 3 flying days in the Fawn and Avro 504 machines but only one entry in February. March became busy with 6 separate days flying and on the 7th included a curious one-way 4 hr flight from RAF Waddington to Turnhouse in Fawn J7183, which was possibly being ferried back after maintenance. This flight coincides with an entry in Clydesdale's log book for the same date and route which is annotated as including a forced landing at Berwick. It is likely that they were flying together in formation and David McIntyre will also have stopped to assist his fellow officer or possibly bad weather forced them both down, which accounts for the extended time for the journey. On the 27th he recorded a photographic mosaic flight of 1 hour over the City of Glasgow and another over the "Bombing Ground" which was at Clydesdale's home at Dungavel near Strathaven. The 30th was a busy day of 3 hrs flying over 5 flights including a 15,000 ft height test with full bomb load for 1 hr 10 mins and a 25 minute formation flight with the Adjutant and Pilot Officer Horsburgh. The following day he recorded a navigation training flight with three up in the Fawn practising "the three course method".

In April a new entry appears: 'bombing obscura', which is the art of bomb dropping in cloud or reduced visibility. There was also a delivery flight to RAF Waddington to bring back a (new to 602) Mk III Fawn J7769 to Renfrew. RAF Waddington was the home of No 503 Reserve Squadron who were also equipped with the Napier Lion powered Fairey Fawn cast off's from the regular Air Force Squadrons. It is possible that these two units exchanged machines from time to time or 602 had maintenance and repairs conducted there which explains the fairly steady traffic, which can be observed between the two units.

May was a particularly busy month with nearly 30 hrs flying on 12 days with aerial gunnery practice and aerobatics predominating. On May 26 there was an unusual jaunt where he flew as a passenger with Assistant Adjutant Barwell in the Avro J9255 to Ettrick Bay on the island of Bute, where he returned piloting Fawn J7770, carrying the recently joined, P/O Mitchell and AC Muir, to Turn-

house. From here he then flew to Renfrew in Fawn J7980. No explanation is suggested for this odd journey, but perhaps the Fawn J7770 had made a forced landing or had run out of fuel, and this was a simple rescue mission.

He was chided by Barwell for the untidy manner in which he recorded his Log Book at this time and Barwell asked him to explain one entry on May 25th, which recorded "Dual Slow Rolls", in the Avro J9255 with Pilot Officer Horsburgh on board. There is no evidence of an answer to this question and no adjustment to his log. June continued a busy schedule of practising including a forced landing competition with LAC Poole on board again.

The Westland Wapiti was a development from the DH9A and first flew in 1927. Some 550 were produced for general purpose and day bombing duties. Powered by a 480hp Bristol Jupiter engine it managed a top speed of 135mph. 602 Squadron were equipped variously with 20 of these aircraft between 1929 and 1933.

Westland Wapiti IIA of 602 Squadron in Hangar at Renfrew 1931

July brought the annual camp at Leuchars where some Army co-operation joint manoeuvres are recorded involving armoured cars and a 'bombing raid'. Clydesdale's log book for this occasion is more explicit and mentions combining with No 56(F) Squadron and the destinations for the raids being Kinross and Montrose. On July 23rd when flying Fawn J7222 David McIntyre's log book reads 'Camera Gun, Esher Trophy' involving a 40 min flight at 2000ft which shows he was one of the team involved in this event. Later in the year, 602 Squadron were the first to be presented with the Esher Trophy at a ceremony at the Glasgow City Chambers by the Marshal of the Royal Air Force, Viscount Trenchard for being the top Auxiliary Air Force Squadron (of which there were 20 throughout Britain). This award was all the more remarkable since 602 were

Caterpillar Club badge presented to DFM after his parachute descent

considered no-hopers by the other squadrons, being the only ones still kitted out with the old and cumbersome Fawn bombers, and it says a lot for the skill, training and determination of the 602 Squadron crews. The final entry at the Leuchars camp was David McIntyre's initial flight in the first of 602's Westland Wapiti bombers, J9094 which he flew solo on 25th July, returning to Renfrew in the Fawn J7222 the following day. This is the point when the Fawns are at last being phased out and the Wapiti takes over as the operational bomber for the Squadron.

Back at Renfrew in August, David McIntyre journeyed down to the Westland Aircraft factory at Yeovil in Somerset, presumably by train, to pick up a new (to 602) Westland Wapiti J9597. This he ferried back to Renfrew via Andover and Catterick on Aug 8th in 6 hrs 35 mins flying time. On 5th September he flew down with Flying Officer Mitchell in a Wapiti J9592 to Gosport via Worthy Down arriving on the 6th and returning via Catterick on the 9th. Since Gosport and Worthy Down were primarily training units for the RAF at the time, it is reasonable to speculate that there was a training session involved during the trip. In October he flew a Fawn down to Hawkinge in Kent via Cranwell in 4 hrs 50 mins but there is no return flight recorded and it is likely this trip was to return the now obsolete aircraft to the RAF. For the remainder of the month and in November he recorded flying on seven days, mostly in the Wapiti, but also a couple of aerobatics flights in the Avro 504.

The year ended in December with a single days flying on the 15th in the Avro 504, J2975 where his first 20 min flight was doing aerobatics. He then took off with Pilot Officer Hors-

burgh in the front seat and proceeded to do some more aerobatics whereupon he was seen to have fallen out leaving Horsburgh to land the Avro while he descended by parachute. His log book reads, *"harness carried away, landed by parachute"*. The telegram from the Caterpillar club, founded by Leslie Irvin the parachute maker, recorded the descent by David McIntyre as being the first by an Auxiliary Air Force pilot. The Squadron folklore attached to this incident suggested that he had ejected on purpose to give the chutes a live test before any of his fellow pilots were required to use one in earnest. David McIntyre had now logged a total of 308 hours of which 282 were solo.

# LEAP FROM 'PLANE.

## THRILL FOR PAISLEY CROWDS.

# AIRMAN UNHURT.

Several hundred persons who, taking advantage of the ideal weather yesterday afternoon, were enjoying a walk through Barshaw Park, Paisley, were thrown into a state of considerable excitement when a man was seen to come hurtling out of an aeroplane, which had been encircling the East End of the town for some time.

As he rapidly descended, many people stood awestruck.

Suddenly a parachute was seen to open out, and the man glided slowly to the ground and alighted in a field to the north of the park.

Most people who witnessed the incident were under the impression that the descent had been pre-arranged, but it is stated that such was not the case.

An officer was despatched from the Renfrew Aerodrome by motor-car in search of the aviator, who, it was feared, had been injured. He was making his way back to the aerodrome with the parachute tucked up under his arm when he was met by the motor-car.

Cutting recording DFM's parachute descent in 1929

Westland Wapiti of 602 Squadron cropped at a jaunty angle as presented by David McIntyre in his photo album

## 1930 — Flight Lieutenant McIntyre

The first three months of 1930 brought David McIntyre to the runway at Renfrew on only six occasions, where the flights were of aerobatics and local formation flying with his contemporaries McNab, Farquhar and Land on board. The latter newly joined in March and having the misfortune to be involved in a fatal mid air collision only a year later. Activity hotted up in April with one day recording 11 separate flights. On the 12th he recorded a Mr Service being taken on a 1-hour passenger carrying flight and there was a family connection here. It is probable that this was Ronald Service, later to become his brother-in-law.

The Service family were involved with shipping on the Clyde and David McIntyre with his brother James ran a stevedoring business also on the Clyde so the two businesses were connected and the directors likewise. About this time he acquired a Morgan open tourer, which he used to drive around the countryside taking friends and family for picnic jaunts into the hills and he was also reputed to fly down to land on Ayr's Bellisle golf course for a quick meal with his parents at the Durdans. There is no record of these flights in his service log book and it is possible that he, like Clydesdale, kept a separate log book for his civil flying trips.

One entry on April 20th related to David McIntyre having made a forced landing through engine failure in Wapiti J9603 at Houston with Corporal White on board. It is clear there were no injuries since the day continued with David McIntyre recording 5 further flights with others on board including the unfortunate Corporal White. The day after

this, he recorded a crash landing at Houston in the Avro 504, J9706 with John Whitford on board. This embarrassing incident was possibly while returning to the scene of the previous day's forced landing to retrieve the Wapiti which was clearly undamaged as it goes on in service until written off in the mid air collision in March the following year. There is however no further record of David McIntyre having flown that particular Avro again and it may have been a write-off. His only interesting flight in May, on the 26th, carried the comment 'War Load Test to 15,000' in Wapiti J9598 with AC Smith on board. Presumably this flight was testing the height ceiling of the Wapiti with a full bomb load, gunner and ammunition.

In David McIntyre's album are a number of photos of the Squadron officers having some fun and games during a picnic at Gleneagles according to the comments he has written on the back along with the names of those participating but no clue as to the occasion or exact date. This is one of several examples of the camaraderie, which was evident amongst the Squadron members and observed in a number of David McIntyre's letters mentioned in later chapters.

602 Squadron picnic at Gleneagles - David McIntyre on the right

602 Squadron shared the use of the aerodrome facilities at Renfrew with the Scottish Flying Club (SFC) which had been formed by some ex WW1 enthusiasts at around the same time as the Squadron. The Club was very active and grew rapidly with many of the 602 pilots being members of the SFC. They had excellent training facilities and by 1928 had established a public air show or Pageant as it was called, in which 602 Squadron would usually be asked to perform. The SFC became the breeding ground for many successful pilots

who later made important contributions to the nations civil and military aviation progress.

June was another busy month with a lot of practice in formation flying and preparation for the annual camp competitions as well as ferrying a couple of redundant Fawns down to Hawkinge. On the 7th, he recorded taking part in a flying display performed by the Squadron at Renfrew and his log book for this day showing 2 hrs flying Wapiti J9602 in an *"Esher Trophy Mosaic"* as well as 40 mins forced landing practice in Wapiti J9600. These flying displays for the public had become a regular event and David McIntyre referred to them in his correspondence in 1934 as having a reputation for being dogged with bad weather where *"our guests are invited to paddle about*

602 Squadron contingent lined up in front of the Wapiti day bomber while at their annual camp at Leuchars in 1930

Aerial view of Renfrew Aerodrome during SFC Pageant in 1931—note water-logged airfield conditions. 602 Squadron aircraft getting ready for formation display. (MOF)

*in the mud and eat damp cake while the Squadron flaps around in the skies getting itself wet".* His parents and other family members were in attendance at this and other of the squadron displays.

Adam Cairns Smith of the Scottish Flying Club was a keen amateur moviemaker and recorded a number of the Squadron activities on film as well as providing an aerial platform in the Club's aircraft for a number of the local press photographers. Cairns Smith was to become a good friend of David McIntyre and made an enterprising flight to Basra in the Persian Gulf, later in 1934 with the assistance of David McIntyre who had flown the route during the Everest flight. There was a good deal of mutual assistance and friendly relationships between the Squadron and the Flying Club while at Renfrew aerodrome.

The July 1930 annual camp was held at Leuchars for the last time and here, in addition to the usual intensive training routine, David McIntyre was involved in escorting the Air Officer Commanding in formation across to the Northern Ireland aerodrome at Aldergrove in Wapiti J9600, returning the same day with an average flight time of 2hrs 15 mins. A ground collision was recorded in David McIntyre's log book on 29th July without any injury being noted. From the sketch of the incident, which David McIntyre has recorded on the back of the photograph, it does not appear to have been caused by him. It is of note also that he has annotated himself as "Flt Lt McIntyre" suggesting that his promotion to this rank had taken place sometime earlier in 1930.

At the end of the Leuchars camp on 1st August, the squadron returned to Renfrew in formation as was customary. The rest of the year followed a now standard pattern of reduced activity except that David McIntyre has been involved in more cross country trips, Dunbar, Hendon and Northolt featuring. David McIntyre's Hendon trip appeared to coincide with the occasion when the squadron

Two 602 Wapiti aircraft involved in a ground collision at Leuchars in 1930.

Example of a HP Hyderabad bomber in which DFM flew during navigation training at Northolt in 1930 (P Jarrett)

competed in the RAF's Laurence Minot bombing competition at the RAF North Coates Fittes bombing range where his stable mate Douglas Farquhar was runner-up. This result came, after four days of competition, as something of a surprise to the regular RAF pilots who had not rated the Auxiliary pilots as serious contenders. It was said at the time that the 602 practice had been conducted on the "Bombing Range" at Clydesdale's estate at Dungavel. There is no evidence however to indicate that David McIntyre was involved in this event. His Northolt trip was recorded as navigation practice and showed David McIntyre being instructed by a Flt Lt Stainforth on one flight in an Avro 504. (Whether this was the same Flt Lt Stainforth who was to set the world speed record at 406 mph the following September in the Supermarine S.6B and who won the Kings Cup air race in a Gloster Grebe in 1929, is not certain.) On that trip he also flew in a Handley Page Hyderabad twin-engined heavy bomber on one of his navigation training flights. By the end of the year he had added some 120 hrs to his flying total.

## 1931— Plans a long distance record & meets Marjorie Potts

Unlike previous years, the early months of 1931 were particularly active for David McIntyre and this continued throughout the summer. In that period David McIntyre recorded having piloted two of the Squadron's younger Officers, Pilot Officer Land and Pilot Officer Phillips both of whom died shortly afterwards in a mid air collision on 7th March near Port Glasgow. There was also another entry of a passenger carrying flight with a Mr Service on 1st Feb, thought to be the same Ronald Service whom he had flown the previous year. The

activities were varied with a lot of formation flying mixed in with wireless testing, camera gun and a number of cross country flights to Hendon, Greenlaw, Stranraer, Leuchars, and a few trips to Turnhouse. In May he recorded a trip in the Wapiti J9601 with Flt Lt Redman to Hawkinge via Waddington and Hornchurch possibly in preparation for the Annual Camp due to be located at Hawkinge that year. Then, having dropped Redman off at Hendon, he picked up another Wapiti J9596 for the return flight from Hendon direct to Renfrew in 4hrs 10mins. One year later in a Hawker Hart he would record doing a similar journey in half that time.

The squadron had been concentrating in developing formation-flying skills and this is evident as David McIntyre recorded 40 flights in May alone listed against this activity. It demonstrated the serious intent of the Squadron to become as professional and disciplined in their flying as possible and is a feature of the attitude fostered by Clydesdale, McIntyre and the other Flight commanders to show that an Auxiliary Squadron can be every bit as good as, if not better than, their RAF counterparts who were at times inclined to look down on their "Part Time" neighbours. In June he recorded a flight with Clydesdale to Strathaven presumably giving him a lift home to Dungavel since he returned to Renfrew alone. Also in June again on the 7th there is a record of an Air Display at Renfrew in which David McIntyre took part in the formation flying demonstration for which the squadron conducted a 40 min rehearsal two days beforehand. An extract from the Scottish Flyer magazine of the Scottish Flying Club who organised the Pageant in adverse weather, reads, "The City of Glasgow Bomber Squadron was, in our opinion, equal to anything we have ever seen, even at the Hendon Royal Air Force Displays".

On 7th July, shortly before heading south for the 1931 annual camp at Hawkinge, there is a curious entry in David McIntyre's log book, which showed a 1hr 40min flight in a Wapiti recorded as being a wireless test and a reconnaissance with the Royal Navy battleship HMS Warspite. In the book on 602 by Douglas McRoberts "Lions Rampant" there is a reference relating to a Wapiti flight in which Pilot

Officer Brian Smith was chosen, "due to his superior navigating skills", to support Royal Navy Fleet manoeuvres far out to sea. It is possible that David McIntyre was associated with this same rendezvous since there were clearly Naval manoeuvres taking place in the Clyde at the time of this flight. David McIntyre flew the Squadron's Avro 504, J9253 to Hawkinge (near Deal on the Kent coast) on 13th July in preparation for the camp, routing via Turnhouse, Catterick, Waddington, and Hornchurch taking a total of 6hrs 5mins. He will probably have returned by train since his next recorded flight was from Renfrew in a Wapiti on 17th July when the squadron flew down to Hawkinge via North Weald in 5hrs 5min for the annual camp.

The activities at the annual camp included four Air Defence of Great Britain exercises and were recorded against flights from Hawkinge to London and back lasting about 4hrs each. These may have been simulated bombing raids on London to test the capital's defensive systems in place at the time. Clydesdale's log book is more detailed and recorded the objective as being the West India Docks and was flown in formation with 604 Squadron.

During the camp there were the now familiar Esher Trophy competition events, including spot landings, formation flying and air efficiency exercises. While at the camp, he recorded having had a flight in a Gloster Grebe — a small fighter biplane nearing the end of its service life. He was probably taking it up for a spin as a bit of light amusement and to experience the characteristics of a fighter aircraft compared with those of their bombers. Clydesdale's log book for the same day also recorded a 15min flight in Grebe J7395, likely to have been the same aircraft, probably of No 25 Squadron stationed there at the time.

A quote from the Aeroplane magazine in June 1931 reads: "No 602 Squadron is as good as the best squadron in the Air Force so far as the handling of its machines is concerned. Judging by a close inspection of those machines on the ground, it is equally good in its care and maintenance. However although the London squadrons pride themselves on their smart appearance they certainly will not beat Glasgow".

Example of the Gloster Grebe fighter aircraft flown by David McIntyre while at Hawkinge camp in 1931.

At this time David McIntyre was the commander of 602's 'B' Flight where he is reputed to have given his pilots a looser reign than his contemporary Lennox in 'A' flight emphasising the development of flying skills, which resulted in 'B' flight being considered to have the finest aerobatic skills in the squadron. Clydesdale was the 'C' flight commander at this time. David McIntyre returned to Renfrew from the Hawkinge camp on 30th July via Cranwell and this was to be his last visit to Renfrew for a while as he had obtained a years attachment to the RAF's No 12 Squadron at Andover. At the end of July his log book is annotated by the Adjutant John Whitford as being 'above the average' proficiency.

There is evidence that David McIntyre, after 3 years developing his flying skills with 602 Squadron, was looking for something more challenging, and during 1930, he started planning for a record-breaking trip to Australia to depart on 11th May 1931. He was possibly inspired by the book he obtained in 1928 by Sir Alan Cobham recounting his epic 1926 Australia trip by seaplane. In this book, David McIntyre has annotated some comments, and he also made use of the map and account of the journey to formulate ideas for his own attempt.

David McIntyre had corresponded with Vickers seeking their assistance in providing a suitable aircraft for his planned attempt on the distance record to Australia. Initially it appears that the use of a Vickers Viastra 10 seat passenger airliner powered by three Lynx engines was proposed but Vickers wrote to him on 12th Jan 1931 to say that they were not proceeding with this development. In the same letter they indicated that they were however, considering adapting the Vickers Vellore for a range of 2,500 miles carrying a pilot and one passenger. They enclosed a memorandum outlining the

DFM's copy of Cobham's 1926 Australia flight account

of the Bristol Engine Co, were proposing to install Bristol Jupiter VIII power plants in the twin Vellore which they considered "the most suitable" on account of their reduced fuel consumption. This was expected give a range of 2,500 miles at 120 mph cruising speed with a 300 yd take-off run in zero wind. David McIntyre's detailed journey plans show that he was attempting to make the trip to Darwin in a little under 4 days (3days 16hrs). Cobham had taken 36 days in 1926 and by 1930 the record time for the journey had been reduced to 9 days. His takeoff point was to be Lympne near Dover on the South coast of England on 11th May 1931, stopping at Constantinople, Jask, Calcutta, Singapore and Port Darwin, with each leg averaging roughly 2000 miles. His unresolved query at the time was whether there were night landing facilities at Singapore. Tantalisingly his papers do not disclose whom he was expecting to provide the finance nor who if any of his Squadron contemporaries he had been planning to fly with. It does not appear to have got much further than the late planning stages and probably evaporated due to lack of finance. It does perhaps give an

scheme for a Vickers Vellore II aircraft to be powered by two Bristol Jupiter engines, which they were proposing for the trip, cruising at 120 mph.

Bristol appear to have undertaken to conduct a series of fuel consumption trials to assist with the planning where the scheduled stopping places are important because of the type of fuel being available and David McIntyre was asked for details of his route. Bristol were also anxious to know which Fuel Company he was going to contract with. This governed the type of fuel as if it was to be the Pratt Co they could supply Ethyl fluid whereas if it was Shell it would be Benzol mixture and Borneo fluid for the special taking off supply. It was proposed to use a higher performance fuel for the full throttle take off, supplied from a separate fuselage mounted fuel tank. David McIntyre also enquired about the availability of a "Pilots assistor" which was probably some form of early auto pilot system.

A little later at the end of January, the correspondence indicated that Vickers, having conferred with Mr Fedden the Chief Designer

The Vickers Vellore I was designed as a single engined freight and mail carrier which first flew in 1928. This 76ft span biplane exceeded many of its design targets on completion, and was re-engined for a long-range flight to Australia. Flown by two RAF pilots of Australian origin wishing to return home, it left Lympne in March 1929 and eventually crash landed at Darwin towards the end of April with engine problems and was a write off. Vickers did not proceed with the Vellore I and moved on with a twin engined version initially designated Vellore II but latterly redesignated Vellore III registered G-AASW which first flew in June 1930 and competed in the Kings Cup air race in July 1930. Although a second Vellore II was built and a third airframe with a wider 10 seater fuselage was completed, named the Vellox, no further development of the type was undertaken.

Vickers Vellore II/III  proposed for long distance flight by DFM to Australia in 1931 (R.T Jackson)

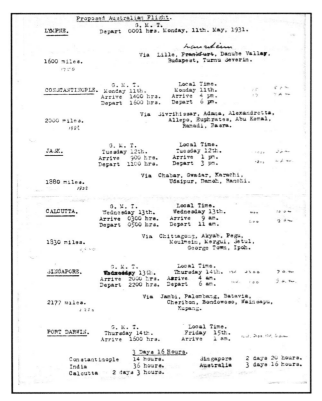

DFM's planned itinerary for his attempt at the England—Australia distance record in 1931

insight into his aspirations to excel at his chosen career and to make aviation his full time business.

## 1931 — Joins No 12 Squadron

The Andover based No 12 (bomber) squadron was known as 'the Shiny Twelfth' and was considered at the time to be one of the RAF's premier units. It had been the only one equipped with the Fairey Fox two-seat day bomber, which led to the Squadron emblem featuring a fox's head.

At the time David McIntyre joined as a Flight Commander in August 1931, 12 Squadron had converted to the new Hawker Hart advanced light day bomber. The Hart would in two years time replace the Wapiti in 602 Squadron since the Auxiliary Squadrons were at the time only considered worthy of the RAF cast-offs, a practice which was to change in 1939 when 602, having been converted to a Fighter Squadron, were one of the first to be equipped with Spitfire Mk 1 aircraft before many regular RAF units. David McIntyre moved to 12 Squadron to learn about the latest experimental bombing techniques and the use

of new gyroscopic instruments to help with blind formation flying in cloud. He is quoted on his return as saying "I soon showed 'em how to do it" and his ability is recorded in his log book at the end of the attachment in October 1932 by his Squadron Commander in one word, "Exceptional". From Sept 1931 to Oct 1932 while with 12 Squadron, David McIntyre recorded 340 hrs flying in the Hawker Hart.

After a short break on return from the 602 Squadron 1931 annual camp at Hawkinge, David McIntyre spent a few days at the North Cotes Fittes RAF bombing and gunnery range near Grimsby, familiarising himself with the area and flying a military DH60 Gipsy Moth K1220 for the first time. This aircraft he ferried across to RAF Halton in Bucks on 23rd August and made his way to Andover where his first solo flight in a Hart K1446 is recorded on 27th after 20 min dual instruction. His next flight was in this same aircraft on 7th Sept to North Coates Fittes for an intensive four-week bombing and gunnery course returning to Andover on 10th Oct. His log book recorded him as being Flight Commander of 'C' flight and back at Andover he spent the rest of the month

David McIntyre has a log book entry in February 1933 which shows that he conducted a solo 1hr 30min altitude test flight in the prototype Fairey Fox IIM biplane J9834 of the RAF at Farnborough to 30,000 ft. This was presumably to test the oxygen and other equipment for the Everest flight. Two days earlier he and Clydesdale individually had conducted two flights of 10 and 15 minutes at Farnborough to familiarise themselves with this same aircraft. The Fairey Fox IIM was a development of the Fox I day bomber produced to compete for a new light bomber specification which lost out to the legendary Hawker Hart. The prototype built in 1929 was used as a demonstrator here at Farnborough, and was probably ending its days as an experimental aircraft as it was withdrawn from service a month after David McIntyre's flight.

Fairey Fox IIm flown by DFM at Farnborough on height test just prior to leaving on Everest flight.

conducting tests of air gunners. In November among the varied training tasks was interspersed an escort duty for Sir Philip Sasoon from Andover to Boscombe Down, Old Sarum, Upavon, and back with a Flying Officer Guinness on board, each leg being between 10 and 15 mins. Also he recorded a single flight in a Wapiti J9613 to Hendon on 7th Nov but no note of a return flight.

The 22nd of November 1931 was to be a memorable date for this was when he made his first contact with Marjorie Potts. He referred to this in a letter of the same date in

The Hawker Hart light day bomber was introduced in 1931 and immediately proved faster than the fighters of the day. No 12 Squadron was the second to receive these new bombers. Powered by a 525 hp Rolls-Royce Kestrel engine it had a top speed of 184 mph. It had a forward firing Vickers machine gun, a cockpit mounted Lewis gun and carried up to 520 lb underwing bombs.

Hawker Hart of 602 Squadron at Abbotsinch c 1935 (MOF)

1934, which is headed *"three years after Andover"*. His log book for 22.11.31 shows no flying and nothing unusual however to suggest what the event may have been. On November 21 1934 he wrote to Marjorie Potts:

*"Many, many happy returns of tomorrow and give Andover a wave from me as you pass on your way to Thruxton."* Also in a letter two days later he remarked, *"Have a pleasant journey down and give my love to Andover as you pass if you can spare any. Cancel that and give it my regards instead, all my love is for you Marge with none to spare.".*

Since Thruxton is only a few miles out of Andover it is likely that Marjorie Potts had a friend or relative living in the area whom she was visiting and during some social occasion she had met David McIntyre and formed what was to become a lifelong attachment.

No 12 Squadron Hawker Harts of 'C' Flight from Andover in 1931 - DFM's Log-book shows him to have flown all three of these aircraft

Formation practice was his main activity in December and a return to Renfrew for the Xmas & New Year break allowed him to have one formation flight in the old familiar Wapiti with his colleague Pilot Officer Rintoul on board. His total solo flying hours to date were 684 indicating that he added 256 hrs in 1931 which was more than double his annual average over the previous four years.

## 1932 — Professional excellence

After his Xmas holiday season break in Scotland with his family, David McIntyre travelled down to London in early January to take part in the wedding of Ronald Service and Doreen Potts. David McIntyre had been invited to be an Usher but it is not known if this invitation was from Ronald Service or as a result of his newfound attraction for Marjorie Potts who was Doreen's older sister. The friendship between the Potts and the Service families first

Part of No 12 Squadron group photo of 1932 showing Flight Lieutenant David McIntyre seated 2nd from the right

became established when they met while on a cruise to the West Indies in 1930 and later the friendship continued through sailing holidays in the Western Isles of Scotland. The Service family business was in shipping in Glasgow and David McIntyre had got to know them some years earlier through their connection with his stevedoring business. Ronald Service and Doreen Potts were married in London on 6th Jan 1932, where Marjorie Potts was one of the bridesmaids. David McIntyre although an usher, could not have lingered long after the reception, for the next day his log book records him flying from Andover on a navigation exercise to an airfield, Church Honeybourne in the Vale of Evesham.

Example of ice build up on the struts and rigging of a Hawker Hart during cloud flying exercises of No 12 Squadron at Andover.

The first name to appear in David McIntyre's log book in 1932 on 7th Jan is that of Flying Officer Capper with whom he undertook four flights, two of which were recorded as 'Air Pilotage Test' in a Hawker Hart (air pilotage being the term then used for the skill of visual navigation by map & compass only). This is almost certainly the one and the same Noel Capper who joined David McIntyre as an instructor when the flight training school opened at Prestwick in 1935 and Cap's unmistakable features are clearly seen in the No 12 Squadron photo of that year.

At the end of January he completed a 10 day blind flying course at Andover concluding with a 55min triangular course 'under hood' via Newbury and Basingstoke. From February to mid March he undertook a very varied collection of solo and formation exercises at Andover. The more unusual included, a Sutton harness test (by 1935 the Sutton Harness was the standard seat restraint shoulder harness used in the Tiger Moth and many other aircraft and may at that time in 1932 have been about to be introduced into the Hawker Hart for which a test was required) and what was called 'Formation Zogging'. (This being a method of inter-aircraft communication to signal a change of direction in a wing drill exercise by the observer/gunners raising their arms in a predetermined code.)

The estimation of wind speed & direction (WS&D) was clearly a topic of some interest for he recorded several alternative methods being tested including the 'Sumers method',

Wedding of Doreen Potts to Ronald Service. Marjorie Potts is the first of the adult bridesmaids. David McIntyre is Usher 2nd right   6th Jan 1932

Hawker Harts of 12 Squadron in formation probably off the Lincolnshire coast when stationed at NCF south of Grimsby at the mouth of the Humber estuary

the 'three course' method, the 'quick turn' method, the 'reverse drift' method, 'W.S &D on balloon', 'W.S &D on bomb sight', and latterly the testing of a 'Drift Sight'.

In mid March he obtained a lift to Northolt from Andover in a Hart where he picked up a 602 Squadron Wapiti and flew it back to Renfrew. Here he spent a couple of days flying with his 602 buddies and then returned to Andover in a Wapiti flown by Clydesdale (an air pilotage flight) whom he then dropped off

Example of 'Formation Zogging' being conducted by a Squadron of Hawker Harts at an air display (Aeroplane)

at Old Sarum in a Hart before returning to Andover. His next four months were spent in a pretty solid menu of pattern bombing, formation flying in cloud, dive bombing, and bombing in cloud. At the beginning of July he was involved in demonstrations of pattern bombing and as 'C' Flight Leader conducted a squadron cloud flying raid of 9 aircraft on Southampton during an Imperial Defence College visit to Andover.

The instructions for the days flying are amongst David McIntyre's papers which show that there were 7, I.D.C. students taken on this cloud flying demonstration bombing raid seated in the rear Air Gunners cockpit of the Hawker Harts duly fitted out with flying suits and parachutes with a map showing the track from Andover to Southampton. However it seems doubtful that flying in cloud would have given them much chance to verify where they were except through the voice link to the pilot.

Immediately after this, David McIntyre is one of three senior No 12 Squadron pilots assigned to a 4 day exercise taking place over the Watchet Range about 88 miles to the West of Andover on the Bristol Channel. David McIntyre's briefing papers for this exercise

| Date and Hour. | Aeroplane Type and No. | Pilot | Passenger(s) | Time | Height | Course | REMARKS |
|---|---|---|---|---|---|---|---|
| | | | | | | Time carried forward :— | |
| 1. 7. 32 | K.1439 | Self | L.A.C. Hull | .45 | 6.000 | Southampton Return | Cloud Raid. |
| 4. 7. 32 | K.1439 | Self | Cdt. Cullen | .35 | 3.000 | Local | Pattern Bombing. Imperial Defence visit. |
| 4. 7. 32 | K.1439 | Self | Captain Rumway. R.N. | .40 | 6.000 | Southampton & Return | Cloud Raid |
| 4. 7. 32 | K.1439 | Self | Cdt. Cullen | .15 | 3.000 | Local | Pattern Bombing. Demonstration. |
| 5. 7. 32 | K.1439 | Self | A.O. Hamblin | .30 | 5.000 | Local | Cloud Flying. |
| 5. 7. 32 | K.1439 | Self | L.A.C. Edwards | .25 | 4.000 | Local | Formation Cloud Flying. |
| 11. 7. 32 | K.1439 | Self | A.C. Tansau | .15 | 1.000 | Local | Weather Test. |
| 11. 7. 32 | K.1439 | Self | P.O. Gough | 1.25 | 3.000 | Southampton Coventry Andover | Cross Country Recco. |
| 11. 7. 32 | K.1425 | Self | A.O. Hamblin | .15 | 2.000 | Tangmere | { Cross Country |
| 11. 7. 32 | K.1425 | Self | A.O. Hamblin | .20 | 2.000 | Andover Caddington | |
| 14. 7. 32 | K.1439 | Self | L.A.C. Hull | 2.00 | 14.000 | Caddington & Return | High Altitude Balloon Trials |
| 14. 7. 32 | K.1439 | Self | Cdt. Cullen | .30 | 4.000 | Local | Pattern Bombing. |
| 15. 7. 32 | K.1439 | Self | Cdt. Cullen | .10 | 3.000 | Local | Pattern Bombing. |
| 15. 7. 32 | K.1439 | Self | Cdt. Cullen | .30 | 4.000 | Local | Pattern Bombing. |
| 15. 7. 32 | K.1439 | Self | Sgt. Holdway | .20 | 2.000 | To Farnborough | Cross Country. |
| 15. 7. 32 | K.1427 | Self | Ballard | .20 | 2.000 | Return Andover | |
| 18. 7. 32 | K.1439 | Self | P.O. Gough | .45 | 6.000 | Local | Test Leader Zone of fall method for Cloud formations. |
| 18. 7. 32 | K.1439 | Self | L.A.C. Hull | 2.45 | 13.000 | | |
| 19. 7. 32 | K.1439 | Self | Maj. Palmerston | 2.00 | | | |
| 19. 7. 32 | K.1439 | Self | Cdt. Clews. | 1.30 | 5.000 2.000 | | Low Raid. Leading Squadron. |
| 20. 7. 32 | K.1439 | Self | L.A.C. Hull | 1.05 | | | |

TOTAL TIME :—

Example page from David McIntyre's Log-Book during his secondment to No 12 Squadron at Andover in 1932.

show this to be a 1932 re-assessment of an experiment first tried in 1919, which was a method of determining the wind strength and direction (WS&D) at an altitude above cloud through the use of Anti-aircraft (A/A) shell bursts. Knowing the correct WS&D was essential for navigation above or in cloud at the time and his log book shows several different methods being practised. In this method the theory was that if shells are fired at 30 sec intervals to burst at a given height and the pilot flies at a constant 120 mph downwind along the line of bursts, timing the interval between 5 bursts, the time in seconds directly represents the number of mph at which the wind is blowing. The direction of the line of bursts being the wind direction.

The services of the 1st Air Defence Brigade at Watchet were engaged to fire the shells and a mobile RAF wireless telegraphy station was driven from Andover to Watchet to provide ground to air communication between the pilots and the gunners. The first day was a test in clear weather to allow the pilots to do two runs each to make the WS&D calculations, compare these with the other two methods used (the three course method and the 90° method) and make the return flight to Andover, navigating by using the new A/A burst method to check its accuracy. The second day was to be flown

No 12 Squadron Harts conducting a formation exercise in cloud from Andover c 1932

12 Squadron Hawker Harts at Andover during formation flying training c 1932.

with a cloud layer between the ground and the A/A bursts, the aircraft being positioned 2,000 ft above the shell bursts for safety at the start, calling up two ranging shots at the desired height so they could see where to expect the bursts before calling up the sequence of 20 bursts to allow the WS&D to be calculated.

The return flight to Andover was conducted above cloud, breaking cloud at the expected arrival time and any navigation error being recorded. On the third & fourth days the rendezvous at Watchet was to be above cloud without first checking at ground level, and to try to pick up the A/A bursts on arrival at Watchet at a specific time. An involved set of coded radio messages were devised to let the ground station know if the bursts were seen or not and to allow repeats. There are no notes or clues in David McIntyre's log book to indicate how effective this rather Heath Robinson method turned out to be or whether any use was made of the experiment!!

David McIntyre's last entry in his log for July on the 21st shows a return flight to Hawkinge and since the Auxiliary Squadron's camp was taking place there at the time, it suggests that he may have been taking the opportunity to have a rendezvous with his 602 colleagues, before taking some leave himself.

He returned from leave arriving at Andover on Aug 18th when he flew with the rest of 12

Squadron to North Coates Fittes in Lincolnshire for another intensive period of Bombing and Gunnery practice which continued through to 7th October when the Squadron returned to Andover. His only breaks in this period were one trip with the Hart to Renfrew with a Flying Officer Kippenberger on board where he stayed overnight on the 18th Sept conducting one flight of 1 hour at Renfrew before returning, and an ambulance flight with a Corporal Herridge to hospital, landing at Cranwell on Sept 14th. The return to Andover effectively concluded his secondment to 12 Squadron, as there are only a couple of more entries in his log book for this period. One of these show that Corporal Herridge must have recovered from his hospitalisation since he accompanied David McIntyre on a flight in the Hart K1427 to Renfrew and back on Oct

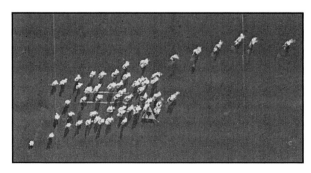

Results of bombing practice by Hawker Harts of 12 Squadron when stationed at NCF . The triangular target can be seen amongst the lower bomb blasts.

27th. Interestingly the northbound leg of this flight annotated *"S.W. W/T. Experimental Test"*, took 2 hrs 55 mins and the return leg back to Andover took 1 hr 55 mins, a full hour less. The direct line distance between Renfrew & Andover is about 350 miles, which gives a ground speed of 175 mph roughly, and the Hart had a max airspeed of 174 mph at 10,000 ft, so it can be concluded that there must have been a pretty strong northerly wind component blowing that day.

The skills and disciplines David McIntyre acquired during his year with 12 Squadron, were to be of immense use to him in his future aviation career. Having the responsibility of a Flight Commander and developing the techniques for pattern bombing in cloud and the precision needed to fly in formation in cloud were coupled with the management and instructing experience valuable in many circumstances later on. It is probable that this intensive year of full time flying brought his skills and experience to a standard which he would have taken a lot longer achieving in the part time activities of his 602 squadron routine. A newspaper report at the time, recorded that he was offered a permanent commission in the RAF after the Andover secondment but that he had turned it down.

David McIntyre continued his 602 Squadron flying at Renfrew in November flying in the old Wapiti biplanes for a couple of days and then towards the end of the month flew himself down to Old Sarum, Hendon and Henlow before returning via Waddington to Renfrew on Nov 26th. The single days flying he undertook in December brought his total flying hours to just over the thousand at 1018 showing that 308 hrs were added in the year, the most active of his career so far.

The next six months of his flying career would require all his experience and skill as a pilot, as he faced his greatest aviation challenge thus far — a record breaking flight over Mount Everest.

Formation of 12 Squadron Hawker Harts in flights of three at Andover possibly including 'C' Flight of which David McIntyre was Flight Commander

# 3. Houston Mount Everest Flight

Houston Westland approaching Everest range on the second flight on 19th April 1933

## Introduction

David McIntyre was chosen as the pilot for the second Everest machine in face of keen competition from more experienced RAF officers. At the time of the 1933 Everest mission, he was a commissioned Flight Lieutenant in 602 Squadron Royal Auxiliary Air Force based at Abbotsinch aerodrome near Paisley, and appointed the Squadron's 'B' Flight Commander with Douglas, Douglas-Hamilton, The Marquis of Douglas & Clydesdale (Lord Clydesdale) being the Commanding Officer. Both David McIntyre and Clydesdale joined 602 in the spring of 1927 and had become close friends during the first 5 years of their Squadron life. David McIntyre's recent one-year secondment to the RAF's No 12 Squadron had earned him a reputation as an exceptionally gifted pilot.

Colonel Blacker, who conceived the Everest Expedition, and Colonel Etherton, established a Committee to develop the project with the backing of the Royal Geographical Society. This comprised a number of eminent names including John Buchan the author. John Buchan, a fellow MP, was instrumental in bringing Clydesdale onto the committee as the Chief Pilot and when it was decided that there should be two aircraft to fly the mission, Clydesdale wrote to his friend David McIntyre (Mac) to see if he was interested in taking up the 2nd pilot position. The first record of David McIntyre's involvement is this letter from Clydesdale on 13th Nov 1932 suggesting he got a move on to apply and advised him that "there are one or two fairly good applications in already". That the Committee elected to put their trust in two relatively unknown Auxiliary Air Force pilots rather than more experienced RAF officers is remarkable and provided the two Scots pilots with a determination to prove the Committee's choice to have been a sound one. He made the application and, was advised by Etherton on 1st December 1932, that he had been successful. David McIntyre, in accepting the position, undertook the venture without pay and with the life insurance policy offered of £2,000 (the equivalent in year 2001 money is £115,000). He was required to undertake a pressure test, which he successfully conducted at Farnborough on Dec 15th. Clydesdale's November letter indicated an expectation that the expedition would be completed by March, but in the event they did

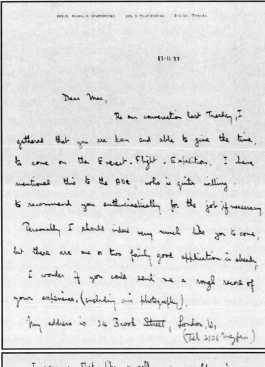

Clydesdale's letter to McIntyre urging him of the need to progress his application to join the Everest Flight team as 2nd pilot.

not leave until February and returned home in May 1933. Lady Houston funded the expedition after some effective persuasion by Lord Clydesdale.

Aircraft capable of carrying two people and the necessary oxygen and camera equipment with sufficient power to sustain at least an hours flight at 33,000ft were not immediately available, so Westland were persuaded to participate along with Bristol the engine makers to provide a suitable pair of aircraft.

## Preparation

David McIntyre's main task was to concentrate on the photographic objective of the mission and in particular the survey work. During January of 1933 he made several trips to Farnborough including a fortnight course in aerial photography conducted in Westland Wapiti aircraft. Air Commodore Fellows, the expedition leader joined one of the flights and the two observers Blacker and Bonnett also partici-

pated in one flight each which are noted in David McIntyre's log book.

Having completed the photographic training in January, contemporary photos show that he was present during the first test flight of the Houston Westland PV3 at Westland's factory at Yeovil at the end of January. David McIntyre also had a call to visit the Westland's aerodrome at Yeovil on Feb 1st, where he was to be present at the first test flight of the "2nd aircraft" the Westland Wallace. He flew part of the way down in The Earl of Selkirk's Moth from Dungavel but the journey was thwarted by bad weather forcing him to finish the journey by train.

The modified Wallace first flew on Feb 3rd piloted by Harald Penrose, Westland's chief test pilot, and on Feb 4th with Blacker as passenger, he attained a height ceiling of 36,500ft. At the start of their descent, an unexpected engine shut down due to failure of the sole fuel pump, required an unscheduled landing at Hamble rather than back at base at Yeovil, and was recorded as the longest engine-off descent achieved at the time. This was to be the only incident of major equipment failure experienced by either of the Everest aircraft during the trip. Westland assigned Frank Burnard one of their best engineers to accompany the Expedition to look after the aircraft and Bris-

The Westland Wallace was a development of the Wapiti, which David McIntyre had flown for a number of years in 602 Squadron and at the time was the latest fighter bomber in RAF service. The prototype PV6 Wallace G-AAWA was modified for the Everest flight with a Bristol Pegasus S3, 9-cylinder radial engine developing 580 hp with a supercharger and specially developed fuel using a high lead additive, which gave the aircraft a top speed at 33,000ft of 120 mph.

Prototype Wallace pre conversion into Everest machine G-ACBR (MOF)

L-R McIntyre, Fellowes, Clydesdale, Penrose at Yeovil for the test flight of G-ACAZ Jan 1933 - Clydesdale assists Penrose with his flying suit. (LEN)

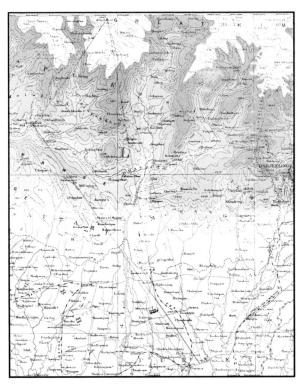

Flying map used by DFM to navigate the Everest Flight. Shows tracks and headings marked by DFM in pencil from the base airfield at Lalbalu .

tol's engineer Cyril Pitt was sent along to nurse the engines.

David McIntyre records that he had not flown the Wallace before they left for India. This photo in Clydesdale's album is annotated as David McIntyre flying the Wallace. However the aircraft still has its RAF markings on the fin showing it to be prior to the departure for Everest so the pilot is Harald Penrose conducting its only test flight.

Other preparatory work included the flight planning for the Everest flight, calculating fuel loads and consumption rates to determine how

long they could afford to run the survey flight legs and get back to base. The survey cameras had a capacity of only 125 frames and a 60% overlap was required for mapping purposes, which meant that only a relatively short distance could be covered between exposures. Detailed planning of the survey photography required to take account of the variation in the height between the aircraft and the ground and its ground speed to calculate the time intervals

David McIntyre ? flying G-ACBR (LEN)

Exposure calculator designed to show the time intervals between exposures of the survey cameras in the various height zones and ground speeds on the route

Selection of AA and Stanford maps prepared for Everest Journey from England to base camp at Purnea.

Bespoke flying maps were prepared for the outward journey to Karachi by the AA, which detailed the routes and headings, required for each leg of the journey. These maps carried on the reverse of each sheet a detail sketch of the local landing ground and the services, which could be expected at each potential stop. David McIntyre conducted the navigation for most of the journey covered by the expedition and received considerable praise and recognition for the accuracy, which he achieved, often in difficult conditions.

A few of his hand-written notes & headings can be seen on some of the maps. Edward Stanford Ltd provided the maps for the 1,500 mile cross India journey from Karachi to base camp at Purnea and onward to Everest. More detailed maps of the country around the base camp and Everest were also used for planning the local journeys on which David McIntyre has pencilled in the tracks and headings to be used at the time. A specially constructed flying map was also prepared for the return leg from Baghdad to Sofia put together as a continuous strip some 11ft long.

for the exposures to maintain the 60% overlap. David McIntyre designed a slide rule to make the calculations easier, the journey having been zoned into average height bands for which, at a range of ground speeds from 80 to 120 mph, the exposure interval was presented. In the event, during the flight, it proved impossible to accurately determine the ground speed and it was not possible to locate the ground control point due to lack of visibility. With these two uncertainties it is remarkable that the pilots and observers between them managed to obtain the successful photographic results that they did.

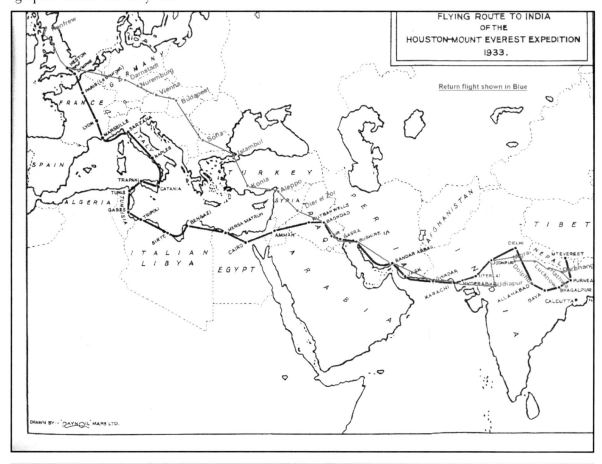

The logbook appears at the top of the page with handwritten flight entries. Printed column headers read:

| Date and Hour. | Aeroplane Type and No. | Pilot | Passenger(s) | Time | Height | Course | Remarks |
|---|---|---|---|---|---|---|---|

Time carried forward :— 1028·80

TOTAL TIME — 1063·35

## Outward Journey to India

Having crated up the two Westland aircraft and seen them set sail from Tilbury docks in London on the SS Dalgoma on 11th February 1933 bound for Karachi, the rest of the party prepared for their own journey out to India. Blacker departed on a Imperial Airways flight, Etherton with Barcas and the film crew and equipment set off by boat, and the pilots with

David McIntyre—in flying suit about to depart on 1st leg from Heston to Le Bourget

Air Commodore Fellows and his wife made up a three aircraft caravan to fly out via North Africa. Three aircraft were obtained for the Expedition to be used as logistical transport while in India. Clydesdale loaned his own Gipsy III Moth G-ABZK, Fry's the Chocolate Co loaned their Puss Moth G-ABWZ and a Fox Moth G-ACCS was obtained, to be disposed of once in India. The Gipsy Moth was the slowest and was piloted by David McIntyre who did the navigating. It had a streamlined canopy over the forward passenger cockpit and was fitted with a metal propeller to improve its speed to a maximum of 95 mph. Fellowes, accompanied by his wife, flew the Puss Moth and Clydesdale flew the Fox Moth with Shepherd of the Times and Hughes the mechanic as passengers.

After a big press send-off, during which they were "subjected to an appalling ordeal by cinema and microphone", they departed on a cold February 16th from London (Heston) heading for Paris for a lunch stop at Le Bourget. The party whose range was four and a half hours made their first overnight stop at Lyons. Having set out for Marseilles the next morning, little did they know it would take them a full week to travel the length of Italy and cross the Mediterranean to Tunis. Italy was a nightmare, the usual landing grounds after Marseilles, at Pisa or Florence were closed forcing them to stop overnight at a small un-serviced military strip at Sarzana on the coast some 70 miles

Postcard of snow covered Mt Etna collected by DFM while delayed at Catania

south of Genoa. Missing Rome, the next day's stop was Naples where their cameras were impounded and the film confiscated for photographing Mount Vesuvius from the air, (hence David McIntyre's only record of Italy is via postcards). Their cameras were later returned sealed against further use in Italy. The following day the trip to Catania in Sicily resulted in them being apprehended by the police for innocently over-flying prohibited territory. The ensuing delay forced an overnight stay and then a three-day spell of stormy weather prevented them, in spite of two at-

Shepherd and McIntyre leaning on the wing of the Gipsy Moth with two companions at Cairo for a 25 hr inspection and service of the engines.

tempts, reaching Trapani 150 miles south at the toe of Sicily until 23rd Feb. In order to get permission to leave Catania, David McIntyre is recorded as having had to convince the Commandant that the tide-line of mud on his boots from walking over this Italian airfield was much lower than that which they frequently experienced back home at Renfrew.

McIntyre in Gypsy Moth flying over the Persian Gulf from Bushire March 6th

Baghdad March 3rd. DFM has noted on the reverse "Self, Barwell, Clydesdale, Martyn" Moth G-ABZK behind

Having conducted the 150 mile Mediterranean crossing from Trapani at 60 mph due to head winds, Tunis was reached on the 24th to a warm welcome from the sun and the French Air Force officers at the airfield.

Five stops were required along the North African coastline during the legs from Tunis to Cairo where the aircraft were due to have a routine 25 hour engine service. The crews not only over-flew the Pyramids at Gisa on arrival at Cairo, but also paid them a personal visit during their 2-day stop over. David McIntyre

Baghdad March 3rd. DFM has noted on the reverse "Barwell acquires a Long Cross Country Beard" - Barwell is being dressed in the scarf by McIntyre while Clydesdale looks on.

conducted most of the navigation over the mainly featureless desert landscape and was given much praise for the accuracy of this in the absence of the normal landmarks and with the limited-scale maps they had available. He is reputed to have flown low over camel trains to see in what direction the robes of the drivers flowed to judge the relative crosswind direction. The next legs were to Amman in Transjordan and on to Baghdad via Rutba Wells. Much of the later legs were conducted in a sandstorm and it was only by flying at 100

Refuelling at Gwadar on 6th March. Fuel was delivered by donkey cart and hand poured through handkerchiefs by the pilots. DFM notes that he slept the night on two trestle tables seen here in front of the aircraft

ft above the oil pipeline that they were able to find their way. A delay in Baghdad to sort out permits allowed David McIntyre to pick up some more postcards before setting out again across the deserts of Iraq. Here more dust storms forced them to follow railway lines at 100ft and eventually they had to force land at a railway halt at Batha. They were advised by the stationmaster to move on 20 miles to Ur so David McIntyre proceeded ahead while Clydesdale in the Fox Moth waited. In half an hour David McIntyre sent a telegraph back to say that the way was safe however when Clydesdale landed, the visibility was still less than 500 yds. The next day 5th March saw the party reach Bushire on the Persian Gulf where they found the weather unexpectedly cold. An uncomfortable session with the customs officials at Bandar Abbas after refuelling from petrol drums on donkey driven carts in intense heat, convinced the party that it would be best to avoid a further stop in Persia and set off on another long leg to Gwadar in Baluchistan. That day they recorded 8hr 15mins flying time leaving them with a dusk arrival at a field 8

Clydesdale in the Fox Moth being welcomed by Fellows on arrival at Karachi after the 18day journey from London on March 7th

miles from the nearest village. An eventful night was spent sleeping under the stars, but they had managed to conjure up an evening meal and some bedding organised by a friendly official who they phoned at the Gwadar post office. The final leg to Karachi was to take only 3 hours and so the outward flight was completed on 7th March having lasted a total of 18 days. In "The Pilots' Book of Everest" there is a reference to David McIntyre's contribution to the trip from Clydesdale as follows, "His forethought and ingenuity were to be of immense value to us in the job we had in hand, and other members of the party were impressed with the wisdom of choosing him as second pilot in the course of that rather difficult journey to India".

McIntyre and Clydesdale with other members of the Everest party in the surf at Manora island

Their arrival at the civil airport at Karachi was welcomed by many people including Fellowes who had arrived first in the Puss Moth. Coincident with their arrival was the docking of the SS Dalgoma on the same day whereupon the aircraft crates were unloaded onto railway wagons and shunted along the 9 miles of railway track to the RAF depot at Drigh road where they were to be assembled and tested.

**Reconnaissance**

The first exercise for the pilots was a reconnaissance flight across India to the base camp at Purnea to check out the 1,500 mile route, which they would shortly be flying in the Everest machines. McIntyre flew the Fox Moth and Clydesdale flew his Gipsy Moth. The route was over the Sind desert through Uterlai,

Local workers at Lalbalu landing ground building canvas hangers for the Westland aircraft under supervision of Mr H.G. Came (right) District Engineer.

staying overnight on the 9th March at Jodhpur as guests of the Maharaja, and on to Delhi on the 10th where they picked up Blacker for the next leg to Alhallabad. After an overnight stay at Alhallabad hosted by Mr Justice King, they flew on to Gaya and Bhagalpur where on the

Reconnaissance party at Lalbalu on March 11th I-r, Dain, McIntyre, Etherton, Clydesdale, Came, Blacker, ?. Gipsy Moth and Fox Moth behind

11th they collected Col Etherton and flew on to the base airfield at Lalbalu, situated 9 miles east of Purnea. From Lalbalu, Clydesdale & McIntyre took the Gipsy moth on a 1 hr 40 min flight to Forbesganj to inspect the forced landing ground site, which had been chosen.

Fox Moth at Alhallabad after its 100 yd storm driven dash across the airfield in an overnight tropical storm on March 12th while returning to Karachi from Lalbalu.

This was approved and the canvas hangars and other preparations at Lalbalu were also inspected to their satisfaction.

That evening McIntyre flew the Gipsy Moth back to Bhagalpur where the party stayed the night as guests of the Commissioner, John Dain. The next morning McIntyre returned with Etherton to Purnea where the Gipsy moth was hangared at the Darbhanga

Westland Wallace G-ACBR in the final stages of assembly at the RAF Depot at Karachi

bungalow. Driving over to Lalbalu, McIntyre joined Clydesdale and Blacker as passenger and they then returned in the Fox Moth to stay the night at Alhallabad en route to Karachi. A severe tropical storm broke over the town overnight which wrecked the Fox Moth in spite of stout picketing. There was nothing then to be done other than to salvage their luggage and make the remaining 1,100 miles of the journey by train. At Delhi, Clydesdale and Blacker were able to hitch a lift from a local pilot in a Puss Moth to Karachi. David McIntyre however had to pay 100 rupees for a seat in the Royal Indian Air Mail plane amongst the mailbags, which by all accounts was a most uncomfortable journey, made worse by the overnight stop at Hyderabad. David McIntyre by the middle of the night, having been unable to sleep in a makeshift bed, awoke the pilot and persuaded him to continue the journey to Karachi in the dark arriving there as dawn was breaking.

### Karachi Flight Testing

By the time the Reconnaissance party had returned to Karachi, the Everest machines had been reassembled and were ready for flight-

Hand cranking the inertia starter of the Bristol Pegasus engine on the Wallace

testing. This was a most important period for both the pilots, who had not had any chance to familiarise themselves with the aircraft before leaving England, as well as for the aircraft and equipment. The Westland Wallace G-ACBR was first to be tested on March 15th with McIntyre & Bonnett taking the machine up to 34,000ft in a 90 minute climb where the temperature was recorded as -45 degrees C. The total flight time was 2 hrs 25 mins and equipment was working to their satisfaction. A design oversight had put heating elements in the knees of the flying suits which when wearing shorts or kneeling down caused blisters and had to be altered. David McIntyre

McIntyre and Bonnett setting out on an altitude test flight from Karachi on March 14th to 34,000ft. Men and machines reported satisfactory.

made a second short 10 min flight that day to do a rigging test with the mechanic Fletcher on board. The following day he piloted a 1hr 25 min flight with the cameramen Sydney Bonnett and Arthur Fisher on board which his log book records as a 'camera test'. At the same time Clydesdale and Blacker were conducting an altitude test in the Houston Westland PV3, G-ACAZ, which was taken up to 35,000 ft on a 3hr flight without problems. That concluded the testing at Karachi and the plans for the trip across India to Purnea were put into action.

### Indian Cross Country

The preliminary preparation was to ferry out to each stopping point on the route, a sufficient store of the specially mixed fuel needed for the Everest machines. This was conducted by Ellison and Gallimore of the Burma Shell Co

Fellows receiving a can of petrol to refuel the Puss Moth on the journey across India

in an old aircraft of the Karachi Flying Club, which was loaned to the expedition as a substitute for the Fox Moth, wrecked earlier by the storm at Alhallabad. This accident also meant that the two Westland aircraft had to carry two passengers and a load of baggage on the cross India trip. The total journey was around 1,500 miles and the fuel plane was scheduled to keep about two stops ahead of the Everest machines, which were accompanied by Fellowes in the Puss Moth with his wife and Shepherd of the Times as passengers. The RAF at Karachi had provided the expedition with 6 aircraftsmen to assist with the management of the aircraft at the base camp, and who, with the equipment and spares went on by rail.

McIntyre flew the Wallace with Bonnett and Burnard of Westland as passengers leaving on 20th March for the first stop about 1 hr away at Hyderabad. Clydesdale flew the Houston Westland with Blacker and engineer Hughes.

Refuelling the Everest machines at Hyderabad , the first stop on the 1,500 mile journey from Karachi to Purnea base camp.

Refuelling at Hyderabad did not take them long and they then headed off for the 3hr flight conducted at heights, which varied from 4,000 to 10,000ft over the wastes of the Great Indian Desert to Jodhpur where they stayed the night, hosted by the Maharaja at the old palace.

The next day took them in a little under 3 hrs to Delhi where they were to pay a call on the Viceroy to acknowledge his assistance in

McIntyre and Blacker beside their chauffer driven transport at one of the overnight stops en route across India

the preparations for the Expedition. The Viceroy inspected the Everest aircraft on the afternoon of their stay, the party having first been welcomed by their friends at the Delhi Flying Club. The party was variously accommodated by their hosts the Viceroy, the Director of Civil Aviation and the Commander in Chief.

The final day of this stage took the party from Delhi to Alhallabad for lunch having had to take care en route to avoid the hazard presented by columns of kites and vultures circling in the thermals, one of which "whizzed past apparently only a yard from our wing tip". A collision with a bird of that size

would almost certainly have been very serious if not fatal. The final leg from Alhallabad to Lalbalu took a little under 3 hrs where they arrived on 22nd March.

## Purnea Base Camp

Typical of the co-operation and assistance which they had received across India was the loan of his Purnea bungalow to the Officers of the expedition by the Maharajah of Darbhanga. A near neighbour, the Raja of Banaili, had made a fleet of cars available to the expedition, which was also of great help in the daily transport of the party to and from the airfield at Lalbalu where the Everest aircraft were housed. The Bungalow had a small landing ground adjacent to it, where the Gipsy Moth had been housed while the party was at Karachi but it proved unsuitable for regular use, being both too narrow and liable to be thronged with locals as soon as an engine was heard. Transport to the airfield 9 miles hence was conducted by car along some pretty rough roads. This would have been a journey of 1 hr 30 minutes should it have had to be done by pony cart, the standard native taxi service. The Bungalow was situated next to a golf course, across which stood the long thatched building of the Planters Club where the party were made honorary members, and where most evenings were spent.

While a swimming pool had been made available to the party by the Maharajah some 10 miles away, which doubled as the bathing pool for the locals and their elephants, it was too far away from the camp to be really useful.

The Darbhanga bungalow where the party were housed . Tents for the Aircraft Technicians were moved to the airfield 9 miles away for greater efficiency.

Swimming party at the newly prepared pool close to the airfield. DFM annotation "L-R, Rosher (agent in India), Came (District Engineer), Ellison, Shepherd, McIntyre"

David McIntyre was instrumental in encouraging Mr Came the district engineer, who enlisted the help of some local fishermen; to clear the reeds from a weed infested pool, which had been spotted behind a bank on the edge of the airfield. A diving platform was constructed from bamboo poles with a ladder to climb back up out of the water and steps were cut down the bank for access. This facility gave many hours of "amusement and

DFM supervising some construction adjustments at the diving platform.

mischief, as well as refreshment", David McIntyre being responsible for much of the mischief by all accounts. After a few days of innocent fun it was discovered that the pool had become the home of a crocodile, which was eventually shot, and the local fishermen came into use again as lookouts when bathing was taking place.

From the time of their arrival at the base camp a daily check on the suitability of the weather for the flight over Everest was monitored and for almost two weeks it proved unsuitable. The film crew took many opportunities to film the various scenes of activity around the camp and in the surrounding locality, finding the conditions of extreme heat and all pervading dust a severe trial. The only truck in the neighbourhood had been hired by the film crew who also had obtained use of a shabby motorbus for additional transport. Typical of their efforts were shots of an Elephant parade being conducted past the hangars where the Westland biplanes were housed on the airfield at Lalbalu. A contemporary report from the Glasgow Herald describes this occasion as follows: "Meanwhile the members of

A parade of Elephants passing alongside the Westland aircraft hangers at Lalbalu. The aircraft being parked outside for the occasion.

the Expedition are allowing themselves a respite from their strenuous preparations. Today they took part in picturesque scenes, the oriental flavour of which was enhanced by gaily caparisoned elephants and weirdly attired Santhals (aboriginal tribesmen), who evinced the keenest interest in the sound filming of exercise flights. Santhal women, dressed in vivid red and green with paper flowers in their jet black tresses, and men with green leaves behind their ears joined in folk dance to the accompaniment of drums, cymbals, and bamboo flutes. Seven elephants, carrying on their

Geoffrey Barcas with his film crew on the back of a truck on the airfield at Lalbalu. The aircraft canvas hangars can be seen in the distance.

Westland Wallace being wheeled out onto the flying field at Lalbalu under the watchful eye of some local inhabitants

backs gold and silver howdahs, headed the procession. They were followed by Santhal tribesmen bearing bows and arrows and dancing a wild war dance as they moved along."

Meanwhile the mechanics kept a daily vigil on the status of the aircraft subjected to swings of temperature of 20 degrees C or more and the need for protection from the ever-present

Clydesdale and McIntyre standing at the wing tip of the Wallace while parked at the airstrip at Lalbalu.

dust. There were also frequent tropical storms with fierce hail, which created havoc on the Hangar tents, which were far from new, and every few days required new rents to be stitched back together. The RAF mechanics camped at the airfield were also flooded out by thunderstorms on a number of occasions but as they had been able to rig up a small generator were able to furnish themselves with electric light not available elsewhere in the village or the bungalow and so maintained their morale. David McIntyre during one flood, undertook to assist an injured pony whose

owner could not afford to help and finished up having to be shot by the local vet whom he had paid 6 shillings to attend to. He was subsequently ribbed by the crew for having spent 6 shillings on a meal for the vultures who quickly reduced the beast to a bleached skeleton.

David McIntyre's log book shows only one flight in the Westland Wallace between arrival at Lalbalu and the 1st Everest flight and this was a flight to check all was okay after a 25hr engine service needed after the journey from Karachi. There were a large number of photos of the aircraft taken during this flight preparation period and there are accounts of a number of flights to satisfy the needs of the film crew who required continuity shots to be mixed in with the shots of the Everest flight itself. The film included scenes for fuelling the aircraft, starting the engines, loading the oxygen cylinders and camera equipment ready for the Everest flight on the day itself.

The planning of each day's potential flight over Everest sometimes took place outside the Bungalow at Purnea and required the input from the meteorologist Mr Gupta for whom a met station was built where he could set up his theodolite and balloon equipment. The theodolite was used to track and measure the progress of hydrogen filled met balloons as they rose into the upper air giving a wind speed measurement at the higher altitudes. They were used in conjunction with daily weather reports telegraphed through from Calcutta to predict the following days likelihood of a flight. Early each morning Air Com-

The Wallace in its hangar being prepared for flight. It took about 20mins to get the aircraft out of the canvas hanger and onto the field.

modore Fellowes would take the Puss Moth up to an altitude where he could see the distant Everest range and report on the extent of cloud cover over the mountain. On his return these findings, together with the met reports and local wind speed recordings, would be considered and a decision reached whether or not the flight could proceed. An initial assessment had been made that a flight should not be undertaken if the wind speed at the summit was above 40mph, but during the

Clydesdale with Gypsy Moth and elephant on a visit to home of Raja Banaili to provide a flying display for his tea party guests.

first ten days or so at Lalbalu it had never been less than 100mph.

The Gipsy Moth and Puss Moth aircraft were used for general transport and David McIntyre's log book shows him flying the Gipsy Moth to Bhagalpur on two occasions before the 1st Everest flight, once to collect the District Engineer, Mr Came, and on another to collect the District Commissioner Mr Dain, to visit the camp at Lalbalu. These journeys were often made in rain, wind and low cloud forcing him to fly low over marshlands where an emergency landing would have been hazardous. Ellison and Clydesdale also made the occasional trip away from base during this period.

The party were able to repay some of the generosity shown by the Rajah of Banaili when they attended a tea party at his estate nearby, which he had arranged for his guests. Here they performed an aerobatic display in the Moths for the entertainment of the assembled company. Another overnight trip was made to visit the Maharaja of Darbhanga who, since there was no landing ground near his estate, had one constructed on an adjacent paddy

field so that the party could land. There they were entertained to a lavish banquet having first been paraded through the estate in a procession of the Maharaja's 40 elephants.

After 12 days of waiting, the persistent storm period broke and on the 3rd of April, conditions were at last favourable.

## First Everest Flight

This account of the first flight is reprinted from David McIntyre's own hand-written (unedited) notes: -

*"The morning of the 3rd of April saw us all up and scurrying about the bungalow at daybreak. Air Commodore Fellowes left after a hasty breakfast for the aerodrome in order that he might make an early recce flight in the Puss Moth and be back with his results by the time we had the aircraft out and prepared for the big flight. Gupta had released a balloon with the first glimmer of daylight but unfortunately had lost it in the dust haze before it had reached a useful height.*

*We saw him working on his second balloon as we passed on our way to the aerodrome. Silhouetted against the dawn with his eye glued to his theodolite, surrounded by his assistants who were writing down the readings as he shouted them out. It took a balloon something like an hour and a half to reach 35,000 ft so a car had been left to rush him out to Lalbalu with the completed wind findings. We bumped down those nine miles of shady but dusty track, each clutching a camera or one of the more delicate instruments in an endeavour to make our bodies absorb as much of the shock from the bumpy track as possible before mounting the delicate mechanisms.*

*The ground staff were already busy on the aircraft on our arrival. The canvas hangers were open and the machines were being manhandled out onto the aerodrome. The bottles of oxygen were carefully placed in their stowage and connected to the complicated system. The great vertical cameras were fitted and tested. Aircraft and engines inspected and tested in every detail, all ready to start up and away on the word go. Pilots and Observers fussed around their equipment, trying on oxygen masks they had tried on many times before. Adjusting straps, heating*

Houston Westland being refuelled outside hanager. Special leaded fuel was carried in drums seen here on the ground and hand pumped into the aircraft.

cables and oxygen feed pipes that were already adjusted to a nicety. Rechecked the carefully planned navigation allowing for the increasing wind speeds at varying heights.

Everyone trying to keep themselves occupied during that tense half hour of waiting for the recce machine to return. There had been so much preparation for the flight, and there was still so much of the unknown about it, that crews could not avoid being slightly affected by the general excitement. Waiting is always unpleasant and everyone was relieved to see the Puss Moth diving down through the dust haze.

At the same moment a dust covered car swung through between the stalwart Indian guards at the aerodrome entrance bringing Gupta and the high altitude wind findings. A hurried conference was held in the shade under the wing of the Puss Moth. The AC brought useful news though he had been unable to climb above the dust haze, he had been able to see the mountains dimly though the top of the haze in a cloudless sky.

This was splendid; Gupta's news was not so good. He had found the wind to be 67mph at 28,000ft. We were not supposed to go if the wind was greater than 40mph but this was the first time we had found the wind below 100mph. We worked it out and found that if we spent not more than 15 minutes at the mountain the wind of 67mph would allow us to get back on our petrol endurance. We might wait for days and not get another opportunity especially with the monsoons due to arrive anytime now. The AC weighed up the whole position and gave the word 'GO'.

Struggling into our heated clothing required time and care. It was necessary to go slowly to avoid perspiring, as this would have added to the cold and discomfort over Everest. First the heavy wind, water and fireproof flying suit lined with electrical heating elements over which we drew on the boots also with heating elements along the soles, up the legs and connected to the suit by a plug and socket at the knee. The headgear gave more trouble with its many leads and connections.

A leather helmet with earphones padded over the ears, goggles surrounded by a fur mask and having tiny electrical elements placed between two layers of triplex glass to prevent ice forming and obscuring the vision, and then the worst and most important of all a great heavy oxygen mask with a metal combined microphone and oxygen feed. This had looked rather like a nosebag and had to fit tight over nose, mouth and chin. It covered over the fur mask on the goggles and had a flap, which came round and under the chin to be held firmly by the helmet strap.

It was all intensely uncomfortable and made it almost impossible to move the head without displacing some vital part of the equipment. The three cables from the telephone, microphone and goggles were led round the back of the head, through the shoulder strap and plugged into sockets on the breast of the flying suit. The flexible metal oxygen feed pipe was led over the back of the helmet, anchored to the shoulders and led under the pilots right arm to a bayonet mount on the dashboard where it would be in easy view. All electrical leads from boots, gloves, goggles, telephones and microphone were led

Clydesdale. Fellowes (with long scarf), McIntyre and Blacker discuss the weather situation on the return of Fellowes having completed his daily high altitude cloud survey in the Puss Moth

down through the suit to two multiple plugs on each side and were attached to sockets abreast of the pilots seat in the aircraft.

Meantime the enormous Pegasus engines were started and the crews climbed on board. The Everest mail was placed in 'Akbar', a few last minute instructions from the AC and then we were off. The course was set on 342 degrees and the machines climbed slowly until they were over the Nepalese border east of Hogratha, gradually the visibility decreased as we climbed up through the dust haze. At 16,000ft the plains were invisible and we could just see the foothills looming up through the dust particles. Clydesdale and McIntyre had arranged that at this height we should have satisfied ourselves that aircraft and equipment were working perfectly and to signal to each other that every-

David McIntyre— ready for the first Everest flight

Pilots and Observers getting dressed in the equipment tent with Etherton looking on prior to first Everest flight

thing was in order to go ahead. McIntyre was a little doubtful about his survey camera control but he signalled the OK to Clydesdale and was relieved to receive an OK in return.

At 19,000ft we suddenly came out over the top of the dust haze. It was absolutely level at 19,000ft and it appeared as though we were peering over the edge of a tremendous round table of brown ground glass and at the opposite end of the table about fifty miles away two virgin white peaks were peering over at us. Makalu clear and dazzling in its snowy whiteness and Everest with its long plume stretching past Makalu and away to the east. We were now in the strong westerly and we continued to climb heading well to the west of Everest. As we rose, the table became smaller and more peaks appeared over the other side until suddenly the table became the horizon and all the Himala-

yan peaks above 19,000ft sticking through its surface.

The altimeter was now showing 30,000ft and we should be somewhere over Komaltar, the trig point in the Arun valley which was to be the start of our survey. However it was impossible see down through the haze and we had to make a rough guess at the starting point and trust that the filters on the survey cameras would penetrate through the dust.

Clydesdale climbing aboard the Houston Westland for the first Everest flight

Clydesdale's machine seemed to be climbing rather better than McIntyre's probably due to Bonnet's heavier cine camera and film. He was gradually being left behind and below. Everest loomed closer and as we passed to the right of Chamlang it seemed to tower above us. We began to realise that we should have started to climb sooner but we reckoned we would clear the summit by perhaps a thousand feet. The wind was obviously much stronger than we had been told. The plume from Everest was streaking away over the twelve-mile range to Makalu at hurricane speed. We were approaching Lhotse the southern most peak of Everest when McIntyre realised that the aircraft did not

Wallace appearing above the dust haze with Everest in the distance

Houston Westland with Clydesdale and Blacker on board in the foreground, McIntyre and Bonnett in the Westland Wallace behind prior to taking off on the first Everest Flight

appear to be climbing just as well. McIntyre though heading to the left of Everest found himself being blown onto Makalu, which had been level with him, a moment ago but which now appeared to be a thousand feet above him. A hasty glance at the altimeter showed a steady decrease in height when there should have been a steady increase.

We were in a down rush of air and though the machine was climbing well it was being carried down many times faster than it could climb. 3,000ft it lost before the down rush cushioned itself on the glacier bed. We were in a most serious position, the great mass of Everest towering above us to the left, jagged Makalu downwind to the right and the connecting range dead ahead with a hurricane wind doing its best to dash us on to the shear knife edge sides of Makalu. Hemmed in on all sides although there was air space behind us, it was impossible to turn back. To turn to the left meant going back into the down current and the peaks below. To turn downwind to the right

would have taken us instantaneously into Makalu at 200 mph. There was nothing we could do but climb straight ahead and hope to clear the lowest point in the barrier range. The machine was almost on its absolute ceiling and very tricky to handle. The slightest error in flying meant a loss of height and there was very little control. With the aircraft headed almost straight into wind we crabbed sideways onto the ridge. A fortunate wind swirl arrived just at the edge of the ridge and we scraped over with a few feet clearance.

Once over we had a view straight down the sheer range face into the glacier cradling the base of Everest. Everest still towered above and we had to turn carefully towards it and over the ridge again, this time with a little more height and face the same flight all over again to avoid being blown back onto Makalu on the one hand and yet having to approach dangerously close to it in order to have sufficient space for a slow gentle turn and at the same time avoid meeting that fatal down draft. Naturally it was impossible to see the down draft, one had to try and imagine its swirls and position from the topography. McIntyre swallowed hard before deciding to risk that turn towards the down rush and crab

Approaching the summit of Everest from the South East

over the ridge once more. Three times we had to repeat this performance before we reckoned we had sufficient height to venture round the north side of Everest and over the top.

All this time Bonnett was working hard at his cine cameras, making the most of the wonderful opportunities afforded by this close encounter with the mountain. McIntyre often wondered if Bonnett fully appreciated the position. They have never discussed it but it is almost unbelievable that a man could carry on working his camera and watch the highest mountain in the world rushing straight at him. From future action one could believe him capable of this coolness. As we swept round the north of Everest and swung to the left to come over the top he went below in order to have a full camera for the summit. While crouched down in the cockpit he unfortunately placed his right foot on his oxygen pipe and on rising pulled and fractured the pipe near the connection.

The first he knew of it was that he had weakened to such an extent that he could not

Summit of Everest through the plume as the aircraft struggles to gain height in downdraft and needing to clear the North East ridge on the right.

support the weight of his camera. He sank down onto the floor and with his remaining consciousness felt for the leakage and bound a handkerchief over the fracture. He made another valiant attempt to struggle up into the slipstream with his heavy camera but there was not sufficient oxygen to support the effort. He collapsed into unconsciousness on the floor. McIntyre saw him slip below and decided to lose height as quickly as possible after registering the summit of Everest on the survey clip. (We slipped over some five hundred feet above it). To counteract his anxiety about Bonnett, McIntyre was relieved to see Clydesdale's ma-

Clydesdale circles the summit of Everest—no sign of Mallory or Irvine

chine on the north side of the mountain. This was the first time he had seen the other machine since they were separated by the down draft. As McIntyre turned he saw it clear the top of the mountain on a southerly course.

A hurried glance at the summit before it disappeared under the aircraft showed a tiny platform that appeared to have standing room for about four men. As McIntyre was saying to himself "well we are over but what a failure from a survey point of view" when he felt freezingly cold about the nose and mouth and imagined that the oxygen heating had broken down.

This was serious as it was only a matter of time until the water content froze and stopped the flow. Actually the complete nose piece carrying the combined microphone and oxygen feed had dropped from the mask and was lying in his lap. He quickly tried to stick it back in position but found this impossible.

The first sixty miles of the return flight was most unpleasant, holding the his oxygen feed against the mask with one hand, flying with the other and at the same time regulate engine temperature, oxygen flow and altitude control, Bonnett lying unconscious or dead in the cabin and trying to lose height faster than was safe to see if the figure of Bonnett would come to life again with the lower altitude, not a movement until we were over Forbesganj at 8,000ft."

Both aircraft returned together with Blacker taking many photos of the retreating mountains before descending again into the dust haze, and by the time that they reached Forbesganj at 8,000ft, the natural oxygen content of the air had allowed Bonnett to recover, much to David McIntyre's relief. Once back at the airfield and the debriefing

Etherton, Clydesdale, Fellowes, McIntyre, Bonnett discuss the outcome of the first Everest flight on arrival. Blacker is still in the Houston Westland behind, unloading the reels of film and equipment.

had been completed, David McIntyre lost no time removing what he described as his *"abominable flying suit"* and diving into the swimming pool.

The following day David McIntyre flew the Puss Moth with Mr Rosher their agent to Dum Dum airfield at Calcutta to have the two rolls of survey photographs processed by the Indian Air Survey Co. These were developed and they returned with the news that, as suspected, the film was of no use for survey purposes.

## Kangchenjunga

With the failure of the Survey cameras on the 1st flight, the primary objective of the mission was unachieved and as the weather was suitable, a second high altitude flight was authorised to adjust and test the survey cameras in operating conditions prior to a 2nd attempt on Everest. On 4th April while David McIntyre was en-route to Calcutta with the survey film, Fellowes flying the Houston Westland and Ellison flying the Wallace with Fisher and Bonnett as camera crew, set off for the 3hr round trip to the Kangchenjunga massif which lay some 100 miles east of Everest. This target was chosen, as it did not require a flight over Nepal, over which the expedition only had permission for 2 flights. Neither pilot had flown these aircraft much before nor had they had experience of the use of the flying suits or oxygen equipment. The mountain, which had been clear of cloud during the early part of the

flight, became increasingly cloud covered as they approached and prevented any photography over the mountain peak but had permitted the checks to be conducted on the survey cameras, which had proved satisfactory. Fellowes and Ellison while circling the mountain peak experienced some severe turbulence and narrowly avoided a mid air collision which resulted in their becoming separated. Ellison returned to Lalbalu at the expected hour but there was no sign of Fellowes who had returned on an incorrect heading and was committed to a forced landing next to a railway halt some 60 miles East of Purnea due to shortage of fuel. He was able to telegraph his whereabouts back to base and the aircraft was recovered without any damage. This incident however alarmed the Committee in London and resulted in an embargo being imposed preventing the expedition from conducting another Everest flight. In spite of many protests they had been unable to get the sanction lifted.

Houston Westland on the Kangchenjunga flight

## Second Everest Flight

Notwithstanding the embargo, the Pilots were determined not to leave without achieving the purpose of the mission and persuaded the Air Commodore, who was laid low with a fever, to allow a final high altitude flight for the benefit

Distant view of the Houston Westland as it approaches the Kangchenjunga range. Cloud build up over the summit already becoming evident.

of the film crew but remaining within gliding distance of the base airfield. Thus empowered and unable to wait any longer due to the imminent recovery of Fellows, they embarked on the 2nd flight on 19th April unannounced to all but the few essential crew members. The day had produced a met balloon wind speed estimate of 110 mph at 34,000 ft against the aircraft's maximum air speed of 120 mph and a preliminary high altitude aerial cloud cover survey as would had been done in normal circumstances was out of the question.

From the experience of the first flight David McIntyre determined to do something about the cumbersome headgear and chose to fly without the heated goggles and special oxygen mask but rather use a smaller oxygen mask and no goggles. He also had taken particular care to ensure that his vertical survey camera was in perfect condition. Building on the experience of the first flight he had conceived a strategy which routed them at 2,000 ft for 100 miles heading to the west of Everest where at this low altitude the wind would be less of a struggle and then they would climb rapidly after turning right directly towards the mountain to the north east with the increasingly strong west wind on their port beam.

The day was unhelpful as a cloud layer of unknown depth covered the route as they headed westwards. Although it was not as far west as they had intended Clydesdale elected to start his climb when he saw a sufficient gap in the cloud to avoid the risk of ice accumulation and was surprised to find that he had reached 18,000 ft before they broke clear into the sunshine and spectacular mountain scenery. He judged that it would be possible to get a survey strip over the last 20 miles to Everest

and made the decision to continue.

Oxygen, which was now in short supply, was not switched on until 21,000ft had been reached. By the time they reached 31,000ft, the cloud below had cleared at about 30 miles from the summit of Everest and they were able to set the survey cameras running. It was becoming increasingly difficult to combat the drift downwind to the east while at the same time attempting to make headway to the north towards the mountain, but at a range of 15 miles McIntyre, positioned a little behind and west of the Houston Westland, was able to let Fisher obtain what were to become the classic photos of the Everest flight.

Clydesdale at this point had a problem with the heater plug of his oxygen system and had to call up a screwdriver from Blacker his observer to spread the pins and secure the plug. While this was being dealt with, the momentary distraction caused him to drift too far east to maintain a course to the summit without getting under the lee downdraft so with about 3 miles or so to go he broke off the course to the summit and headed for a turn towards Makalu and home. McIntyre meanwhile battled on towards the summit electing to stay on course rather than follow Clydesdale but with the increasing wind strength at 34,000 ft was barely making headway. He succeeded in reaching the summit with his survey camera still running and by keeping a steady return course while descending through the 15,000 ft thick cloud layer, eventually reached Lalbalu 3hr 50mins after take-off.

This account of the second flight is reprinted from David McIntyre's own handwritten (unedited) notes:-

*"Our Committee at home and our backer Lady Houston at this time became very concerned about our safety and many wires were received instructing our leader to prohibit a second flight over Everest. Many depressing meetings were held and our leader had decided that he could not ignore these instructions and gave the orders to pack up our equipment and prepare for the return home.*

*This meant the almost complete failure of the Expedition and the loss of putting into practice the valuable experience gained on the first flight. All our careful training and lengthy* preparations were to be thrown away on the orders of a few people who were at too great a distance to realise the actual conditions. The air became surcharged with conspiracy. Pilots and Observers could be seen whispering in the mango groves outside the Residence, at other times deep in thought in odd corners - failure weighing heavily on their young shoulders. Guy Fawkes would have found us splendid companions at that time. The whole place fairly reeked of a gunpowder plot. Fortunately an ill wind came along and struck our gallant leader down with fever and as he lay sick-a-bed a conspiracy took shape and form. Clydesdale, McIntyre and Blacker decided that if we sneaked off on a second flight while the AC (Air Commodore Fellowes) lay ill we would be guilty of gross insubordination but reckoned that we could live

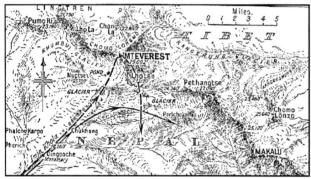

Map showing detail tracks of the aircraft on the 2nd Everest flight. McIntyre in the Wallace is on the left, Clydesdale in the Houston Westland on the right.

that down in time. Shepherd was called in to give his opinion on the conspiracy and agreed that this insubordination would remove all blame and responsibility from the AC and provided we returned safely, there was very little they could do to us on our return home. Moreover we all felt the AC would be quite pleased unofficially to hear on his recovery that we had made a second flight and crowned the Expedition with success.

We warned the troops to have the machines prepared for a final high altitude camera test and prepared our equipment in the greatest secrecy. In India the very furniture has ears and we were frightened news of our intentions might leak through to the servants or Mrs Fellowes who was nursing her husband the AC. We had a grim time wondering, which would improve first, the weather or the AC. On the 17th it looked like the weather, on the 18th the AC showed a very definite improvement and we

were forced to take a chance on the 19th. Bonnett very generously offered to forego his position in McIntyre's machine in favour of Fisher our second cine operator observer.

We stealthily crept out of the bungalow at daybreak on the 19th and made our way down to Lalbalu feeling rather ashamed of ourselves. Everything was ready on our arrival with the exception of McIntyre's survey camera. After its failure on the first flight he had insisted on looking after it himself. He had satisfied himself that it was working perfectly in every detail, taken it down to the machine and tested it in the aircraft then carefully wrapping it up in silk and paper and locked it up in a vermin and dust proof steel uniform trunk alongside the aircraft.

He particularly considered the survey photography to be the cream of the whole expedition and was determined there should be no repetition of the failure on the first flight. That he attributed to the bumping of the cameras to and from the bungalow and too many people handling it. He even went to the extent of setting approximate drift and switching on the main controls before leaving the ground in order to remove the necessity of his observer even touching it during the flight, His theory was proved correct as his Williamson Eagle III was the only one to give a perfect unbroken survey strip. As it was all ready, it was fitted to ACBR in a few moments and the machines were ready for the second attempt on the secret places of Everest.

It was a rather foolhardy attempt, the necessary secrecy had prevented our usual careful preparation and the AC's rapid recovery from fever forced us to make an attempt in almost impossible wind conditions. That morning our Met Officer Mr Gupta had managed to follow a balloon to 24,000ft and observed the wind to be 88mph from N.W. From previous experience we realised that this was likely to give a wind of about 120mph at 34,000ft. In fact a headwind equal to the speed of our aircraft, which meant we would be stationary at that height and unable to make any progress directly towards the mountain. Also tremendous down currents unless we kept well above the mountain.

Eventually we worked out all the possibilities and reckoned that instead of making an obvi-

Nearing Everest on 2nd flight. Much higher wind strength causing longer plume over the summit around 20 miles distant.

*ously futile attempt to fly straight to Everest, if we flew at right angles to Everest, due West near the ground taking advantage of the Easterly surface wind, for 100 miles and then climb steeply heading well to the West of Everest on a Northerly course, the strong upper wind would carry us back the 100 miles we had come West and at the same time the aircraft would have made sufficient forward progress Northerly to bring us crabwise over Everest at least 5,000ft above it.*

*It took a great deal of careful and complicated calculation, working with assumed wind speed and direction, which was increasing rapidly at height until it equalled the airspeed of the machines at 34.000ft. At the end of our workings we were all surprised and delighted to find that using this strategy we could just do it inside our fuel and oxygen range. Another difficulty that beset us was the fact that the country from the foothills north was covered by an enormous cloud bank extending up to 18,000ft. This meant that when we turned to come home from Everest we would be faced with 100 miles of flight over clouds with nothing to guide us and at the end of this sea of cloud the almost featureless plains of Bohar and somewhere Lalbalu. If we were going to reach Ever-*

*est there would be no petrol to spare for anything except a straight course back to Lalbalu. All this had to be considered before we started. We approximated a wind speed and direction to cover the enormous changes of speed and direction we would meet as we lost height on the return journey and fixed on a definite compass course for the return flight. This we noted in large figures as something we could concentrate on, as one could not be certain how the mind would act after a prolonged effort at height. We had already seen the effect of what we termed*

David McIntyre piloting G-ACBR approaching Everest on the second flight.

The classic view of the Everest flight showing Clydesdale in the Houston Westland as the aircraft approach to 12 miles from the summit

*high altitude baby mindedness. All this settled, we untruthfully warned the ground staff that our camera test might last until near the end of our endurance. We climbed into the aircraft for the second flight, Clydesdale and Blacker as before in the leading machine 'Lucy' and McIntyre and Fisher in 'Akbar'.*

*The morning was beautiful as we took off. The heat of the sun was making a slight haze against which a fresh Easterly breeze was fighting. We flew down this breeze passing low over the maidan and the crocodile infested Losi River. Ahead stretched that no mans land South of the Nepalese border, to our right lay the threatening cloud layer, towering up to 18,000 ft and obscuring the foothills.*

*We made good speed on the low Westerly track and turned north in a steep climb over the edge of the cloud layer. Near Chileutar again we were doomed not to see that great extent of the mountains south of Everest. Everything below 18,000 ft was buried in cloud and everything above stood out in dazzling clearness,*

*bright reflection from the clouds on brighter frozen snow covered peaks making the sky a peculiar dark blue in comparison. As we came closer to Everest we appeared to come on a strange new land. When thirty miles away the country was mostly above the cloud sea and we prepared to start the cameras. After starting the camera mechanism McIntyre moved over to the left of the leading machine to allow Fisher to obtain an excellent photograph with the leading machine in the foreground and Everest towering ahead of it fifteen miles away. We had required to keep altering our course farther and still farther to the left as the wind threatened to carry us to the down wind side of Everest and once there we could not have fought our way back.*

*At twelve miles distance the leading machine suddenly turned right and disappeared down wind in an incredibly short time. McIntyre was left undecided whether to break off and follow his leader and his duty or continue the survey of the mountain. Some instincts are stronger than a sense of duty and when they are the outcome*

| Date and Hour. | Aeroplane Type and No. | Pilot | Passenger(s) | Time | Height | Course | REMARKS |
|---|---|---|---|---|---|---|---|
| | WALLACE | | hv. | | | Tabbali hv. Everest | |
| 3·4·33 | G. ABCR | Self | Bennett | 3·10 | cor. 30.000 | Tabbali. | First hr Everest Flight |
| 4·4·33 | PUSS MOTH G. ABNZ MOTH III | | hv. Kosher | 5·20 | | Tabbali. Dum Dum Tabbali. | To Calcutta. To have Survey film developed by Indian Air Survey Co. |
| 13·4·33 | G. AB2K | | cal. Ecklerton | 1·00 | | Tabbali. Darbhanga. | |
| 13·4·33 | G. AB2K | | - | 1·30 | | Darbhanga. Tabbali. | |
| 18·4·33 | G. AB2K | Flt/o Clydesdale | Self | 1·10 | | Tabbali Darbhanga. | |
| 14·4·33 | G. AB2K | Self | | 1·20 | | Darbhanga. Tabbali. | |
| 14·4·33 | G. AB2K | | | 1·00 | | Tabbali Darbhanga | |
| 14·4·33 | G. AB2K | | hv. Shepherd | 1·10 | | Darbhanga Tabbali. | |
| 15·4·33 | WALLACE G. ABCR | | hv. Bennett | 1·00 | | Tabbali. Tabbiarpanj & Return | Photographic Flight |
| 18·4·33 | PUSS MOTH G. ABNZ | | L.A.C. Young | ·20 | | Tabbali. | Local. |
| 19·4·33 | WALLACE G. ABCR | | hv. Fisher | 3·50 | cor 34.500 | Tabbali. hv Everest Tabbali. | Second hr Everest Flight |
| 20·4·33 | PUSS MOTH G. ABNZ | | cal. Eckerton | 1·60 | | Darjeeling & Return | Photographic Flight |
| 20·4·33 | W. WESTLAND G. ACAZ | | L.A.C. Hensley | ·30 | | Tabbali | Formation |
| 20·4·33 | WALLACE G. ACBR | | hv. Commophis | ·10 | | Tabbali | Formation |
| 20·4·33 | G. ACBR | | Commophis L.A.C. Young hv. Bain | ·20 | | Tabbali | Formation |
| 24·4·33 | PUSS MOTH G. ABNZ | | Dr. Bennett Maj. Ben. Police | 1·10 | | Tabbali Baghalpur & Return | |
| 24·4·33 | G. ABNZ MOTH III | | hv. Camp | 1·10 | | Baghalpur & Return | |
| 26·4·33 | G. AB2K | | Camp | 1·00 | | Forbespanj & Return | |
| 27·4·33 | G. AB2K | | cal. Eckerton | 1·00 | | Tabbali. Darbhanga | |
| 27·4·33 | G. AB2K | | cal. Eckerton | 1·25 | | Darbhanga - Hathwa. | |
| 28·4·33 | G. AB2K | | cal. Eckerton | 2·15 | | Hathwa Lucknow | |

of months of concentrated training they naturally take the lead. McIntyre decided to push on towards the mountain, altering course even more to the left and being blown even more to the right. The altimeter was now reading 37,000 ft and in his amended headgear he was feeling more or less comfortable. Small oxygen mask was doing well and perfect vision without goggles. Everest still appeared to the right of the nose and an odd glance away from the instruments showed the enormous pinnacle of the world, the bright morning sun glinting on the frozen snow showing the darkness of the great cliff faces, some of them a sheer 8,000ft and more, into strong relief.

The machine appeared to be making no headway and loosing ground rapidly to the right. The next fifteen minutes was a grim struggle. The great peak with its enormous plume swirling and streaking away to the South East at 120 mph seemed to be almost underneath us and refusing to get right underneath. Gradually it disappeared under the nose and McIntyre determined to hold the present compass course until just over the mountain. Petrol was getting low and there would not be suffi-

cient to go beyond Everest. It was out of sight 5,000 ft beneath the aircraft for what seemed to be an incredible time. Quick anxious glances behind to see if we had passed over then suddenly an enormous bump. Just one colossal impact such as one might get flying low over an explosives factory as it blew up. We were thankful for the strength of the Westland aircraft. It felt as if the wings should snap off at the roots but a hurried look round showed every wire tight - no slackness anywhere. It was a relief in a way

Survey frame showing summit of Everest taken from the Wallace on 2nd flight.

The last lingering look at Everest and Makalu from the Houston Westland on the homeward journey with the impenetrable cloud layer to negotiate ahead

*as it indicated the summit and with a sigh of relief, McIntyre started a gentle careful turn to the right and settled the compass on the predetermined course for home. He had grave doubts that insufficient allowance had been made for the wind but knowing how incapable the mind is of rational reasoning at altitude, he decided not to alter it.*

*The great spans of Makalu which had been such a frightening time on the first flight slipped past on our left. Chamlang with its many glacier beds was left behind on the right and straight ahead a seemingly endless sea of clouds. Loosing height gradually until we were brushing the billowing cloud mass wondering if we would be able to recognise our position when we came to the plains. Unfortunately we came out over featureless country with nothing to recognise but sandy scrub covered hills and dry riverbeds. McIntyre tried to check up on his drift and found he was steering too much to the right. Altered course 5° and decided to carry on holding that course until he either recognised his position or got down to his last 10 gallons of fuel. He came to a winding muddy river which he felt certain must be the Kosi but as it had been known to alter its course as much as 30 miles from year to year, he paid no attention and hung on grimly to the compass course. Then a tiny village appeared ahead and to his relief he recognised it as Darana, a village he had passed over in a tropical thunderstorm on his way back from Darbhanga a few days before. This made us about 15miles west of Lalbalu and we joyfully turned east and flew low back to Lalbalu to discover that the leading*

*machine had arrived back some twenty minutes before us. We had made our gamble against disobedience and had succeeded. All that remained was to develop and print our survey strip to see if the expedition was complete and had justified itself."*

## Survey Results

After their return, the Pilots and Observers spent an anxious afternoon and evening waiting for the survey film to be developed. Due to the unscheduled nature of the flight it was decided to process them in the dark room, which had been established in the bungalow and where aircraftsman Fraser had been expertly processing all the expedition's photographs. Both reels of 125 frames were successful and at last justified the whole expedition and the many risks taken to obtain them.

They had some good fortune with the survey results, for Clydesdale's camera jammed at a point 5 miles west of Makalu at the very

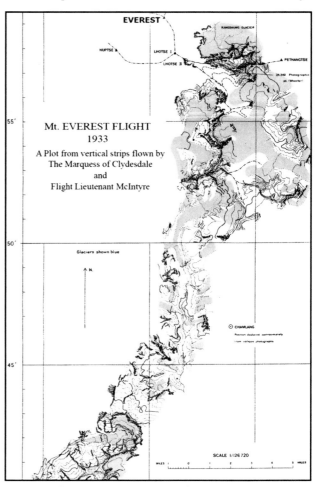

Map created from vertical survey photos of the 2nd Everest flight. Green areas are glaciers.

same spot where McIntyre's film ran out. This allowed the two strips to be joined up and be accurately positioned, giving excellent results. Two new glaciers were identified and had to be transposed onto the maps, which previously had been incorrect.

One feature which caught McIntyre's attention was the evidence of a hot lake at 18,090 ft and he proposed that this should be named Loch Everest to leave a permanent reminder of the Scottish connection with its discovery. The suggestion was however thought likely to mislead and was in conflict with the normal practice of using native language names. In the event the Nepalaese Government named it Parvati Tal (the Lady of the Mountains) in recognition of Lady Houston's patronage.

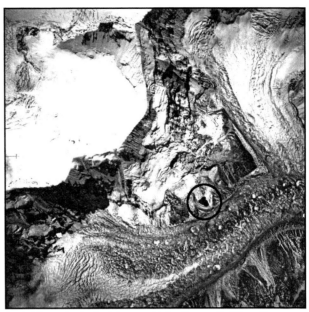

Vertical frame showing hot lake located below the summit of Lhotse II

Many telegrams of congratulation were received to add to those at the time of the 1st flight including one from Sir John Salmond, Marshal of the Royal Air Force, that provided tacit official approval of their constructive insubordination.

**Return Across India**

Once the 2nd flight was completed David McIntyre's log book shows that the following day was spent flying Col Etherton to Darjeeling in the Puss Moth where a filming session had been scheduled, and taking some of the aircraft mechanics who had supported the flight (LAC Helmsley, LAC Young and TD Connachie of the film crew) on sightseeing trips in the Wallace and Houston Westland, to a height above the dust haze where the Himalayas could be seen in all their splendour. The Everest machines were then flown back to Karachi by Clydesdale & Ellison to be crated up and shipped back to Westlands at Yeovil.

David McIntyre, meanwhile, supervised the packing up of the camp at Lalbalu while waiting for Etherton to return from Darjeeling. In that period he recorded having made a couple of journeys to Bhagalpur in the Puss Moth ferrying the Commissioner Mr Dain, Dr Bennett and the District Engineer, Mr Came back to their headquarters. On the 26th he flew the Gipsy Moth with Mr Came to Forbesganj for a crocodile shoot and also to decommission

the emergency landing ground, which they had established there.

On April 27th David McIntyre left Purnea for the last time in the Gipsy Moth with Etherton as passenger in the company of Fellows and his wife in the Puss Moth. They travelled to Darbhanga, Hathwa, Lucknow, Dolphur and Agra, paying their respects to, and being feted by, the local dignitaries. On the next leg to Jodphur they encountered a fierce dust storm and had to beat a hasty retreat back to Agra arriving just in time to shelter the Moth and were forced to stay the night. Jodhpur was reached the next day where they were again hosted by the Maharaja. David McIntyre's log book records a reception, a swimming party and visits to several palaces.

Next stop was Udaipur where Boar versus Tiger fights were witnessed. This location clearly became cemented in David McIntyre's memory for in his personal correspondence to his fiancée he describes a dream in which they both visited this most attractive city. They then flew on to Karachi on 2nd May were David McIntyre had to wait for his permit for the return flight through Persia until May 5th. Here his time was spent mainly bathing at Manora island and packing up the remaining heavy luggage for return shipment home.

Composite Infra red panorama of Everest and Makalu taken from 100 mile range at 21,000 ft on afternoon of 19th April after 2nd Everest flight. Note afternoon cloud build up.

### Return Journey Home

The prospect of better weather during May, when the return journey was scheduled, enabled them to obtain insurance for the shorter route through the Balkans. This had not been the case at the time of the outward journey in February when they were restricted to the longer Mediterranean crossing to Tripoli. On this part of the journey David McIntyre was accompanied by Ellison who was returning home from his RAF posting in India and they flew Clydesdale's Gipsy Moth in the company of Fellowes and his wife flying in the Puss Moth.

They departed from Karachi for Gwadar on 6th May, had a snack lunch and flew on to Bandar Abbas where they stayed overnight at the British Consul's house and bathed in the Persian Gulf. The next day they flew for 11hrs stopping for fuel at Bushire and Basra along the Persian gulf before landing at Hinaida in Iraq having had to overfly Baghdad, their planned stop, due to a dust storm. That night was spent in the RAF Depot Mess with a reference in David McIntyre's log book indicating they met up with their ex-602 colleagues Martyn and Barwell who featured in one of the photos. Their next port of call on the 8th May was a refuelling stop in Syria at Dier-Ez-Zor, an airfield occupied by the French Air Force who could not afford the petrol to fly their smart fighter aircraft. McIntyre and Ellison undeterred by the lack of fuel

visited the local bazaar where they purchased several four-gallon cans of petrol and hired a man with two donkeys to carry them back to the airfield.

After a night stop in Syria at Aleppo, the next day saw them reach Turkey with a refuelling stop at Konia where a contretemps with a customs official over a clearance certificate was to cause problems later in Istambul. Here David McIntyre's camera was found by customs to contain film which was confiscated again, and he had to resort to buying postcards to have a record of his stay in Istambul. One of the postcards he collected shows warship and submarine activity in the Bosphorus straits, probably German Naval activity. They were well entertained by the British Ambassador and the Consul General staying over at the Royal Hotel on the 10th May, but were advised on the morning of the 11th that they were being sought by the customs officials who, having

Postcard of Istambul and the Bosphorus straits collected by DFM in Turkey where his film was confiscated. Whose warships might these have been?

processed McIntyre's film, viewed it as suspicious, so they had to make a quick getaway without formal clearance, and move on to Sofia in Bulgaria.

After Sofia, the next day's flying in rain and mist brought them to Budapest in just under 5 hours. From here they flew the next day under low cloud up the Danube valley at tree top height to Vienna, only two hours flying but in the difficult conditions in an open cockpit, probably enough to call it a day. The next stop on the 14th was at Nuremburg, reached in 3hr 20mins of flying through bad weather. David McIntyre continued his photography of aircraft on this part of the trip, some of which

Early 3 engined Junkers Airliner of Lufthansa photographed by DFM possibly at Nuremburg on return journey.

Arrival at Vienna having flown up the Danube valley all day in poor weather.

were taken at Nuremburg where he also noted with some concern the overtly military attitude displayed by the officials. They were also warned to avoid any groups of citizens giving the Heil Hitler salute for lack of response could lead to violence. They had a sense of unease over the enthusiasm, which the German flying club pilots were showing for the new Nazi regime. The final day's flight to London via Brussels was diverted to Darnstadt due to bad weather, which delayed their arrival in London until 7.15 pm. Here representatives from the Times and other officials welcomed them.

David McIntyre then flew Clydesdale's Gipsy Moth back up to the Squadron base at Abbotsinch, leaving on 16th May and having to stop overnight at the Auxiliary Air Force aerodrome at Castle Bromwich due to bad weather. The next day, after stopping at Liverpool and Blackpool en-route due to fog, he reached Ayr where he visited his parents for a

day, landing at the old racecourse at Ayr or according to some accounts at Cambusdoon. He may have taken his mother up for a flight in the Moth while he was at Ayr and later he was photographed here doing an engine check before returning to Abbotsinch on 19th May 1933.

Little has been said of the piloting skills shown by McIntyre and Clydesdale in handling the two unique Westland biplanes, but it was considerable. The pilots had not been able to test fly the aircraft and become familiar with them before arriving in India. The many modifications and extra equipment meant so many things had to be done while flying that they had to develop a set memorised programme to avoid some important function being forgotten. His notes record:

*"At that time we ate, slept and drank Everest, oxygen, temperatures, seconds interval, survey camera exposure, and of course every landing and take off was fraught with the knowledge that during the run on the ground there was only eight inches clearance between the tip of the enormous high flying propellers and the ground. The tail being raised the tiniest*

David McIntyre with Gipsy Moth at Ayr old racecourse while stopping to visit his parents en route to Abbotsinch on return from Everest trip May 17, 1933

*bit too high would mean irreparable damage to these precious aircraft".*

During this Everest trip David McIntyre added 226 flying hours to his log book which accounted for about one fifth of his flying experience by that time. It is estimated that the whole trip for David McIntyre amounted to something in the region of 18,800 miles, most of which were flown in the Gipsy Moth at an average speed of around 80 mph. There are some 100 stages or flights included in this trip covering 58 different landing grounds in 17 different countries as recorded in his log book. The expedition accounted for fully six months of his working life, which was to have a profound influence on his future career. There are a number of occasions in the two contemporary accounts of the expedition where David McIntyre's drive, initiative, ingenuity and playfulness are commented on as having been of immense value to the success of the project, and there were probably many more examples which do not get a mention.

## Aftermath

Both McIntyre and Clydesdale were later awarded the Air Force Cross as a result of their Everest achievement for which they were highly delighted. David McIntyre recorded this in a letter to his fiancée:
*"They don't hand out A.F.C.'s in bunches and one to an expedition as civilian as the Everest flight is a very good show indeed. I should think Clydesdale's is partly C.O of 602 and partly Everest in any case we are all frightfully bucked*

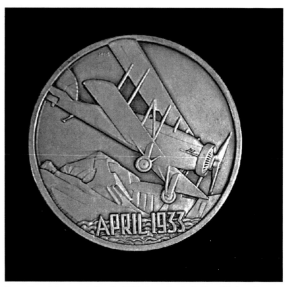

Everest medal presented to David McIntyre by the Duke of York on 1st June, 1933

*about it."*

The two Everest biplanes were reassembled on their return and featured at the 14th Royal Air Force display at Hendon Aerodrome on 24th June 1933, flown along with the Fairey Long Range monoplane in which Squadron Leader Gayford had broken the world long distance record and the biplane of Cyril Uwins which held the world altitude record (44,000 ft) at the time. In all some 200 aircraft took part in the display to demonstrate the strength and lead achieved currently by the British Aircraft industry. It is thought that the show was attended by the Everest pilots themselves. The two aircraft were returned to Westlands where the Wallace was reissued to the RAF in standard form and the PV3 continued in the development work of the company.

# 4. Post Everest & World flight Project

## May / June 1933 — Public recognition

The fame brought about by the Everest Flight made many demands on David McIntyre's time following the return from Everest, on top of resuming his 602 Squadron duties and his stevedoring business. A rough diary of his social calendar show the next few months to have been very hectic. He was invited to a Conversazione organised by the Royal Society in London in honour of the Flight on May 17th. On 20th May 1933, David McIntyre and Lord Clydesdale flew in to attend the Scottish Flying Club Pageant at Renfrew as Guests of Honour at which the Scottish Flying Club Vice Chairman, Sir Eric Yarrow, presented them with mementoes of the Flight. The presentation was followed by a reception in the Town Hall hosted by Provost Michie of Renfrew at which watches were presented to the two Everest fliers by the East Renfrew Conservative association. At the end of the event David McIntyre gave his Everest watch to the Provost as he later recounted in a letter to his fiancée.

The Times newspaper, arranged a welcome Luncheon for the members of the expedition on 1st June 1933 in London. The paper's owner Major Astor who had arranged for commemorative medals to be presented to the main participants by the Duke of York, the future King George VI, hosted this occasion. The lunch was also attended by Lord Trenchard and Air Marshal Dowding.

EVEREST HEROES AT RENFREW AERODROME

Lord Clydesdale and Flight Lieutenant M'Intyre received a tumultuous welcome on their arrival at the Pageant from their historic flight over Mount Everest. They are here seen in company with an official walking round the aerodrome after the official welcome.

Clydesdale and McIntyre at the Scottish Flying Club Pageant at Renfrew with Mr G.F Luke and Provost Michie after the Presentation.

David McIntyre (2nd left) and Marquis of Clydesdale (right) receiving mementoes from Sir Eric Yarrow of the Scottish Flying Club at the Renfrew Pageant (LEN)

Also in June there was a Dinner on the 3rd arranged by 602 Squadron in honour of their pilots who had brought such renown and prestige to the Squadron. The seating plan for this occasion included David McIntyre's brother James who was clearly one of the gang. Among other names of note in addition to the Squadron pilots and past CO's were Captain John Houston the legendary CFI of the Scottish Flying Club and the Lord Provost of Glasgow. On the back of the envelope containing his seating plan, David McIntyre had scribbled out the staging points for the flight

David McIntyre and other members of the Everest party at the Times luncheon.

out to Karachi with the distances for each leg, in preparation for the speech he made at the Dinner.

The importance of the Flight resulted in a celebration Dinner in honour of the achievement on the 14th of June in the House of Commons attended by more than 50 M.P.s including Winston Churchill. A No 12 Squadron 'at Home' and flying display at Andover followed this the next day. He was invited by Clydesdale's mother The Duchess of Hamilton to a reception at Dungavel the following day and to stay the weekend. The next week he was occupied in London with additional filming and making the sound recordings for the 'Wings over Everest' film and that week also included invitations to an 'At Home', and a dinner at the Ritz. David McIntyre had renewed his acquaintance with Marjorie Potts during these visits to London as there is a note written on the back of one of David McIntyre's many Everest function invitations in June 1933 which reads 'Brookmead 5pm', a reminder that he had been invited to visit the Bookmead home of Mr & Mrs Potts at Frinton.

Gaumont British film crew at work on Wings over Everest film at Lalbalu airfield

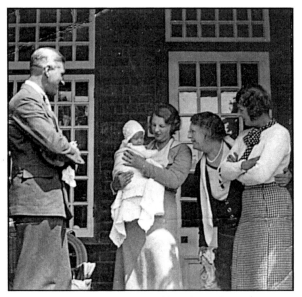

David McIntyre visiting Brookmead in 1933.   Marjorie Potts Right, Mrs Potts looking at 1st child of Doreen Service

The 1,500 ft sound movie 'Wings over Everest' produced by Geoffrey Barcas from the 80,000 ft of negative taken out by the film crew, came in for a fair degree of criticism by the pilots. They expressed the view that as well as being badly edited and mixing up shots of the two flights in the one apparent sequence, they felt that the serious point of the survey mission with much of the film's scientific value and photographic uniqueness had been discarded onto the cutting room floor and lost to the world. Since there had been a considerable effort expended in obtaining this film record at the time of the expedition, they felt that a most short sighted view had been taken at the time of its editing.

The film however was the recipient of the 1935 Academy Award for best Novelty Short Subject film and the directors Geoffrey Barcas and Ivor Montague went on to become well known in film and literary fields. It also carries the only known recording of David McIntyre's voice still existing.

On June 30th he attended the Prize-giving at Ayr Academy after much persuasion by his sister Annie who managed to overturn his initial refusal to participate. His speech notes for this occasion acknowledged that he was once a pupil there and he recorded his debt to the School for the education he received.

## July 1933 — World flight project launched

The 1930's were a period when many flyers were making long distance flights to break various records for the quickest journeys across significant tracts of the globe. These being more easily organised than attempts on height or speed records as they needed little specialised recording equipment to homologate the record. The distance tasks usually requiring only some suitable arrangement to cram on board as much fuel as could be carried and still allow the aircraft to take off. In some cases specialist aircraft were built such as the Fairey long-range monoplane and in other cases the idea of refuelling the aircraft in flight was attempted. Other arrangements such as carrying the long distance aircraft piggyback on a larger launch aircraft to a starting altitude were also given a go. Problems that had to be overcome were the choice of suitable landing grounds en route with the correct refuelling facilities and the difficulty of keeping the pilot awake and competent as the stage lengths increased. The latter problem introducing the early forms of auto pilot system. Weather forecasting and navigation facilities were still very limited at the time, making these attempts particularly hazardous.

There is extensive correspondence in David McIntyre's archive of personal papers showing that the Everest Team had hatched up the bones of an idea for a round the world flight some time during the Everest expedition or shortly after their return. The first evidence of David McIntyre's involvement in what was initially titled the "Non-Stop Flight" is in a letter to him from Col Etherton dated 4th July 1933. Etherton was the Hon Secretary of the

Everest Flight and one of its main Organisers and in this letter he invited David McIntyre down to his Goodwood home for a house party from July 25th to 29th. He proposed to discuss the project fully with David McIntyre, having developed the scheme sufficiently to be considering an announcement. It is not clear if David McIntyre attended this get together or not but he was invited to a party in London on the 25th July by the Duchess of Hamilton which he may not have refused and so being down South, could have gone on to Goodwood the next day. Additionally it was during the fortnight of the 602 Squadron annual camp at Hawkinge and David McIntyre may have allowed himself a short diversion from the Squadron's main flying occasion of the year.

A World Map with Etherton's name on it shows a round-the-World route marked out in David McIntyre's hand with this table of

| London–Karachi | 4,000 miles |
| Karachi–Darwin | 4,500 miles |
| Darwin–Yokohama | 3,000 miles |
| Yokohama–Vancouver | 4,300 miles |
| Vancouver–London | 5,500 miles |
| Total | 21,300 |

@150 mph = 142 Hrs/24   = 6 Days

places, distances and times written on the back.

He received two garden party invitations in July, one a Government affair at Hampton Court and the other at Buckingham Palace. David McIntyre is on record as having an aversion to this type of occasion but it is not clear if he managed to evade these ones as the Everest Organisers were keen to have their unwilling 'stars' appear at as many events as possible.

David McIntyre continued his 602 Squadron activities, now located at Abbotsinch where the Officers Mess had been established at Abbotsburn House on the edge of the airfield, the home of the former CO, Squadron Leader Fullerton. Clydesdale was the Squadron CO and David McIntyre the 'B' flight commander at the time. 602 Squadron had since 1929 been flying the Westland Wapiti biplanes and were not to convert to the later Hawker Hart day bombers until February 1934. David McIntyre had however spent the year of 1932 flying Hawker Harts with No 12 Squadron and it is possible that having to revert back to flying the old Wapiti for the next year may have dampened his enthusiasm a bit during the early part of this period.

The 602 Squadron July annual camp in 1933 took place at Hawkinge in Kent and David McIntyre as 'B' Flight Commander was present on this occasion, taking over temporarily from Clydesdale on the trip down from Abbotsinch when Clydesdale made a detour en route, arriving at Hawkinge the following day. David McIntyre was involved at Abbotsinch during June in some pre-camp training and practising with his flight, making ready for the Esher Trophy events and other exercises planned for the fortnight's joint manoeuvres with the other Auxiliary squadrons. He no doubt found it difficult to fit these in between the numerous Everest publicity appearances demanded of him. He recorded attending ground gunnery courses for the Vickers and Lewis guns at this camp on 15th July and his scores of 385 out of a possible 540 were not as good as the 491 he had managed the previous year. Perhaps being sandwiched between two garden party events, the first only two days earlier, had made concentration more difficult than before.

602 Squadron Wapitis flying over Renfrew

## Sept - Nov 1933 - Friendship blossoms

Following the July camp there were continued Squadron activities including co-operation

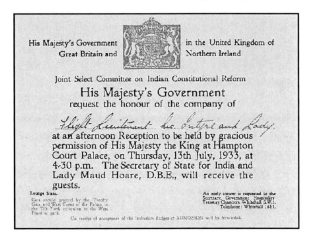

Garden Party invitation for David McIntyre and Lady

with fleet manoeuvres in September. A letter from his friend Shep of the Times recorded an event on Sept 2nd in Edinburgh which they both attended. Clydesdale suffered from a period of poor health after this and he spent 3 months in Egypt and Switzerland for a "cure" in early 1934 which, as he wrote in a letter to David McIntyre, "I am told will speed up my recovery". Clydesdale's military log book has no entries from 19th September 1933 until 7th April 1934 when he recorded his next flight in a Hart as "Flying practice".

In October David McIntyre was pressed, after much initial resistance, into attending a City Livery Lunch in London attended by the Lord Mayor and the US Ambassador about which Etherton later commented, "I thought the American Ambassador's speech was five minutes of real oratory and carried a genuine thrill."

David McIntyre had managed to arrange further meetings with Marjorie Potts during his visits to London including their joint attendance at the dinner of the Royal Empire Society on 7th November and in one October letter he wrote *"You converted my last visit to London from a tiresome duty to a visit of real pleasure and I am now looking forward to the next one".* Also in November he attended an Auto and Aero Engineering Society dinner, and a Times Everest Photo Exhibition launch, all in London.

## Dec 1933 - World flight project consolidates

Instructed by Etherton to bring a long overcoat and black tie for the occasion, he boarded an Air France flight from Croydon to Paris for a reception held at the Sorbonne by the French Geographical Society. He wrote to Marjorie Potts on the Friday night Dec 7th from the Hotel Lotti in Paris, thanking her for her letter carrying an invitation to a later stay at 54. Elsworthy Road, the Potts' family London home. In this letter he commented,

*"This is not Paris, just a gathering of old men and women with the most peculiar names and titles. I am going to escape as soon as I get a moment to myself but there is not much hope of this before the noon plane on Saturday. Dinner with President tonight. Whoopee!".*

His Paris trip had further ramifications, as in his next letter from the 602 Mess on 12th Dec to Marjorie Potts in London, he wrote:

*"You are a very independent young lady but your party last night was wonderfully pleasant and thank you very much. Messrs. Frost and Fog are now my friends for life.".*

Clearly he had been delayed by wintry weather in London after his journey from Paris before returning to Glasgow allowing them unexpectedly to meet up. This letter speculated that their next meeting could be before Xmas for he noted:

*"Clydesdale has arrived in London to have an operation or two carried out on his nose (four times broken) so with any luck it might be before."*

This suggested that he was expecting to act as a ferry pilot to fetch Clydesdale back from London by plane once his operation was over, but there is no record of this having happened.

The "Non-Stop Flight" correspondence continued through to December 1933, by which time Etherton had enlisted the help of Air Commodore Chamier as Technical Advisor. Chamier had been from 1927 to 1929 the Director of Technical Development at the Air Ministry and was currently the Chairman of the Air League of the British Empire. He passed on some notes of the problems he foresaw with a "Round the World flight" to Etherton, which were forwarded to David McIntyre. At this time Col John Buchan had also been brought into the Committee and David McIntyre was spending a lot of time developing the necessary flight plans, navigation routes, calculating stage lengths and preparing the requirements for the type of

aircraft needed to accomplish a round the World flight. He sent specifications of the project requirements to a number of Aircraft Companies asking them if they could provide, or were prepared to produce, a suitable aircraft. In January, David McIntyre received a letter from Blacker, the chief Observer on the Everest flight, who was also involved in some way in this project. In this letter Blacker commented that Chamier seemed to be setting up for a £50,000 project which would take 18 months to launch and which posed novel refuelling requirements, and asked David McIntyre for his opinion on these proposals. This is one of two letters David McIntyre received from Blacker where he expressed his concern that this new project might "damage the prestige of the Everest flight" and possibly as a consequence, was not too enthusiastic about it.

David McIntyre's Everest lecture burden continued in December with talks in Glasgow to organisations such as the Giffnock Unionists and the Giffnock Scouts and he gave several more lectures locally in Scotland which continued into February. By March however the lecture burden had lifted and it is evident that he found this need for public appearances somewhat tedious both in respect to time and cost. He made it clear in one reply to a letter from Blacker, wanting him to attend a series of meetings, that it cost him around £10 to give a lecture in the South of England and as the normal fees for such events were usually a pound or two, that he could not afford to take them on. It was probably only due to his growing attraction to Marjorie Potts that he attended as many as he did.

## Jan 1934 — In temporary charge of 602 Squadron

David McIntyre recorded returning from Brooklands to Abbotsinch on 2nd Jan 1934 in what must have been one of the first Hawker Harts to join 602 Squadron, writing to Marjorie Potts after visiting her in London, *"The new aircraft is a wizard. Even with the head wind it brought me here in time for lunch at 1.30.".* He had earlier in November invited Marjorie Potts to the Squadron *'beer & banger'* dance at the 602 Mess on 1st Dec while she was staying with her sister who lived at 'Claddoch' on the shores of Loch Lomond. During this event she clearly took note of the state of the ladies lounge for he wrote to her in February:

*"As PMC (President of the Mess Committee) I have the pleasure to convey the thanks of this Mess for the two - too beautiful lamps you have presented for our Ladies Room. As D.McIntyre.Dot. I think it is very charming of you and I am sure you will be just as delighted as we are - when you see how much they have improved the appearance of the room. I nailed them down with my own fair hands and everyone has rushed upstairs to admire them.".*

Later on in Dec 34 she made a donation of a cigarette box for the Ladies lounge at the Mess and was well thought of by the Squadron as a consequence.

David McIntyre in Clydesdale's Moth G-ABZK

Clydesdale while he was out of action, left his Gipsy Moth G-ABZK in David McIntyre's care for the use of the Squadron for the first three months of 1934, and it is evident that David McIntyre had used it from time to time to visit his girlfriend Marjorie Potts in Frinton. In his letter to her on 15th Jan he mentioned that Clydesdale had made his Moth available and he wrote:

*"so you can have the 'Stunts' any time you care, and/or if you contemplate coming North to check out the extensive alterations at Claddoch, I shall be delighted to come down and bring you up by air. P.P.P. (Pa Potts Permitting)".*

Marjorie had clearly expressed a wish to partake of some aerobatics on an earlier occasion. In another letter to her on March 34 he wrote, *"I dislike your Frinton farmers, they must*

*be a very bad type to refuse you anything. I think it would be a good thing if you pin-point the field on the map for future guidance".*

He has been in the habit of flying down to Frinton, sometimes with Ronald Service, and finding a suitable landing ground is clearly what was under discussion here. In later years his wife used to describe how she was sent out to inspect Frinton fields to be sure they were free of rabbit burrows, which were not easy to spot from the air. David McIntyre did later fall into this trap and bent a propeller on a landing at Frinton in July 34 while in Clydesdale's Moth, so the hazard was real and on that occasion it required him to do some fancy footwork. This earned the admiration of his Squadron colleagues, for by pulling a few strings, he managed to acquire and fit a replacement propeller at short notice during the weekend so that he could be back at the Lympne Camp on time for the parade on Monday morning.

David McIntyre was left to handle Clydesdale's 602 Squadron CO duties while he was absent, one of which was to follow up in early Jan 1934, the offer made by the past CO, Squadron Leader Fullerton, to present, in Clydesdale's words, "such a splendid shield" for an annual competition between the Squadron and the Scottish Flying Club. Fullerton's letter to Clydesdale proposed, "for two years out of three, it should take the form of a Flying Competition and the third year should be devoted entirely to sport".

He remarked that the objective of the Trophy was "an endeavour to bring the Service and the Civil side of Flying closer together, both being imbued, to a very great extent, with the same idea, viz: - Air Mindedness."

Clydesdale replied to Fullerton acknowledging his generosity and concurred with his objectives but with a cautionary note saying "but it needs some careful consideration as to how this can best be brought about, and an annual competition in some purely sporting event might much help in this way."

Clydesdale continued: "It would not, however, be practical to hold a Flying Competition between the Squadron and the Club, and such an event would certainly not receive official sanction." He finally noted that he was

Fullerton trophy event at Renfrew May1935—602 Squadron pilots on left—
Scottish Flying Club pilots on the right (DC)

"leaving the matter in the hands of McIntyre" during his absence. Clydesdale's covering letter to David McIntyre however indicated that his real attitude to Fullerton's suggestion was much cooler. In a letter to David McIntyre a couple of weeks later, just before he departed for Egypt, Clydesdale remarked, "I hope Fullerton is not unduly offended at my attitude concerning his shield."

There is evidence to show that Clydesdale and McIntyre were doing their best to instil flying discipline and precision into the Squadron and possibly felt that a Flying Competition might undermine this rigour and encourage a reckless attitude, which they had been trying to discourage. However the Fullerton Trophy did go ahead but on an unofficial basis and it is likely that Clydesdale's reservations were probably unfounded. From this dialogue it is evident how close the relations between McIntyre and Clydesdale were and the extent to which Clydesdale trusted his Everest partner to manage things in his absence.

Etherton wrote to David McIntyre on 19th Jan saying he was trying to arrange a meeting with him on the "Non-Stop Flight" later in the month and he was clearly enthusiastic for he remarked "This is going to be the greatest thing ever attempted in aviation and I am getting together a splendid band of workers." Towards the end of January 1934, David McIntyre received replies to his enquiries from the De Havilland Aircraft Co, Airspeed Limited, and the Blackburn Aeroplane Co regarding the provision of an aircraft with which to make their "Non-Stop" flight. These first replies were generally supportive but necessarily rather cagey.

## Feb 1934 — 1st meeting of World flight project committee

The first meeting of the "Non-Stop Flight" organising Committee took place on 1st Feb 1934, in the House of Lords, which David McIntyre, although invited, did not attend but sent his comments and support as requested. Etherton wrote to him after the meeting to say that it was just as well that he had not come down. The Committee having decided that it needed more expert advice and required first to settle on the type of Machine to be used. Blacker, meanwhile had arranged to "discuss the 'new project' & some ideas connected therewith" with David McIntyre on a lecture visit to Glasgow in February.

## England - Australia Race

Towards the end of February there was a reply to David McIntyre from De Havillands relating to their plans to build up to a maximum of six "Comet" racing machines for the MacRobertson International Air Race from England to Australia, and that in view of his recent enquiries they felt obliged to keep him informed of

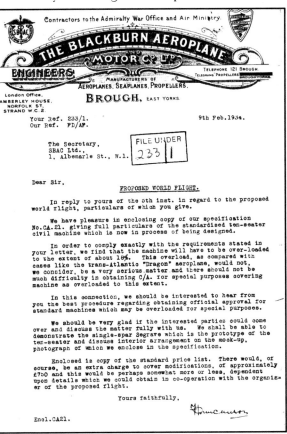

Initial letter from Blackburn relating to World flight Project

The de Havilland Comet was essentially a private manufacturing venture by Sir Geoffrey de Havilland to avert the risk that Britain should loose the prestige afforded by this race, due to there being no suitable competitive aircraft made in Britain at the time. The need was for a machine, which could fly for 2,000 miles at 200mph. It was reported that each 'Comet' aircraft was purchased for £15,000 although it was estimated that they cost de Havilland's £50,000 each to build & prepare for the race (a cool £2.8m in year 2001 money).

Painting of the Grosvenor House Comet, winner of the England to Melbourne race in 1934. In the family collection due to DFM's interest in the race

their order book position which was about to be filled. The letter also states, "Naturally we are anxious for you to pilot a de Havilland machine, and we sincerely trust that we shall have the pleasure of preparing your entry". There is little in the correspondence to indicate exactly what was being considered here, but it suggested that there was an interim scheme being hatched to enter David McIntyre in the MacRobertson race. The race was described in the Encyclopaedia of Aviation of the time as "probably the greatest International air race yet held". A letter from Etherton to David McIntyre on March 1st reported that Cathcart-Jones had come to see Etherton anxious to compete in the Australia race, and he wrote to David McIntyre, "I think we ought to have a go at it and I should like to hear what you have to say; it would be better if we could go into this and the other flight as early as possible," Etherton also commented that he was making progress with securing experts for advice on the "Non-Stop Flight". On March 6th a letter from Etherton to David McIntyre was trying to set up a meeting between the two on 11/12th March in London. In this letter he commented "we ought to go all out for the Australian race as a preliminary to the non-

stop" and in a separate paragraph, "Please return Cathcart-Jones' papers. It may not be necessary, or advisable, to bring him in with us on the Australia thing". In Etherton's next letter to David McIntyre on March 12th there was no mention of the Australia race and nothing in any later correspondence to reveal the reason for it not going ahead. David McIntyre showed a continued interest in the race, referred to it a couple of times in his letters, and kept a water-colour painting of the winning Grosvenor House Comet aircraft as a reminder.

The race took off from Mildenhall in Suffolk on 20th Oct 1934, with three Comets only in the starting blocks, these presumably being the three firm orders quoted in De Havilland's February letter to David McIntyre. One was flown by CWS Scott and Campbell Black, one by Mr & Mrs Jim Mollison, and the third by O. Cathcart-Jones and Kenneth Waller. Scott & Black were the eventual winners arriving at Flemington racecourse Melbourne in 2 days 15hrs 35mins, more than halving the previous record.

Of the 70 entries for the event only 20 finally started. Cathcart-Jones and Waller were 4th overall but third in the open event. Second place went to a KLM Douglas DC2 airliner flown by two Dutch pilots Parmentier & Moll, who were awarded the first prize in the handicap event rather than 2nd in the open event. The prizes for the event were furnished by Sir William MacPherson Robertson, a citizen of Melbourne and were held as part of the Mel-

Report on progress on the MacRobertson Race

KLM's Douglas DC2 airliner—2nd in the MacRobertson race but placed 1st in the handicap section

bourne Centenary celebrations. It is interesting to note that a few years later, just as Holland was being over-run by the Nazi forces, the same Captain Parmentier was the KLM Captain who gave Noel Capper his familiarisation flight in the Fokker F22 at Schipol airport before Cap flew the airliner back to the UK to prevent it falling into enemy hands.

David McIntyre in his correspondence on 23rd Oct to his fiancée recorded, *"Scott and Black have put up a cracking show in the Air Race. I am as thrilled about it as if I had been with them. All the old grey heads will begin to think that perhaps there is something in this Aviation game after all. I still raise my hat to the Dutchmen with their load of mail and passengers in a really useful type of aircraft."*

David McIntyre, like other observers at the time, is recognising here the significance of this KLM achievement for the long term future of passenger transport.

## March 1934 — World flight project gets into gear and DFM goes skiing

In early March Etherton enlisted the support of Sir John Salmond the son-in-law of Lord Desborough one of the Project Committee who he reported, " will do everything to make the non-stop a success". In this letter he added a postscript that Sir John Salmond had a machine for David McIntyre to look at "which might do the job". He was also trying to set up a meeting with Chamier, Salmond, himself and David McIntyre. Another contact Ether-

It is possible that Salmond's machine may have been a diesel engined version of the Fairey Long range Monoplane that in May 1933 had achieved a record 5,400 miles flight from Cranwell to Walvis Bay en route to Capetown. Sir John Salmond was Marshall of the RAF at the time and in 1934 the Air Ministry, who funded the Fairey machine, were considering another attempt on the long distance record which had since then been extended by the French to 5,600 miles. This was to be in a modified version of the earlier record breaking Fairey monoplane fitted with a German Junkers Jumo diesel engine to increase the range. At an estimated £12,000 cost, with a 7,500 mile range, the Ministry considered this a less favourable option than a totally new design targeting a 10,000 mile range, however nothing came of this.

Fairey Monoplane used for long distance record in 1933 by RAF (Flight 7886)

ton suggested in his letter was Oliver Simmonds who manufactured the Spartan biplane. There is no record of this contact being followed up.

In mid March, Etherton organised a meeting, which included a refuelling expert, a designer from the Blackburn Aircraft Co, and the Secretary of the SBAC. He also recorded having instructed a contact in the Ministry of

In 1931 a three engined, low wing, mail-carrying aircraft G-ABLI with a range of 1,200 miles was built. It was used for a long distance 5 day flight to India in 1932. Later it was developed into the Spartan Cruiser and this pedigree may have led Simmonds to propose it for the World flight project.

Saro-Percival A24 Mailplane forerunner of the Spartan Cruiser (AJ Jackson)

David McIntyre and Clydesdale at Basel Airfield—April 1934 while en route from a skiing holiday

Civil Aviation to furnish David McIntyre with details of Pacific landing sites. David McIntyre was then left the File on the "Non-Stop Flight" to manage affairs while Etherton is away for a two-week holiday jaunt in Europe. A few days later the Pacific islands information arrived, however they were very scanty and did not look as though they could have been of much help. At this time David McIntyre had some initial contact with Blackburn, who

**Die Mount Everest-Flieger in Basel**

Photo Aviatik beider Basel.
Von links nach rechts: Lt. Mac Intyre, Lord Clydesdale. Flugplatzdirektor Charles Koepke.

Die beiden berühmten englischen Flieger Lord Clydesdale und Mc Intyre, die als erste voriges Jahr den Mount Everest überflogen hatten, statteten Basel einen kurzen Besuch ab. Von Innsbruck, aus dem Wintersport kommend, erreichten sie am 29. März abends unseren Flugplatz. Sie übernachteten in Basel und flogen am folgenden Tage von hier ohne Zwischenlandung direkt nach London. Diese mehr als 700 km lange Strecke legten sie in zirka dreieinhalb Stunden zurück.

McIntyre and Clydesdale with the Basel Airport Director

indicated that they could provide what was needed and he forwarded to Etherton, his plans for the project, detailing the targets as - Setting the world's long distance record, - Achieving the first non-stop flight to the Cape, - Breaking the London - Cape speed record, all to demonstrate the capability for high-speed mail carrying flight. A three-man crew was envisaged.

Towards the end of March 1934, David

David McIntyre and Clydesdale at the Hafelekar ski slope restaurant near Innsbruck in March 1934 (LEN)

McIntyre and Clydesdale met-up in Austria for a winter sports holiday. This was immediately after Clydesdale completed his rest cure in Egypt, and coincided roughly with his acquisition of the Puss Moth G-AAXO, which he may have been giving its first long distance outing. A press cutting in the family archive shows that they stopped in Basel on 29th March before flying direct to London and positions other photos of them with G-AAXO almost certainly at the same stop. A photo of the two of them together on skis although not annotated was probably taken during this winter sports holiday, and a photo in Clydesdale's album shows them drinking grog together at the Hafelekar hotel on the ski slopes north of Innsbruck. In Clydesdale's log book there are two entries which confirm this trip, recording on 29th March 1934, a 2 hr 10 min flight from Innsbruck to Basel with David McIntyre as pilot and Clydesdale as passenger, and on the following day a flight from Basel to Lympne, again with David McIntyre as pilot, in 3hrs 40

David McIntyre and Clydesdale on skis—probably in Austria 1934

min. Clydesdale then piloted the plane on to Hendon the same day. There is no record to show how the aircraft G-AAXO got to be in Innsbruck, although it is likely that David McIntyre flew it out there earlier in March to collect Clydesdale after his convalescence and to enjoy a few days skiing himself.

## April-June 1934 — Blackburn support for World flight — DFM courtship begins in earnest

By March of 34 David McIntyre's relationship with Marjorie Potts was becoming a little closer, for his letters are now addressed *"Dear Marge"* rather than the earlier more formal *"Dear Marjorie"*. They met for a couple of days in April 34 when his flight down to Hendon with Clydesdale, having struggled through rain and snow to get there, was delayed on its return by bad weather.

During April & May there was an exchange of "Non-Stop Flight" correspondence with Blackburn relating to the specification and performance options on the aircraft in which they suggested that the requirements might be difficult to meet. David McIntyre was looking for stage lengths of around 7,000 miles and Blackburn indicated that 3,000 miles was much more attainable with their current knowledge and experience. Etherton at the time concurred with a 3,500 mile range option. There was also a passing comment from Blackburn's designer to the effect that he considered the airframe requirements and cost would be much more attainable if the alternative of in-flight refuelling was the chosen option. This comment gives a clue to the possible underlying reason for the lengthy delays that followed.

David McIntyre probably visited Blackburn Aircraft works at Brough on the Humber around this time and one of these letters confirmed the scheme to fly direct London - Cape Town non-stop as a test flight prior to the World flight. Etherton, by June 8th, had concluded a funding agreement with Theodore Salveson and thanked him for his generosity in putting up the £20,000 needed for the project. Then a meeting between Etherton and the Blackburn directors took place in early June

A Blackburn twin-engined monoplane type CA21, initially proposed for the World flight project. The ten seater monoplane used a Duncanson spar wing design, where the fuel was carried in the hollow tubular metal wing spar. (BHG)

where he had advised them that there was only a maximum of £15,000 to spend on the aircraft and he reported to David McIntyre that he believed, from their replies, that Blackburn would be able to meet their requirements within that sum. David McIntyre was left to continue the negotiation with Blackburn while Etherton headed off to South America with Dr Eckner in the Zepplin for the rest of June and most of July.

During the same period, David McIntyre is looking for any opportunity he can get to fly down to see Marjorie Potts at the weekends. One such visit was especially memorable which he commented on in a later letter, for at the end of this visit he flew Marjorie Potts up to London where they lunched at the Washington Hotel before he returned to Glasgow. Later he bemoaned the fact that he was unable to remember the exact date of this event for it was one of his *"Big"* dates which he wished to permanently acknowledge, describing it in a letter on 19.11.34 *"I wish I could remember the date in June when we lunched at the Washington as it is one of the most important dates in my young life and the birthday of the present D. McIntyre.dot. We shall celebrate that day next year and it is fun to conjecture where, when and how."*

In another visit on 1st July he described, *"Sunday was the most wonderful day in my young life, so far, every moment of it from eight to eleven with the exception of that quarter of an hours depression before leaving Brookmead".* He had, late that evening, been driven up to London by Marjorie Potts in her open MG and worried about her late night drive back alone to Frinton. In this letter he indicated his

intention to fly down the following weekend to make arrangements for the Squadron's annual camp at Lympne, writing *"am trying to scrounge a civil aircraft in which case I shall drop Ronald off at Frinton and call back for him later."* It is not clear if this arrangement materialised.

## July 1934 — DFM gets engaged - 602 Squadron at Camp

David McIntyre's 602 activities in the summer of 1934 were concentrated on practice for the two-week annual camp to be held at Lympne. The Squadron was now fully equipped with Hawker Hart day bombers and the Camp at Lympne followed a familiar pattern with Formation Flying for the Air Defence Commander's and Commander in Chief's inspections, also the Esher trophy exercises which the AAF squadrons competed for annually. For David McIntyre however the camp held much more important memories for it was during the last weekend of the camp that he proposed to Marjorie Potts and was accepted. His letter of 27 July from the 602 Mess is probably best left to speak for itself.

*"My Dear Marge, All back safely in 'Bonnie Scotland'. We left Hendon at six this morning - only one hour late - and had a perfect flight over to Lympne, everything all still and 'early morning-ish', you would have enjoyed it. The trip up here was even bumpier than the one we had up to Hendon yesterday afternoon. I made up some of the lost sleep by roaring straight off to bed immediately after my goodnight telephone call. I hope you did likewise and have recovered from all the flying and excitement of the last two days. I am afraid I haven't.*

*The whole way up from Lympne today I paid very little attention to leading the Squadron North. All my time was spent trying to make myself believe that it is not just another of my 'Castles in the Air' and that you will not regret or anything like that before this cad is in a position to fix things definitely. I do not know what would happen if you did. - Probably some super and foolish flying record of some kind. However the old nose goes down to the grindstone early tomorrow morning plus brain at full throttle - all doubts cast aside in case they have*

602 Squadron Harts in formation with Loch Lomond in the background (602M)

602 Squadron Group at Lympne Camp in 1934. Front row L-R - Hodge, Feather, McIntyre, Allan, Clydesdale, Baldwin, Sutherland, Farquhar, Smith, ?. Back row L-R - Hodson, Shewell, Law, Grant, Rintoul, Howell, Robinson, Selway, Bell, Horstmann, Pinkerton.

*a retarding influence. Yours, David."*

He makes further references to this weekend, one in which he records the 26th July 34 as one of *"our dates"*, and another a month before their wedding where he describes the 26th as:

*"that perfect and astonishing day at Hythe when you agreed to take a chance on this poor hoot as a husband, tho' I have lost most of my confidence and feel even more unworthy than I did then - I still feel certain that you will never have cause to regret it seriously. Our only worry, Ways & Means Ltd, we shall enjoy overcoming together and then everything in the garden will be perfect and the green grass will grow all around Skiff Cottage."*

This confirmed that David McIntyre proposed to Marjorie Potts and was accepted when they visited Hythe that Thursday although the engagement was not officially announced until 1st September once David McIntyre had persuaded George William Potts, Marjorie Potts's Father (GWP) that he was a worthy son-in-law and had overcome some surprising early resistance from his own family.

There is an indication that immediately after this they intend to keep the engagement quiet for in David McIntyre's words: *"we must be careful not to bring on the battle while I am still on his down-hill side"*, and a little later in the same letter he remarks *"if the worst comes*

*to the worst and everyone disapproves of me - Let's go to a little country church"*. However he is almost immediately starting to consider places to live in the vicinity of Abbotsinch since they appear to have set themselves a 6 month time scale for the wedding. Keeping things quiet proved difficult and he admitted to having spilt the beans to his brother-in-law Ronald Service by the following Tuesday, and his Squadron colleagues suspected something was afoot for he wrote:

*"When I left the telephone last night, I hung around for five minutes to let the smile die down before going in to supper. I tried very hard to appear normal and thought I was putting up rather a good show until half-way through soup, when Hodge suggested that I would make more progress with a soup spoon. That and a few peculiar looks from the others. All very difficult for our serious member of the Squadron."*

Meanwhile things were progressing slowly with the Long Distance Project and, in spite of the assurances given to Etherton in June, David McIntyre received a letter from Blackburn's Chief Engineering Director saying that it would cost at least £25,000 to build a machine to do the job, that it would not be ready by the required date in summer of 1935, and that at this point in time they did not know if they could guarantee the performance required. Clearly the Engineering department had not been involved in Ethertons' earlier

Studio portrait of Marjorie Potts c1933

meeting with Blackburn.

During mid August, Etherton advised David McIntyre that the World flight Committee, now comprised, the Duke of Sutherland, Earl of Lonsdale, Earl of Lytton, Lord Desborough, Lord Moynihan, and Col John Buchan. He also informed David McIntyre "by the way" that he had been appointed by the Committee, as Chief Pilot, proposed by Buchan and seconded by Lytton. He also gave David McIntyre, Chamier & Salmond the job of selecting the assistant pilot; voicing his own opinion that Ellison should be considered.

The conflict regarding Blackburn's capability to design and build a suitable aircraft for a 7,000 mile non-stop flight rumbled on until 6th September when Etherton wrote to David McIntyre summarising his latest meeting with Blackburn at Brough a few days earlier. A this meeting they quoted him a cost of £30,000 for the 20 seater without a guarantee of the 7,000 mile range and Etherton concluded that they could not do the job. In this letter he congratulated David McIntyre on becoming engaged, the announcement of which had been reported in many papers on 1st Sept 1934.

## Sept 1934 — World flight project unravels - works on Everest book

After the formal engagement was announced, David McIntyre introduced Marjorie Potts to his Parents and sister Bunt, and presumably brother James and his wife Margaret and on 10th Sept he wrote:

*"The 'Old Folks' ask me to send all sorts of kind regards. They are in cracking form and I have never seen my mother look better or happier for years. You must be having a tonic affect on them as they now express anxiety that I should overcome our Ways & Means problems as soon as possible."*

He spent ten days in London with Marjorie Potts during mid September while conducting stevedoring business and work related to the World flight project. In order to continue to see Marjorie Potts in London he *"wangles"* reasons for making a trip whenever there is no legitimate reason either to be away for Squadron activities or Business ones. One trip which he did not consider to be a *'wangle'* saw him travelling down to London by overnight train with Hodson ('Stacy' Hodson was the RAF regular Adjutant at 602 Squadron at the time, and who later became an Air Vice Marshal) for a Friday conference on 12th October and while in London he visited the Air Ministry on the World flight Project, conducted three business meetings, attended the wedding of Dick and Beryl Ellison as Best Man, having first advised Dick to arrange for a substitute in case he could not make it, and met up with Marjorie Potts for the rest of the weekend. MFM used to recall that the Ellison wedding was a bit haphazard with David McIntyre having to collect Dick from a yacht, which had been moored at a dock on the Thames, and with some difficulty shepherded him to the place of the wedding. He wrote to Marjorie Potts before he returned to Scotland:

*"I think you have organised the week-end wonderfully, and I raises me 'at to Mrs Potts (assuming a cockney accent for that expression no doubt) She is a wizard like daughter Marge. I shall never get over this phenomenal luck, and pray that I shall make a success of everything and try to deserve a little of it. Do you think this possible? I am afraid I do not but I shall try very very hard and you know you are loved more*

*than any other girl has been loved before and perhaps that will make up for my failings."*

David McIntyre and Clydesdale set about preparing the material for the 'Pilots Book of Everest', which they had determined to write, being unsatisfied with the account, which was written by Fellowes & Blacker immediately after the expedition returned home. The Blacker/Fellowes book titled "First over Everest" was first published in Dec 1933 and set out the account of the preparations and execution of the Flight largely from the viewpoint of the Organisers. This account dwelt at length on the political and cultural background of the country in which the flight took place in addition to the expedition details itself. The pilots both felt that the aviation and flying aspects of the expedition had been given scant coverage with Clydesdale only contributing a short account of the flight itself. David McIntyre & Clydesdale enlisted the support of Edwin Colston Shepherd (Shep), the aviation correspondent of The Times who had been

the official reporter with the Everest expedition, in preparing the draft chapters from the accounts written by the pilots themselves. There are a number of letters from his friend Shepherd to David McIntyre relating to this work, which as time goes on show him to have become increasingly exasperated with the pilots and their delays in the preparation of the original text. Part of this problem is accounted for by the illness, which Clydesdale experienced during the latter part of 1933 and his absence while recuperating in the early months of 1934.

David McIntyre's day job continued after Everest, being involved with his brother James in an unlimited company he referred to as McIntyre Bros, running their stevedoring "business" and he recorded having to visit docks at Greenock and Ayr as well as Glasgow. It was an unlimited company and was in competition with another stevedoring business, the Clutha. A clear understanding of what this business involved has been difficult to glean, but some idea can be obtained from this newspaper article relating to his engagement announcement, which gives a brief insight into David McIntyre's stevedoring life which reads: - "Everest hero as dock "worker". How many who daily pass along Govan Road, Glasgow, know that working in Princes Dock there is one of the heroes of the Houston Mount Everest expedition. He is Flight Lieutenant David Fowler McIntyre whose engagement has been announced to Miss Marjorie Florence Potts, aged 29, of Chelsea. They are to be married at St Columba's Church of Scotland, Pont St, London. Even before he took part in the epic flight over the world's highest and most inaccessible mountain, Flight-Lieut. McIntyre was associated with the firm of Messrs. John Robertson & Son, stevedores, the Terminus, of which both his elder brother and himself are the two partners. Practically every day now sees this unassuming young airman down at the various basins supervising the unloading and loading of freighters. All the dockers know him, and appreciate his innate modesty, for he always deprecates his contribution to the history-making flight, preferring not to mention it at all. 'Works Day & Night'. Right up to the time when almost all the preparations for the expedition had been made, Flight-Lieutenant McIntyre continued working away at the docks and after the flight, he suddenly appeared at the South Basin again, resuming as if nothing more had happened to him than an ordinary holiday. And because he happens to be Flight-Lieutenant McIntyre doesn't mean that Mr. McIntyre is afraid to work. The dockers, who know a man when they see one, think all the more of the quiet hero who works in their midst. "I have seen him," a docker told a Sunday Mail reporter, "down here at all times of the day and night, supervising the loading of ships, when they had to get a ship away in a hurry." "The men here appreciated his desire for not wishing anything to be mentioned about his part in the flight, and when he slipped away, we just took it as a matter of fact. Even when he returned, we knew his wishes so much that the idea of making a presentation was immediately vetoed, because although we knew he would

One of many Engagement announcement cuttings

appreciate it, he really much preferred to remain in the background, and be allowed to take his part as an ordinary citizen."

Shortly after he proposed to Marjorie, David realised that his ability to demonstrate to his future father-in-law that he had the business sense and prospects to keep his daughter in the manner to which she had been accustomed, were not good. Although the fame of the Everest flight and his other aviation management abilities through his position as Flight Commander in 602 and 12 Squadron would carry some weight, his track record in a business sense through the Stevedoring activities with his brother James were clearly at this point earning him little by way of income or reputation. He determined to do better and shook off the service title of Flight Lieutenant reverting to a civilian title, which he jokingly refers to in his letters as "D. McIntyre.dot" and embarked on a more vigorous attempt to make the Stevedoring business profitable. A term, which he uses to express this current objective in his letters, is "Ways & Means".

The influence which Marjorie Potts had on David McIntyre's outlook and self esteem is from the beginning very substantial and in

Portrait of DFM at the time of his engagement to Marjorie Potts..

particular she had encouraged him to considerably improve his financial prospects, a most important factor in persuading GWP to sanction the marriage. Within a week of getting engaged, David McIntyre wrote,

*"My Dear Marge, You are a wizard. Do you realise that you have made a businessman out of a rather useless type. It is absolutely a grand game and I am enjoying myself. Especially this morning when I swallowed my nasty pride and asked a flying friend for business. Of course ever since I had the cheek to tell you I loved you - this capacity for cheek has been increasing at an amazing rate of knots and it is just what the doctor ordered. With this cheek and such a marvellous objective, business is a most decided pleasure - I think even greater than flying. I am completely amazed and frightfully pleased with myself - and all your doing so you should be very proud and happy at your handiwork."*.

It is not exactly clear what the business might have been which he mentioned, however he does later go on to undertake lectures and Marjorie Potts's influence on the Everest book is also substantial.

David McIntyre had explained to Marjorie Potts about the book and expressed the hope that it would be sufficiently successful to fund their honeymoon trip to North Africa and the East. Personal correspondence between David McIntyre and his fiancée Marjorie Potts in the later months of 1934 recorded that she had considerable influence in motivating him to get on with the book and that she typed up some of the drafts at the home of her married sister at 'Claddoch' on the banks of Loch Lomond. On Nov 17th, David McIntyre wrote that he has received an official letter from Gaumont British offering free use of all their photographs in return for suitable acknowledgement in the book writing:

*"the next time I am in London we will go down to Shepherds Bush and see the film of 'Wings over Everest' and you will help me to choose really good, interesting photographs to illuminate the wherewith all for our honeymoon round the East. That is where I get the kick out of this writing idea and enjoy every moment of it."*

In his letters, David McIntyre recorded how much he welcomed the pressure, which Marjorie Potts puts on him to get on with the book mentioning at one point, *"but for you I would never have had the patience to get down to it"*. During an intensive period while drafting his account of the Everest flight David McIntyre recorded that it had even been percolating into his dreams, when he described to his fiancée:

*"You may not know it but we went swimming last night in the private swimming pool of the Maharajah of Udaipur and you enjoyed yourself a lot. We then insulted H.H by refusing to witness a specially arranged tiger and pig fight and had to fly away in ZK at great speed to avoid serious trouble. We seemed to finish up in a very pleasant desert somewhere enjoying a hearty meal."*

He went on to say that: *"Dreaming is a new experience for me and I am afraid you are responsible once more, but it is grand fun and we are always together. If they mean anything at all - we have a very happy future ahead of us which is exactly my idea of things."*

## PILOTS' OWN STORY

### *Lady Houston's Help*

#### By J. D. S. ALAN

AN airman's dream of spotting Mallory and Irvine, dead but triumphant after climbing cold Everest, is told with unconscious pathos by the Marquess of Clydesdale, who with Flight-Lieutenant M'Intyre, at last gives the world "The Pilots' Book of Everest."

Film, book, lectures, and stories have told about the 1933 flights.

#### STEEP SNOW

At last we have the real stuff by the men best qualified to write it.

"I had always cherished the faint hope that it might be possible, visually or by photograph, to establish that Mallory and Irvine, last seen attacking the final 1,000ft. of Everest, had actually reached the summit" writes Clydesdale.

"As I came over the top I tilted the right wing and looked down. It was not possible to discern any hint of human remains, or of the apparatus.

"I began to realise that it was most unlikely that any trace could be seen from the air. To the east and south was the steep snow face on which they could not have lain, unless they had dropped into the small concave area just below, and there they would have been covered with snow."

#### EXPERT ADVICE

He describes how they had been driven by financial difficulties to contemplate hiring a commercial 'plane from a company that would have provided the pilot and have taken the vital part of the organisation in its own hands.

Then Lady Houston weighed in, and tribute is paid to her for her motherly solicitude and her insistence on safeguarding personnel by taking advice from medical experts and Wing Commander Orlebar, whose opinion she greatly admired.

The book costs 10s. 6d. and is published by William Hodge and Co., whose development from legal to general publishing is comparatively recent.

Scene of Udaipur on return journey from Purnea to Karachi on Everest trip.

With Blackburn failing to come up with a suitable aircraft for the World flight project, in spite of the considerable incentive from the future interest that Imperial Airways and the Air Ministry would be showing in the design for commercial and military transport uses, the Committee turned to Airspeed as an alternative supplier. A letter from Etherton to David McIntyre on Sept 13th recorded that Airspeed had sent full details of their design to Clydesdale a week or so earlier, however Airspeed were unable to meet their needs and he concluded that the only course left, having exhausted all other supplier avenues, was to go back to Blackburn, opting for their 10 seater machine adapted to give a maximum range of 4,500 miles.

It is perhaps of significance to note that during this 1933/34 period, Sir Alan Cobham was developing with Airspeed, of which he was a Director, an experimental in-flight refuelling system specially fitted to an Airspeed Courier aircraft, modified for a 10,000 mile long distance record flight to Australia. Their first long distance attempt on 22nd Sept 1934 to fly non-stop to Karachi in five 1000 mile in-flight refuelling legs got as far as Malta after two successful refuelling rendezvous but he had to force land on the island due to a throttle linkage failure in the engine. This attempt was further blighted by the fatal crash of the first refuelling tanker aircraft on its return to base, and it was said to have set back the case for in-flight refuelling by some ten years. It is probable that the timing of Etherton's request for assistance had come at a bad time for Airspeed who would have been concentrating on the final stages of this costly project and had influenced their response.

## Oct 1934 — World flight project revived - house hunting starts - Everest book progressed

Out of the blue on Oct 5th a letter from Blackburn Aircraft Co is received by Etherton which read "having further studied our position", in which they agree to the production of a one-off design, meeting the 7,000 mile non-stop range at an average cruising speed of 125 mph, to be available before the end of 1935 and costing a (25% discounted) price of £30,000, less the cost of the twin Napier 'Cutlass' diesel engines. This design was to be based on a 20 seater commercial aircraft which Blackburn were planning to develop, and they even offered a £5,000 bonus if the world long distance record was broken. In David McIntyre's personal letters to Marjorie Potts he recorded staying the night with Etherton at Salveson's home at Broxmouth Park, Dunbar, having a jolly party on the night of Oct 5th by all accounts and wrote:

*"Imperial Air Development advanced a goodish step, and really requires an early visit to London."*

It is more than likely that Blackburn's sudden renewed interest in this project was influenced by Cobham's in-flight refuelling set back only two weeks earlier, for it was reported that Robert Blackburn and Cobham were closely involved in a number of aviation interests and this Airspeed/Blackburn connection might have been the reason for Blackburn's earlier vacillation. (i.e. if Cobham had succeeded in showing that in-flight refuelling was the way forward, there would be no future in Blackburn pursuing Etherton's World flight design requirements.)

Galvanised by this change of heart by Blackburn, David McIntyre and the Committee proceed to proposition the Air Ministry to support the project now titled "Imperial Air Development" through financing the £10,000 shortfall in their funding or by arranging for a loan of the engines and in generally supporting the flight so that a better price could be negotiated with the manufacturers.

During the third weekend in October, David McIntyre made a no wangles flight to London to see Marjorie Potts and she came up the following weekend by train to do some house hunting, staying at Claddoch where David McIntyre had also been invited to stay. It was at this point that the *"chicken farm below Torbracken"* (Skiff Cottage) is first mentioned as a possible home but it was not recommended by Torbracken's occupant, Dennis McNab, as being thought to be too damp. They visited Skiff Cottage during the weekend and had initial reservations about it themselves.

Marjorie Potts had typed up some of his draft Everest Book material to send down to Shepherd when David McIntyre's close friend and 602 Squadron mess mate Ozier Hodge, who normally did his typing, was away sick. He recorded that he would not allow anyone else see his draft work. He also made reference to his respect for the contribution, which Shepherd made to the finished product when he wrote, *"by the way, Shepherd has sent up his version of the flight across India etc. which you typed. I shall post it down to you tomorrow. You will be amazed to see how much he has made out of very little and at the same time you will see why I was so careless about the rough idea. It is rather wonderful how he works it all in with odd notes from Clydesdale and his own memories and ideas."* and in another letter, *"I am beginning to think that thanks to old Shep, this book will be a real success even apart from its connection with Everest. Light, thrilling and amusing with some sound serious interesting stuff. With a decent review it should sell like hot cakes."* The publication of the book was ultimately delayed until after the honeymoon and so proved unable to contribute to the funding of the trip. In the event it was not until April 1936 that Ozier Hodge, whose business was in publishing as William Hodge & Co, was able to bring it to the public. A version published in New York was also produced in 1936. No record has been found to show how successful it was in financial terms for David McIntyre. Shepherd later became editor of the Aeroplane magazine from 1939 to 1943, nurtured by Sir Peter Masefield who was on its editorial staff at the time.

## Nov 1934 - DFM seeks pastures new - World flight project teeters

Two situations are mentioned in his letters in the autumn of 1934 which suggested that he had been looking for other business opportunities. One was with a shipping line in Liverpool through a contact with Ronald Service. The Liverpool job involved a shipping company,

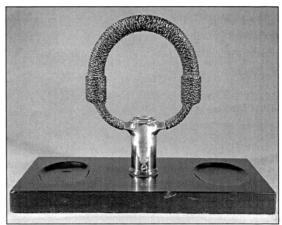

Everest control stick from G-ACBR - birthday gift from DFM to MFP, 5 Nov 34 described by him as being "his greatest treasure".

the Harrison Line, with which the Service family were associated, and he visited Liverpool to meet a Brian Hughs, but there is no further reference to what this job was or whether anything came of it. Also there was a scheme involving the Daily Express which remains obscure which he mentioned in a letter to his fiancée on Nov 17th *"I do not wish to fix anything with the 'Daily Express' until I have had a chat with Clydesdale about it as it might mean retiring from the Squadron and I would like to avoid that if possible. What do you think about it? Personally I am keen to do anything down to bank-robbery if it would help us to get married a little earlier but that might not be good policy."* A few days later he wrote *"I am seeing Clydesdale on Thursday evening about the 'Daily Express' offer and hope we can wangle it through Air Ministry. It would solve our immediate problems."* After he saw Clydesdale he reported back to Marjorie Potts that Clydesdale has agreed to help in any way he could but after this there was no further mention of the Daily Express and it is unclear what the offer might have been.

Details of his 602 activities after the Lympne camp are sketchy and can only be gleaned from his correspondence with his

Photo of Marjorie Potts taken by David McIntyre at East Renfrewshire around 1934

fiancée and relate more to the social events of the Squadron which had a reputation for putting on a pretty good bash. An example:

*"I wish you could have been up here on the 5th of May. The Squadron is throwing a Garden Party, Tea, At Home, Flying Display. On second thoughts it is probably just as well. I remember now that this show always coincides with a couple of cloud bursts and our guests are invited to paddle about in the mud and eat damp cake while the Squadron flaps around the skies getting itself wet."*

And another was the December 'Come Cruising' party, which was an annual event, organised by the Squadron and friends. His brother James's wife seems to have been involved in the painting and Marjorie Potts was asked to bring up some novelty decorations from London. During the build up period he remarked that it would be difficult to make it *"as amusing as last year"* as neither He nor Hodge would be available to get things organised and it would be up to the new Assistant Adjutant 'Mark' Selway (later to become Air Chief Marshal Sir Anthony Selway) to do most of the work. By all accounts the party was a big success for he wrote on Dec 11th *"I tackled Hodge about the date of*

*publication of our book and he says 1st April at the earliest which is not so good, but the silly chap was too keen to tell me how much he enjoyed the 'Come Cruising' party to take a serious interest. Evidently everything went well with him, Anne's* (later to become his wife) *Navy friend retired as a body at the beginning of the party and Hodge is frightfully bucked about it. We shall have to make it a little less drunken next year. When I returned last night I had a quick look through the results of the Cocktail Bar and they are absolutely astounding."*

There are no papers in the file to show how the "Imperial Air Development" Plans were received by the Air Ministry, which suggested that they might not have been too keen about it. Another problem loomed for Etherton by the beginning of November when he reported to David McIntyre that Salveson was being difficult and threatening to pull out unless he was guaranteed an Honour for his contribution. Etherton stated that he had no intention of furthering this aspiration and started to look for other sources of funding. In a letter to Marjorie Potts on Nov 17th, David McIntyre made this reference to Salveson,

*"I am afraid Salveson is packing up on us and I do not know what we are going to do about it. He feels his position is a bit small and unlikely to bring him the honour he would like. His £20,000 seems a trifle compared with the £70,000 involved but his is the only 'uninterested' backing. I can see trouble ahead unless he changes his mind or someone else takes his place. On the other hand it might save you a lot of unpleasantness next November but I doubt if the I.A.D. can be allowed to drop at this stage."*

This reference to "unpleasantness" presumably anticipated that David McIntyre who, by then only recently married, would be away from home on a potentially hazardous venture for some time and that this would not be welcomed by his future wife.

### Dec 1934 — World flight project recovers - dream home purchased

On 19th Dec, Etherton reported that the panic with Salveson had been resolved and he

Skiff Cottage during renovations in Jan 1935

embarked on further negotiations with Blackburn in regard to the cost of the World flight project. Etherton had managed to get Blackburn to lower their price to £25,000 and this left the Committee having to find a further £5,000 to bridge the gap in the finances. He then approached Salveson to see if he could be persuaded to increase his contribution by £5,000 to make up the deficiency.

It was not until mid December that they made an offer for Skiff Cottage. GWP then stepped in to help with the purchase and a March wedding date was suggested. David McIntyre expressed his gratitude for GWP's support many times and this was one example on Dec 14th,

*"I have written to your Father all about it and asked for permission to have the house in your name. As you know anything as wonderful as this is beyond thanks and I am sure they know how tremendously I appreciate it. In fact I still feel very bewildered and overwhelmed by such kindness. I do not think any girl could be blessed with such kind, loving parents. Parents, dog, D.dot, everyone loves you and you deserve every bit of it."*

GWP certainly showed considerable generosity to help them with the purchase of their house at Skiff Cottage but only at the last minute when presumably he had established that the young couple had done what was necessary to manage to finance it themselves.

Over the next three months David McIntyre was assisted greatly by his Squadron friends Ozier Hodge, George Pinkerton (*"the rhubarb farmer"*) Dennis McNab, and others in the alterations to his new home. There are also at least two occasions in the early months

of 1935 when he commented that flying was becoming a nuisance and prevented him getting on with the house which clearly measured its importance to him.

David McIntyre's Parents received his news of a house and a wedding date without enthusiasm, and although he was clearly not surprised by this reaction, he was nevertheless inwardly disappointed. It took him some time before he had convinced them of the merits of his choice of wife and future but by mid February he had settled things with them and wrote,

*"Now it is splendid to know that they are 'flat out' for the 23rd March and us both. They like you tremendously and were bothered about me asking you to live on a small income for your own sake ., you will find them real friends.*

His next letter written later the same day discussed the house plans, Christmas presents and confirmed that his brother James has agreed to be an usher and that he was about to tackle Clydesdale to be best man. Clydesdale later agreed to assist, and he reported:

*"Clydesdale is delighted to give me the final kick into matrimony".*

Skiff Cottage after renovations completed. c April 1935

## Jan 1935 — Near disaster – Making Honeymoon plans

David McIntyre made a 30th birthday trip for three days to London flying there and back, as usual counting the miles on the way down but having to contend with almost lethal weather conditions on part of the route back. His own matter of fact account to Marjorie Potts of this trip reads:

*"The weather people at Air Ministry let me down earlier this morning. From Liverpool North the weather was good on the West coast and they did not tell me, whereas the East coast from Hendon to the Borders was about as bad as I have seen it in this country. Heavy snow storms right down to the deck and if I had known it was clear at Abbotsinch I could have kept up in or over the clouds and saved myself much excitement and telegraph pole hopping.*

*When the visibility was at its worst a stupid old crow smashed the windscreen to our mutual discomfort. This side of the borders it was quite like summer without a cloud in the sky and visibility about forty miles. In one very narrow valley in Yorkshire, almost dark and visibility one telegraph pole, I suppose I was about as occupied as it is possible to be and if you had offered me 'a penny for them' you would have received the same answer."*

602 Squadron Harts flying over Renfrew  (LEN)

He will have been flying a Hart at the time and it is possible that a less experienced pilot might not have survived these conditions. It is also likely that he was concerned to sustain the windscreen damage, for the trip seemed to have been a bit of a wangle. He explained that the flight had been undertaken, as there was a wireless operator in need of experience and that he would not *"be able to leave before about 9.30 in order to allow one or two of the wireless stations to come to life and amuse the operator."* He also said that *"I shall park aircraft with 600 Squadron and John Whitford will not know that I am in town. Low cunning."*

Whitford, who was the RAF Adjutant at 602 Squadron when stationed at Renfrew until Sept 1931, was then in charge of a regular RAF Unit at Hendon. His estimated arrival time at Hendon was 11.30 am, which confirms that he was flying a Hart.

An interesting postscript to this incident is reflected in the letter recording his next return flight from Hendon on Feb 22nd in which he wrote *"I had a very slow flight up today - met the depression within half an hour from Hendon and - true to the new idea - sat down on a private aerodrome for two hours until the worst had passed. Thereafter a strong N.W. wind which held the boy back quite a bit."*

So it appears that a lesson had been taken from the previous near disaster. It also indicates that flying the Glasgow – London route was potentially more hazardous at that time than these pilots were prepared to admit.

By the end of January he was starting to consider the provision of an aircraft for their honeymoon trip, which was loosely planned to follow the outward bound Everest party route along North Africa to Egypt and possibly beyond. The options, which he wrote about in his letters to Marjorie Potts, were the Puss Moth of the Earl of Selkirk, the Leopard Moth of Clydesdale and the hire of a Leopard Moth from an old 12 Squadron colleague, George Walker. He was unable to persuade Walker to let him have his aircraft at a reduced rate which closed off that avenue and he fell back on the offer of Clydesdale's DH.85 Leopard Moth G-ACPK. With the help of Clydesdale's mechanic Hughes (of Everest flight fame) he spent a couple of days in early March giving

Clydesdale with his Leopard Moth G-ACPK lent to DFM for the Honey-moon (LEN)

the aircraft a thorough overhaul and fitted a dual-control rudder bar for his future wife to use. He brought it down to Hendon the following weekend returning in his Hart in 2 hrs 20 mins, which he seems to have left at Hendon from an earlier trip. He explained that the plan was *"while the Leopard is lying at Hendon, John Whitford's chaps could wash it down and make it all bright and polishy for us."*

In another letter regarding his preparations for the honeymoon he casually wrote, *"suddenly remembered floating waistcoats and a metal hot water bottle for our desert rations. I think another one for rum in case we should park down on an Alp or have to float about for a bit. Both highly improbable but we might as well be comfortable."*

Marjorie Potts had shown a great interest in flying and was recorded in the correspondence as having studied flying training manuals as well as having been given a go at the controls by David McIntyre on a number of occasions as this comment in a letter of Feb1st records,

*"Geordie Hamilton will be over for the guest night and I shall ask him if his aircraft is free at the end of March and beginning of April. Unfortunately it is even slower than ABZK. It is the one you flew back from Gleneagles and surprised me with the natural way you handled the controls. It is incredible what a marvellous girl you are Margie, and a born pilot as well. I would give anything to be sufficiently successful to afford an aircraft and give scope to develop your natural ability. Honeymoon will make a pilot of you and I shall be prouder than ever of Mrs D.F."*

David McIntyre's future business success was never to manifest itself in any significant personal financial reward and he never became the owner of a private aircraft of his own in spite of these early aspirations.

## Feb 1935 - World flight project abandoned - wedding plans finalised

Etherton reported in mid February that he had failed to persuade Salveson to provide the extra funds for the Imperial Air Development project and it appeared from this letter that the project at this point had all but been abandoned for the sake of £5,000. In the personal correspondence from David McIntyre to Marjorie Potts dated 16th Feb 1935, among the various items relating to the wedding preparations he records *"Salveson has pulled the ladder up once more and old PT.Etherton is working on someone else."*

His 602 Squadron activities continued at a low level and he recorded this incident on 25th Feb 1935, *"Today has been quite a thriller. Five of our aircraft went down to Usworth near Newcastle for a rugger match. Ran into snow. Two crashed without hurting anyone and three landed in odd fields so the morning was pretty busy trying to collect them together and arrange about the bits".*

This incident is recounted in greater detail in two of the books on 602 Squadron history and shows this highly understated comment on the event by David McIntyre to be typical of his outward expression of Squadron affairs. Once David McIntyre had announced the wedding day, his 602 squadron colleagues schemed together to have constructed, a clock as a wedding present. The clock face was circular mahogany and of a diameter which allowed the mechanism to fit into the boss of a wooden propeller, thought to be that of a Wapiti.

The noon position carried a brass shield with the original 602 Squadron Glasgow city emblem of an oak tree, bird and the salmon. The other hour positions 1 – 11, were marked with a brass profile of an aircraft in plan view into which had been engraved the signatures of the squadron members who had participated. Their signatures were: Clydesdale (whose name is down twice, possibly as an individual and as CO), John S. Feather, A.D. Selway, S. Hodson, E.A. Howell, T. Brian Smith, A. Milne Grant, A.D. Farquhar, J.H. Hodge, J.M. Shewell, J.P. Hawkes, J.C.H. Allan, A.V.R. Johnstone, Lewis A. Sutherland, Marcus Robinson, George Pinkerton, Andrew

602 Squadron's Wedding present to David and Marjorie McIntyre

As well as his immediate Squadron friends, Dennis McNab, George Pinkerton, and Ozier Hodge who were Ushers, and Clydesdale as Best Man, other members of the Squadron had been invited and he commented about their potential behaviour at the wedding saying:

*"I hope none of my low friends sing 'all the boys will be jealous of me' before Howard gets going on the anthem. From odd remarks in the mess I gather they intend making a party of it. But they are naturally fairly well behaved unless John Whitford or Hodson go all boyish in which case they will be amusing but not so well behaved."*

In another letter he remarked, *"John Whitford will arrange to have it (the Leopard Moth) out and ready for us about five o'clock. No one will be allowed to enter the aerodrome, which is a good thing. Also you need have no fear of being carried out of the Mayfair. Bodyguard arranged and I shall be very sorry for any high spirited guest from the North who attempts to be amusingly rough."*

Rintoul, K.B. Horstmann. Nearly all of these officers were to have notable careers during the war in one capacity or another.

In spite of his efforts, the stevedoring business he ran with his brother James did not appear to have been a particularly successful operation, for by the end of February 1935 he recorded, *"Business appears to have collapsed during last week and I have decided that loneliness plus business worry and depression is a pretty poor mixture. Our Royal Mail hope is not as bright as it was - more wheels within wheels. Lord Evendon is Chairman of Royal Mail Lines and also a Director in our rival Clutha Stevedoring Co which makes it all extremely difficult. However I still believe that the luck I have in every other way will spread to business and everything in the garden will be beautiful once more."*

## March 1935 - Wedding and honeymoon

David McIntyre took the train down to stay at the Hendon Mess on the Sunday prior to his wedding and spent most of the week preparing the aircraft, swinging the compass, preparing route plans, acquiring maps and arranging insurance, for which he believed he could obtain better rates by face to face encounters than by doing it remotely in advance.

David McIntyre and Marjorie Potts at Turnberry 1934.

The church service took place on a wet afternoon at St Columba's, Pont Street, with about 200 guests who then attended the reception at the Mayfair Hotel. The toast to the brides Parents and the bridesmaids, was delivered by David McIntyre's Father in which he reflected among other things on a game of golf at Turnberry which he had played with the young couple some six months or so earlier. It was a most amusing and well-received address, which he was delighted to have been asked to give. This game at Turnberry also had lasting memories for David McIntyre for he wrote in a letter on Nov 17th 34

"*I have just returned from a grand game of golf at Turnberry with Father and Black. I wish you could have been there to make a fourth. I managed, with a little low cunning and a few tactful remarks to persuade them to play on the No2 course - the one we played over with Father. I saw all the bunkers you went into that day. I could picture you scrambling out of them in tweed, yellow top with the little telegram boys bag. We have many happy games on that course to look forward to in the near future.*"

Little else remains to record the wedding apart from the surprisingly few photos and

GW Potts escorting Mrs John McIntyre from the Pont Street Church after the wedding

John McIntyre and Florence Potts leaving Pont Street Church after the wedding

several press reports. In a later letter he recorded that the 602 Squadron contingent found it an occasion, which they had never enjoyed as much before.

There is no record of the itinerary, which the newlyweds followed during their honeymoon trip, and there are few other records remaining apart from a number of unedited photos which show that they did reach Mersa-Matruh and the pyramids. David McIntyre had suggested that Marjorie Potts now MFM would

Wedding group at the Mayfair reception, L-R back row—Howard Potts, Hozier Hodge, James McIntyre, ? , Clydesdale, MFM, DFM, John Whitford, Dennis McNab.

David and Marjorie McIntyre after swimming on the banks of the Suez canal while on honeymoon April 1935

need to sleep in the rear cabin of the aircraft for the first two days of their trip to recover from the exhausting work load which she had undertaken in making the arrangements for the wedding. The honeymoon for Marjorie Potts was clearly imagined to be a romantic and carefree go-anywhere adventure, however David McIntyre mindful of the need for planning and safety, agreed with reservation which is demonstrated in this note in one of his letters: *"Your honeymoon suggestion is a really good one but I do not think we should cut down on time and go as far as we can without a set programme until we find a place we like in the sun. It will be a happy honeymoon whichever way we take it. Certainly crack off for Egypt and go as far as appears care-free and possible"*.

It is known that David McIntyre arranged for visas for them both as far as Egypt. In among the honeymoon photos were two weather bulletins prepared in Tripoli one dated March 26th on the way out for destinations Sirte and Benghazi and the other on April 7th on return showing a Tunis destination. This indicated that they had made very good progress south after the wedding, reaching the North African coast in a little over two days flying. It is probable that they followed the route; Paris, Lyon, Marseilles, Rome, Naples, and across the Mediterranean from Sicily to Tunis. This reflects the better performance of the larger Leopard Moth G-ACPK as compared with the older Gipsy Moth used on the Everest trip. From Tunis

they would have flown down through Tunisia to Tripoli in Italian Libya and along the Libyan coast via Sirte and Benghazi to Mersa-Matruh in Egypt.

## May - June 1935 — World flight project aftermath - 602 squadron reflections

On return from honeymoon they set up home at Skiff Cottage with David McIntyre continuing to work with Brother James and involved in 602 Squadron activities as before though no longer as one of *"The bachelor party"* residing in the Mess. Although it is now less than 12 months before the Flying Training School started up at Prestwick it is a surprise to find no inkling of this venture appearing in any of the correspondence before his marriage. In early July, Marjorie McIntyre travelled down to Frinton for a holiday with her Parents, as David McIntyre was to be absent from home for the two week Squadron camp.

The last letter in the Imperial Air Development file from Etherton to David McIntyre is dated 6th June 1935 where he explained that Salveson had demanded his money back. This Etherton returned in full, explaining to David McIntyre that what he objected to was "the boorish spirit and churlish manner of the fellow". He then recorded that Chamier refused to return the 125 guineas, which he had been paid, and Etherton had to refund this out of his own pocket, commenting that neither he nor David McIntyre have had any payments, which needed returned. Finishing the letter, Etherton said he was trying to get the project

MFM with Jake her English setter in the sitting room at Skiff Cottage after return from honeymoon. The Everest control stick ornament can be seen in the far corner.

financed elsewhere but in the meantime the project was in abeyance and if he could not find the funding, the Committee would be dissolved.

This must have happened, for there was no further record of this project except one. This was in a letter to David McIntyre from Salveson dated 25th July, which in addition to other matters he commented that he was "very sorry that Etherton could not bring off his projected flights". He remarked that Etherton had written to him on April 13th to say, "unfortunately the matter did not materialise as anticipated despite all ones efforts to the contrary". Salveson complained that he had heard through a friend that the cause of Col Etherton's project not materialising was because he had withdrawn his support. Salveson then stated "It is of course absolutely untrue as I have never withdrawn my support and Col Etherton's letter to me of 13th April shows this clearly". A considerable communication gap had clearly developed between the two by the end of the project.

It must have been disappointing for Etherton, who had put in the lions share of the effort on this project, to see it fizzle out as it did after two years of beavering away at it. Whether it was the fickleness of Salveson or the vacillation of Blackburn, which caused the demise, is hard to say, on the other hand it may just have been a bit too ambitious for the technology of the time. As a footnote, the world distance record when they started in 1933 stood to France at 5,657 miles, in July 1937 it was stretched to 6,305 miles by the Russians and it was not until Nov 1938 that the 7,000 mark was attained by Britain at 7,158 miles, and this stood until the end of WW2. So one might conclude that they were perhaps about three years ahead of the time when aviation technology had reached the advancement needed for such a distance attempt to succeed.

Although David McIntyre's expenses incurred in the "non-stop" project may have been recovered, it is clear that he received no payment for the time he devoted to the considerable amount of work he had undertaken. In David McIntyre's correspondence with Marjorie Potts during this period, he did not

mention the project with any apparent enthusiasm but it showed that he had involved her in the details of the project and he commented at one point on the soundness of her help and advice. David McIntyre was by the finish probably not too distressed to see the "non-stop" project fold.

### Life in the Mess

The Abbotsinch Mess was located in Abbotsburn House on the banks of the river Cart close to the Aerodrome and had belonged to Squadron Leader John Fullerton who was the second CO. of 602 Squadron from 1927 to 1932. He sold it to the Squadron when they moved to Abbotsinch in Jan 1933. David McIntyre has a room in the mess, which he described thus: *"This is being written on the floor in front of the fire in my room - back propped against wardrobes A.M. (Air Ministry) Oak, Officers for the use of, one only. I find it more comfortable than the Chairs, Rush bottom. In a few moments I shall look slowly over my treasures and nip into bed."*

He had or possibly shared a batman, took a bath each morning, and ate his breakfast and evening meal usually at the Mess. His bar bill ran to about £4 per month and one of his regular exercises was a game of squash which he also records as having played with Marjorie Potts on more than one occasion. David McIntyre once described one of their Mess games he called 'billiard fives' which involved propelling a billiard ball up the table with the palm of the hand to rebound off the top cushion, meanwhile your opponent/s has sprinted round the table in time to catch the ball with

David McIntyre playing trombone in the Buck Shee Band

the palm of the hand before it returned to the bottom cushion, repeating the throw back up the table in the hope of it returning before you have completed your sprint round the table. David McIntyre in later life had surgery on the palm of his hand to correct tendon damage which he put down to this youthful and very energetic past time. David McIntyre played the piano by ear and was by all accounts involved in a group who called themselves the 'Buck Shee Band' who played for local charity dances although there is no mention of this in the correspondence. One of David McIntyre's regular gripes in his letters to Marjorie Potts was the lack of privacy associated with the Mess phone which prevented him conversing freely and he suggested one or two schemes for the construction of a phone box including one which involved reusing a bath surround liberated during mess reconstruction in this period. In one letter he wrote, *"I wish we had our telephone box. Tonight people were bathing after squash with the door open, Selway was changing right above the telephone and one very quiet man sat in the ante-room."* and in another, *"I have never had so many 'listeners-in' before as I had at our telephone call last night. The Batman was standing alongside part of the time trying to say something, Russell & Smith were arranging supper, chaps were bathing after squash and odd people were scrounging around in the wreckage of the hall for hats and coats."*

Russell and Smith were mess orderlies, and their names appear frequently in David McIntyre's letters, Smith brought him his morning mail, sometimes even when in the bath, and Russell often delivered his letters to the mail train at Central station sometimes even on his racing bicycle.

## July 1935 - 602 Squadron Camp - Scottish Aviation begins

The Squadron set off for the 1935 camp at North Cotes Fittes (NCF) in Lincolnshire on Sat 13th July. He must have met up with his wife soon after arrival on the Sunday, as he recorded, *"Yesterday was absolutely perfect and I now add Huntingdon to my list of really good spots.."*. NCF was a gunnery and bombing

station, which the RAF used for training regular crews and David McIntyre had spent several months there when seconded to No 12 Squadron. 602 were the first Auxiliary Squadron to be given the use of this facility and were reported to have fired 13,600 rounds of ammunition and dropped 529 bombs with great success. His first letter to his wife at Frinton on the Monday reported *"The first day has gone past with a good deal of flapping but I am hoping we will be settled down by tomorrow and that I shall perhaps be able to wangle down to see you in the afternoon."*.

He later explained that by being first off on Tuesday and last off on Wednesday he would have time to stay overnight at Frinton. On the Thursday he wrote of his frustration at being apart from his wife after only one day, he declared his intention to arrange Camp differently next year, and confirmed his intention to be at Frinton over the weekend. This he achieved, and more besides, for on the following Monday he wrote, *"Apart from not seeing nearly enough of you, it was a wizard weekend and from Clydesdale's and the 'B' flight boys point of view - an absolute cracker. I believe Pinkerton enjoyed his first cocktail and opened out under the influence to twice as good a fellow as we thought. It is the first time he has left his shell. Clydesdale 'enthused' in my room for an*

Potts Family group at Brookmead—GWP  front row 2nd left  - c 1934

*hour and a half before going to bed and reckons it was even better than the wedding which is saying a lot. You and the Parents and Howard were marvellous with them and I am sure they never enjoyed anything as much before."*

There can be no doubt that this weekend had a significant bearing on the future by letting GWP obtain a first hand assessment of the sort of chaps David McIntyre, Clydesdale and their squadron companions were, and their enthusiasm for aviation. It will have enabled him to see a little of the potential future for aviation and encouraged him to provide the financial and moral support needed by his new son-in-law in his Prestwick Airport ventures. The extent of GWP's encouragement in the Scottish Aviation development is tantalisingly unrecorded but it was probably most significant as this later comment of David McIntyre's reveals. In an accompanying letter he wrote to GWP in December 1943 when he forwarded to him a copy of their future plans, he added a PS: *"You certainly started something that will go a long way".*

The 1935 camp coincided with the beginnings of the set-up of the Scottish Aviation flying training business at Prestwick and from here on, David McIntyre's active involvement

Newly weds at Skiff Cottage

in 602 Squadron activities started to diminish. He was however continuing to operate as an instructor for the new pilots in the Squadron and this was recorded by Hector MacLean in his excellent book 'Fighters in Defence' when he wrote "I first took to the air on 17th November 1935 in an Avro 504 with David McIntyre as my instructor. None of those I encountered could match his calm and courteous handling of a pupil."

His original log books were destroyed by fire in February 1941, and his continuation log book recorded an estimate of 475 flying hours for the years 1934 and 1935 but the invaluable detail they would have revealed of his flying activities in this period are sadly lost.

David and Marjorie McIntyre spent August holidaying at Skiff Cottage enjoying their newly married life and were busy preparing the garden, cooling off by boating and bathing in the nearby reservoir. Increasingly his daily travels took him south to Prestwick and he gave up his involvement in the stevedoring business, which he had shared with his brother. All his thoughts and activities now were centred on fulfilling his dream to develop a lasting aviation business at Prestwick.

Marjorie McIntyre in canoe in front of Skiff Cottage after return from honeymoon. The Skiff wood and hill can be seen in the distance

# 5. The Prestwick Flying School

## 1935 - Prestwick Aerodrome beginnings

It must have been sometime in 1934 when the idea of setting up a flying training school at Prestwick was formed, at the time when the Baldwin government decided to expand the strength of the RAF as a result of the failure of the Geneva disarmament conference. This immediately produced a need for more pilots to be trained and the lack of Government funds determined that the capital for the Civil Elementary Flying Training Schools would have to come from private sources. David McIntyre and Clydesdale from their 602 Squadron and Everest Flight comradeship latched onto this opportunity and as a result of Clydesdale's connections with the De Havilland Aircraft Co they were able to pull together a scheme to establish such a school at Prestwick. Exactly when the planning for this venture started is not clear and it is surprising that David McIntyre makes no reference to it in any of his letters prior to his marriage in March 1935.

The first recorded mention he makes of Prestwick appears in early July 1935 in a letter

No 12 EFTS Tiger Moth training aircraft outside Prestwick Aerodrome Tiger Hangar c 1936

to his wife from Skiff Cottage where he reported that: "*I am going round the Aerodrome site at lunch time with Clydesdale and Group Captain Leakie who is the Air Ministry man in charge of Reserve Training so I hope to hear how our tender is doing and look forward to telling you all about it this evening.*" This suggested that during the May/June period the Training School project had blossomed fast. In his book "Where no Angels Dwell", Sandy

Aerial view of Prestwick Aerodrome c 1936 - Orangefield Hotel can be seen in the trees on the left.

David McIntyre outside Prestwick Aerodrome watch tower

Johnstone recalls, when a Pilot Officer with 602 Squadron, landing in an Avro Tutor with David McIntyre at the field opposite Orangefield Hotel in June 1935. While standing beside the aircraft he was invited by David McIntyre to join the future Flying School and recounts this conversation: "How about it, Sandy? we hope to have the airfield and the Flying School opened before the end of the year. I'd like you to come and join us.". Johnstone was unable to take up the offer at the time but did so later in 1938 as a training instructor in the Ansons.

Other evidence of activity relating to the flying training business is manifest in the three flights which Clydesdale made in his Leopard Moth G-ACPK from Dungavel to Ayr in June of 1935 and which continued at monthly intervals until November of that year. The next reference occurs in David McIntyre's letter from the 602 Squadron Camp at North Cotes on July 15th where he noted:

*"Clydesdale has gone north this afternoon to try and bring Angus into the Company as Chairman. De Havilland's have not heard anything definite but all are very confident.".*

Financing the purchase of farm land, buildings, hangars and aircraft was a difficulty as neither Clydesdale nor David McIntyre had access to spare cash. Clydesdale's father, the 13th Duke of Hamilton one of Scotland's largest landowners, had put the family fortunes in the hands of Trustees as the previous, profli-gate Duke had mortgaged everything to the hilt, so that Clydesdale could get no money directly from that source. However the Hamilton Trustees were persuaded to purchase the land at Prestwick and De Havillands agreed to take shares in the new company in lieu of the £750 needed for each of the initial 16 Tiger Moth aircraft which were obtained. This number was soon increased to 20. David McIntyre, who had little money of his own, is thought to have provided a £5,000 capital contribution through the generosity of his Father-in-Law, George William. Potts. Contributions were also made by elderly relatives of Stewart Kennedy who was Scottish Aviation's first Company Secretary. Thus the money needed to float the Company in August 1935 was achieved and the Prestwick school was launched as a subsidiary of the De Havilland Aircraft Co.

The Hamilton interests were represented on the Board by Lord George Nigel Douglas-Hamilton, Clydesdale's younger brother 'Geordie', since Clydesdale as an MP was not able to hold office in a Company engaged on government contracts. The Earl of Selkirk was at the time CO of 603 City of Edinburgh Auxiliary Air Force Squadron, and was later to take up residence at 'Eldo' House next to Orangefield Hotel. His wartime activity included that of the Chief Intelligence Officer of

Aerial view of Prestwick Aerodrome c 1939

Tiger Moth training biplane preparing for a training flight at Prestwick c 1936

Fighter Command at their Bentley Priory headquarters. Another early Director of Scottish Aviation was R.L Angus a local industrialist and chairman of the mining business Baird & Dalmellington Ltd, whose estate was close to the new airfield. W.E Nixon of De Havilland was on the Board as Chairman.

David McIntyre was appointed Managing Director and for a short initial period was also the Chief Flying Training Instructor. By September 1935, he had moved into rented offices in the bridal suite of the Orangefield Hotel with the Company Secretary Stewart Kennedy while work was started on constructing the aerodrome buildings at Prestwick. The fields on the north side of the Orangefield Hotel had been used from the early 30's for pleasure flying trips by SMT and others and there is evidence that it may have been used as far back as 1913. Clydesdale's log book shows his first landing at Prestwick to be on 24th September 1935.

David McIntyre and his wife spent the Xmas period of 1935 with the Potts family at Frinton. He returned to his parents home in Ayr in late January and wrote describing his journey in the Austin 7 from Sudbury to Ayr as taking ten hours twenty minutes, having stopped twice for petrol en route. This suggested that he must have been away for longer than was expected which is reinforced by the opening paragraph which reads, *"Everything went to programme in my absence and no harm done. I expect I shall be busy down here all week. I am amazed how much I am looking forward to seeing the cottage again."* He is referring to work progressing on the start up of the Aerodrome and Flying Training School at Prestwick and his prolonged absence may have been due to his wife's illness.

The Monkton site had not been the first choice identified by the company who had initially selected the area, which later became Heathfield Aerodrome also known as RAF Ayr. This was not allowed by Ayr town council at the time in 1935 who had zoned the area for housing. David McIntyre from his 602 experience of flying around the West coast region was aware of the exceptional weather characteristics of the 'Prestwick Gap' and being keen to establish employment in his home patch, reinforced the choice of Prestwick as the ideal location to start the flying school. The company had to overcome some early ignorant Air Ministry opposition that the site was unsuitable and were unable initially to adopt their preferred name for the company, Scottish Aviation Limited, as this name had already been registered by at least two companies with the same name which existed pre 1920. While this problem was being unravelled it was named "the Scottish College of Aviation Limited".

## 1936 — Flying Training starts at Prestwick

David McIntyre invited various of his contemporaries to join the new venture, such as Dick Ellison who had been a reserve pilot on the Everest flight and Noel Capper with whom he had flown when in RAF's 12 Squad-

The Original group of Flying Instructors at Prestwick in 1936. L-R rear - Adam Bailey, Dick Ellison, John Dobson, Noel Capper, Irvine Watson, Front - Harry Cummerford, Mackinlay Thompson, David McIntyre, Pete Barrow, Sailor Gibb.

ron at Andover. Other names which became well-known to the family like John Dobson and Irvine Watson were in at the start. There were eight instructors including David McIntyre who embarked on their first group of 34 students on 17th Feb 1936. On the maintenance side Frank Burnard who had been Westland's support engineer on the Everest flight joined and was later to become a senior manager in the factory during the war.

The Company designed lapel pins depicting this insignia, No 1 being allocated to David McIntyre, and these pins were issued to all the early employees as far as is known. The winged tiger insignia can also be seen on the early letterhead used by the company and was displayed on various buildings constructed by the company.

The first buildings to go up at Prestwick were the Tiger hanger which housed the initial 1936 compliment of Tiger Moth train-

Scottish Aviation Lapel Pin No 1 — issued to David McIntyre

ing biplanes and next to it was built the associated watch tower and office block. The first aircraft arrived in Dec 1935 which, according to an account by Stewart Kennedy, was soon parked on its nose and temporarily put out of action by David McIntyre when landing at Prestwick after a night flight around Ayr with Kennedy on board. Early flying training activity gave rise to a number of complaints from locals objecting to the noise such that it became necessary to fit silencers to the aircraft and Sunday flying was initially constrained out-with the times of the Church services. The aerodrome was accessed from the Monkton - Sandyford Toll road, beside which the hangar and control tower were built. Later on when the war started, this road was closed and became incorporated within the Scottish Aviation factory site.

The Tiger Moth training aircraft provided by De Havilland were finished with orange fuselage and fin with silver flying surfaces and carried the Company winged tiger insignia on the rudder. It is probable that the name of the aircraft type gave rise to the choice of this company logo.

Tiger Moth training biplane model in the colour scheme of No 12 EFTS at the start in 1936

Initially trainee pilots had to find digs in Monkton and Prestwick but later Scottish Aviation erected two large wooden dormitories for their accommodation in an annex to the Orangefield Hotel, which was used as the Mess. David McIntyre applied a strict disciplined regime on the trainees, which they were later to appreciate when they went on to join the RAF. However this did not preclude a reasonable amount of fun and relaxation on Mess nights and David McIntyre had the reputation of removing the rotor arms from the distributors of those cars which belonged to any revellers whom he considered unfit to drive home. Later the accommodation was extended to provide additional facilities includ-

SAL Tiger Moth being fitted with silencer in 1936

ing two squash courts and changing rooms.

With the start of the Prestwick operation, although he was still involved with 602 Squadron at Abbotsinch, David McIntyre found the increasingly more frequent journeying down to Prestwick from Howwood both tedious and unproductive which encouraged him to look for a home in the vicinity of Prestwick. Making use of aerial reconnaissance, David McIntyre

Cushats from the air c1939 looking west. Sundrum on the left and farmer Brown's piggery in the immediate foreground. Walled garden on the right

identified a suitable property at the Cushats, about seven miles inland from the aerodrome, and it was purchased sometime in 1936.

The Cushats had been the dower house of the nearby Sundrum Castle which by then had been converted into an Hotel and was some half-mile distant to the South. The Cushats grounds extended to some 100 acres of which three quarters was woodland through which flowed approximately a mile of the river Coyle, a tributary of the river Ayr. Adjacent to the house was a stable and garage block and the grounds contained an orchard and a large double walled garden.

At the time David McIntyre and his wife moved in to the Cushats, the garden design was minimal and there was a large amount of

The Cushats in 1936  Austin 7 HS8300 seen in the driveway

activity undertaken to landscape the garden by building an extensive rockery with raised beds along the edge of the Sundrum field and to build a swimming pool outside the dining room window. It was said that this work was completed with considerable assistance from members of the Flying School. A terrace was laid outside the south wall of the house overlooked by the drawing room window which later was converted into a french window and the sandstone slabs making up the terrace, were purloined from the top of the walled garden walls which had been capped with these conveniently sized blocks.

When the Cushats was bought, a magnificent Scots Pine dominated the driveway surrounded by a circular strip of grass immediately in front of the house. But this was soon

Aerial photo of the Cushats dated July 1936 when purchased by DFM.

Flypast of three Tiger Moth's of No 12 EFTS over Cushats probably during Christening ceremony for son Dougal c Aug 1937

considered to be a hazard if it should be brought down by a high wind and it cast a considerable amount of shade for the larger part of the day over the house. David McIntyre decided to pre-empt the forces of nature by having it safely removed but left the stump to form a circular seat in the middle of the driveway around which the cars would continue to turn.

The 602 Squadron activities for David McIntyre in the early days of the Flying School period became less and less and he was unable to take part in the 1936 Annual Camp at RAF Tangmere due to the pressure of his duties at the Flying School. Clydesdale relinquished his position as CO of 602 Squadron in September 1936 and handed over to David McIntyre who continued in this role for the next year.

He started his fifth log book from the beginning of 1936 recording his total hours for each month by type summarised from other flying school records. In this year he recorded having flown 155 hours in the training school Tiger Moths instructing pupil pilots. His most active month being February when the first batch of pupils started and coincided with his period as Chief Flying Training Instructor.

## 1937 — Command of the Squadron

Within a year of the move to the Cushats, offspring number one came on the scene in the name of Dougal on 11th Feb.1937 and gave rise to a memorable christening party which is described in Hector McLean's book, "Fighters in Defence". A photo of three of the EFTS Tiger Moths flying over the Cushats

show the event being celebrated and one or two items of silverware also bear witness to the occasion. Clearly a great deal was expected of this firstborn who was photographed incessantly during the next 12 months.

Empire Air Day air shows were a national initiative held all over the country on the same

David McIntyre and his wife Marjorie with infant Dougal – spring 1937. Newly constructed swimming pool and rockery can be seen in background.

day the 28th of May to encourage the public to see what was developing at the country's military airfields and embrace their interest and support. The first of these at Prestwick Aerodrome was organised by Scottish Aviation in 1936. At these events, the resident squadron, in this case the local Flying School instructors, would perform formation flying displays in the Tiger Moth training aircraft, and a visiting RAF Squadron was enlisted to demonstrate their skills in the Hawker Hart and Hawker Hind bombers with formation flying and bombing runs using flour bombs on a dummy target. There would also usually be some individual aerobatic demonstrations with a number of other military aircraft on display having been flown in from other RAF units. A film of the occasion records large crowds attending with Clydesdale and his brother The Earl of Selkirk watching the display. The flying school Tiger Moths are seen flying in formation piloted by David McIntyre and the other instructors.

In the summer of 1937 the training school expanded to take on the pilot training of RAF Volunteer Reserve recruits. This took them up to 'Wings' standard and for this advanced level the school was equipped with Hawker Hart day bombers. David McIntyre's first pupil training flight in the Hart took place in July and he logged around 10 hours in the year in the School's Harts in addition to the 153 hours of instruction he conducted in the Tiger Moth trainers.

David McIntyre along with Clydesdale and other officers in the Squadron attended a Royal Levée in the summer at Holyrood Palace where they were presented to King George VI. The Squadron Camp was held at Rochford near Southend-on-Sea where the Squadron were able for the first time to wear their newly approved Grey Douglas tartan dress uniforms. The Squadron had by this

Hawker Demon bombers returning from a demonstration bombing display at the Empire Air Day show at Prestwick (MOF)

time converted over to the Hawker Hind and the field proved to be rather short and tricky for landing these high performance aircraft. With no RAF accommodation on the airfield, the squadron lived under canvas and David McIntyre was commended by Hector McLean for, "proving himself as a man of infinite resource and sagacity made a messing deal with the Palace Hotel in Southend who did us proud at a very reasonable cost". He handed over the Commanding Officers baton to Douglas Farquhar in Oct 1937 and in his last year it was recorded that the 602 pilots at Abbotsinch saw very little of him which was not surprising in view of the rapid developments at Prestwick and that he had moved his home to Ayrshire .

602 Squadron Pilots at the Rochford camp in 1937. David McIntyre centre seated with Douglas Farquhar on his left.

On the 2nd of December 1937 he attended the wedding of Clydesdale to Lady Elizabeth Percy (daughter of the 8th Duke of Northumberland). The ceremony was held in St Giles' Cathedral in Edinburgh where David McIntyre had been invited by Clydesdale to be his Best Man.

## 1938 — Navigation School commences

David McIntyre and his wife were blessed with the arrival of number two of the next generation named Anne who appeared in March 1938. At this time the Flying Training School at Prestwick was expanding fast and the war was looming, but it was still possible for the Potts family to come up and visit the grandchildren at the Cushats and Marjorie McIntyre visited Frinton with the children in summer of 1938 as evidenced by some of the photos and postcards sent back to Granny Mac from Frinton

At Prestwick the date in May 1938 for the Empire Air Day display was brought forward by a week to avoid the noise of the passing aircraft disturbing the British Amateur Golf Championships being held at Troon on the prescribed date of the 28th. A similar programme as had been adopted the previous year was employed to entertain the large numbers of visitors who attended.

The success of the early Scottish Aviation training operation was impressive, for they more than halved the normally expected time for pilot certification. It brought additional contracts in 1938 to train navigators for which a number of Avro Anson aircraft were acquired and to accommodate these, the Anson Hanger

First expansion at Prestwick Aerodrome with the addition of the Anson Hanger on the left and extended office accommodation in 1938

and additional office accommodation was constructed adjacent to the Tiger buildings. The air navigation school ( No 1 AONS) was put under John Dobson's direction and in the three years of its operation produced nearly 2,000 navigators.

Avro Anson outside Tiger hanger at Prestwick Aerodrome c1939

David McIntyre recorded 12 hours of pilot instruction in the Hart as well as 52 hours in the Tiger Moths in 1938 and he also logged his first training flight in one of the newly acquired Ansons.

## 1939 — Grangemouth 'Central Scotland' Aerodrome opens

There had been only one fatal accident in the school's five-year history, that of an Anson, which got lost and crashed in bad weather in the Galloway hills in January 1939. The circumstances relating to this incident are explained by Sandy Johnstone in his book

David McIntyre playing with children Dougal and Anne on the lawn at the Cushats c 1939

Avro Anson aircraft parked outside Anson Hanger at Prestwick

"Where no Angels Dwell". Sandy had joined Scottish Aviation the previous year and flew as an instructor / pilot in the Ansons while also a member of 602 squadron.

In the spring of 1939 the flying training school obtained Fairey Battle low wing monoplane fighter trainers intended to give the pilots, after their basic training was completed, a preliminary introduction to the new low wing fighter aircraft types such as the Spitfire

Fairey Battle— type used by No 12 EFTS for advanced training in 1939 (MOF)

and Hurricane then coming in to RAF service. David McIntyre recorded taking one of these new trainers up for a half hour test flight in May of this year.

During the period of the flying training school, which opened in early 1936, Scottish Aviation had been maintaining its growing fleet of training aircraft, which were used at the school, mainly the Tiger Moths and Ansons, and had developed considerable experience in aircraft engineering skills. Developing an aircraft engineering and manufacturing side to the business was a long term aim of David McIntyre and as early as 1936 he had considered an arrangement with de Havillands for the sub-contract manufacture of propellers. Also in 1938 there had been discussions with Rollasons of Croydon for sub-contract airframe work, neither of which came to anything as the Company did not want to loose its independence by becoming a subsidiary organisation

Two Fokker F22's and the F36 of Scottish Aviation parked outside the Tiger hanger, used as a flying classrooms for Navigator training during WW2

Grangemouth Aerodrome from the air in 1939. The words 'Central Scotland' have been marked out in the middle of the flying field

which either of these two deals would have meant.

To get the company's manufacturing operations started, David McIntyre organised the first factory building for the repair and modification of aircraft to be set-up behind Orangefield Mains farm using the farmhouse as an office and the farm sheds as workshops. The first contracts in early 1939 were for modifications to Vickers Wellesley bombers, which enabled the company after a shaky start to build a sound reputation for quality output. An interesting aside relating to the Wellesley involves the long distance record-breaking subject, which is mentioned in an earlier chapter. Here it was indicated that the 7000 mile barrier, which David McIntyre's 1934/5 World flight Project aspired to break, had not

Display aircraft performing a formation fly past over the newly opened Terminal Buildings at Grangemouth Aerodrome on 1st July 1939

been reached until 1938 and it was a Wellesley bomber in which an RAF crew flew from Ismalia to Darwin in 48 hours to create the 7,158 mile record.

An airfield was developed by Scottish Aviation at Grangemouth as The Central Scotland Airport in 1939, in the first instance to accommodate the need for more pilot training brought about by the set up in Edinburgh of a Volunteer Reserve training centre for up to 200 pilots and 200 crew members. It was David McIntyre's long-term aim to develop this site to provide both the Edinburgh and Glasgow communities with a joint Civil aerodrome. However while the City Corporation of Edinburgh supported the scheme, the Glasgow Corporation declined to get involved. The site when it was being developed in Feb

Viscount Trenchard performing the opening ceremony at Grangemouth Aerodrome on 1st July 1939. Lord Selkirk is on his right

1939 was quoted in the Times as being the biggest in the British Isles and it was expected to have been used by North Eastern Airways for their Edinburgh to London service, which at the time operated out of the Macmerry aerodrome in East Lothian.

No 35 Elementary Flying Training School was established at Grangemouth by Scottish Aviation and the aerodrome with its handsome administration building was officially opened on 1st July 1939 by Air Marshal Viscount Trenchard. The opening signal was triggered when the propeller of the model spitfire was rotated by Viscount Trenchard and the contemporary report records that the pyrotechnic display thus initiated caused so much smoke that the formation take-off of the demonstration aircraft was obscured from the assembled

Tiger Moth aircraft of Scottish Aviation No35 EFTS Squadron at Grangemouth Aerodrome in RAF livery in 1939 (MOF)

guests and visitors. A Douglas DC3 of KLM was present at the opening ceremony and made a stop at Prestwick en-route, thought to be the first ever visit of a DC3 to either airfield. It was also reported that the German ambassador was present having been flown in by a German aircraft which was suspected of clandestine aerial reconnaissance en route over the Forth naval bases.

The EFTS operation at Grangemouth was short lived, for the RAF moved all flying training overseas for safety, and the aerodrome was then sold at a loss in 1941 by Scottish Aviation to the Air Ministry who used it for fighter deployment and other training activities during the war. After the war it was never used commercially and was eventually engulfed by the Oil and Chemical refinery complex now seen there today.

The first three months of 1939 show him to have done no flying but in May he recorded his first, and by all accounts, only flight in the Fairey Battle. David McIntyre's flying for the

rest of 1939 was quite limited, and included 17 training hours in the Anson, 11 training hours in the Tiger Moth and 12 training hours in the Hart. In October 1939 he took his first flight in the Fokker, which had just been retrieved from Amsterdam.

When war was declared in September of 1939 it effectively closed the first chapter in the life of Scottish Aviation which up to that time had been independently managed without any significant interference from political influences. The war was to change all that and while it provided the catalyst to accelerate David McIntyre's hopes and ambitions to develop an Aviation business in Scotland, he would struggle for the rest of his life to maintain operational independence for his business.

The airfield at Prestwick was to become renowned as a strategic landing ground for American and Canadian built aircraft crossing the Atlantic, and the repair and modification of military aircraft would provide the kernel for his manufacturing aspirations.

# 6. Scottish Aviation in World War 2

### 1939 — Prestwick Aerodrome moves onto a War footing

David McIntyre as Managing Director of Scottish Aviation Ltd was responsible for the running of the Airport from 1936 when it opened until July 1941 when the Aerodrome was requisitioned by the Air Ministry as a military airfield. For the latter part of this period after the outbreak of war, the aerodrome was designated RAF Prestwick and David McIntyre became Station Commander as a Squadron Leader in the RAF Volunteer Reserve, a rank to which he was appointed in April 1938. On the outbreak of war the Instructors were mobilised and Prestwick aerodrome became a Royal Air Force Station.

In 1939, the company undertook the training of wireless operators for the RAF, and David McIntyre incurred the displeasure of a number of local landowners by requisitioning the country houses of Adamton, Rosemount and Dankeith to accommodate a total of up to 400 pupils at a time. Although this scheme

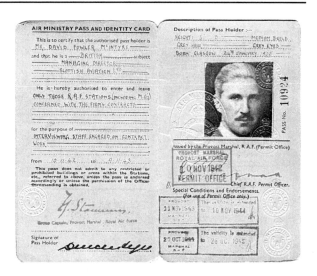

Pass issued to David McIntyre by Air Ministry to allow visits to other wartime installations where Scottish Aviation were at work.

only lasted a year, nearly 1200 wireless operators were trained and contributed greatly to the war effort. The flying school continued to expand in 1939, and the colour scheme of the Tiger Moths, was changed to a more sober standard adopted for all the wartime aircraft.

Prestwick Aerodrome looking south –c 1944 showing numerous aircraft on the north dispersal awaiting onward routing to European war zone.

By this time the Prestwick Flying School's fleet had grown to 120 aircraft and included 45 of these forgiving and robust biplanes.

On the manufacturing front, the Wellesley activity led to more sub-contracted work from Blackburns of Brough (near Hull) which commenced in Oct 1939. This involved modification work on Skua and Roc dive-bombers and continued through to April 1941.

After early negotiations with KLM in August of 1939, Scottish Aviation purchased three Fokker airliners from KLM. Cap recounted undertaking a journey at short notice by train with another Scottish Aviation pilot to Amsterdam in September to rescue the Fokker

Aerial view of the Palace of Engineering at Bellahouston Park, Glasgow during the 1938 Empire Exhibition which was reassembled at Prestwick Airport in 1940.

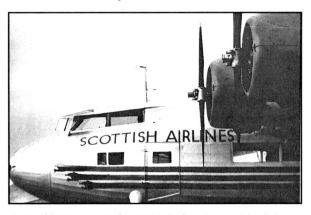
Fokker F22 Airliner used by Scottish Aviation for navigator training during WW2 and later as a passenger Airliner in Scottish Airlines service post war

aircraft shortly before invading German forces overran Schipol airfield. His one familiarisation flight in the Fokker F22 before taking off from Amsterdam was conducted by no less than Captain Parmentier of the Melbourne race fame. Scottish Aviation converted the Fokker airliners into flying classrooms carrying 26 pupils and 2 instructors giving the navigation training, but David McIntyre had initially planned that they should be used for passenger carrying work. In 1939 he formed a subsidiary Company named Night Air Transport, which was planned to run a fast night airmail service between Scotland and London operating out of Grangemouth using these Fokker airliners. Unfortunately the war intervened before he was able to eliminate the inevitable opposition from the existing Imperial Airways operator through their subsidiary Railway Air Services who flew mail and passengers to London out of Renfrew. The large size of the four-engined Fokker airliners needed additional hangar

capacity, more than could be afforded by the Tiger or Anson Hangers so in 1939, a third hanger was built to the north of the Monkton - Sandyford Toll road appropriately named the Fokker hangar.

## 1940 — Palace of Engineering removed to Prestwick

Through the months of 1940, David McIntyre recorded only about 2 hours per month flying, which was mostly in the Tiger Moth just to keep his hand in rather than as any serious contribution to the training effort. In June he recorded having taken up a Hurricane for a 40 min test flight and in the following month a Spitfire was subjected to 40 minutes of his hands at the controls.

The outbreak of hostilities in the autumn of 1939 brought many changes to the family life at the Cushats and while far removed from direct danger such as that experienced in many parts of the country, the wartime shortages,

Marjorie McIntyre with children Dougal, Anne, and Jane (in pram) at the Cushats

rationing of petrol, and isolation were to put much strain on Marjorie McIntyre in her efforts to run the household, manage a market garden and bring up a young family which by January 1940 had swelled to three with the birth of daughter Jane. Marjorie McIntyre is

Example of the Hawker Hurricane type whose rudders were one of the first sub-contract jobs undertaken by Scottish Aviation in 1939. (MOF)

thought to have suffered the first of her two miscarriages during the war in November of 1940. In spite of the many growing business pressures loaded upon him, David McIntyre made a determined effort to be involved with his family at every opportunity.

The manufacture of rudders for the Hurricane fighter aircraft was the next major job undertaken by Scottish Aviation, which followed at the outbreak of war and a contract for the production of Westland Lysanders subcontracted from Westland, was negotiated. Lack of a suitable sized factory building at Prestwick, prompted the company to purchase the Palace of Engineering building which was standing unused at the time in Bellahouston Park in Glasgow. It had been erected to house the engineering exhibitors at the Empire Exhibition of 1938. During the summer of 1940

Spitfire wing section under repair at Prestwick by SAL fitters during WW2

Wartime SAL Calendar depicting Spitfire and Liberator aircraft being repaired in the "Palace" factory building.

Scottish Aviation completed a major feat of construction engineering with the disassembly, uplift and reconstruction of the "Palace" at Prestwick. This building was ideal with a large main hangar door able to accept the largest of wartime aircraft. Almost as soon as the "Palace" was completed the company was chosen as a primary site for the repair of fighter aircraft and the Lysander contract was cancelled before any were produced at Prestwick. Spitfires were the main aircraft to be repaired by Scottish Aviation and a production rate of up to twelve aircraft a week was commissioned with some manufacture of components. At any time from 1940 through 1945, up to seventy Spitfires could be on site at one time and some 1,200 of these aircraft passed through the factory to be returned to active service during the war.

Scottish Aviation's manufacturing efforts expanded to the purchase of Cairds shipyard at Greenock, which was turned into a seaplane, overhaul, modification and repair yard working mostly on Sunderland and Catalina aircraft. This expanded down the coast to Largs where

Short S26 Golden Hind at Cairds shipyard where Scottish Aviation conducted repair and overhaul of Sunderland and Catalina flying boats in WW2

another seaplane station was commissioned to handle American lease-lend Catalina and Coronado flying boats. Scottish Aviation also undertook the assembly of American warplanes at Abbotsinch from components shipped across the Atlantic by boat and unloaded at the Clyde docks. One domestic outcome of this work came about when David McIntyre acquired a spare Sunderland wing tip float, which he had transported to his home at the Cushats, intending to convert it at some time after the war, into a speedboat. However by the time the family moved from the Cushats to Troon in 1950 nothing had

Liberator bombers outside the Anson Hanger at Prestwick undergoing modification for use in anti submarine Atlantic Patrols. (IWM-CH17440)

Scottish Aviation maintenance crew being briefed by John Dobson prior to carrying out work on a B26 Martin Marauder at Prestwick en route to the Allied forces in Europe. (IWM-CH17457)

been done to it and it was eventually disposed of for scrap.

The rapid growth of the manufacturing operation was not achieved without some early problems in the staffing and management of the factory which led to charges being laid with the Ministry of Aircraft Production through the local MP by a group of sacked employees. These malcontents accused the senior management including David McIntyre of serious mismanagement but the charges

Prestwick Airport passenger terminal converted from the Orangefield Hotel became the haven for transatlantic crews and passengers in WW2

were later dismissed by an enquiry as evilmongering and followed up by a further review conducted by the Minister, Sir Stafford Cripps who personally closed the case as unfounded.

The Lease-Lend agreement by which American aircraft were provided to Britain before America joined the war provided much work for Scottish Aviation and prompted the major expansion of the airfield at Prestwick. This commenced when it was decided to fly the aircraft across the Atlantic rather than ship components across for assembly in Britain. Shortly after this hazardous operation commenced, a Hudson aircraft, having lost its way en-route to Aldergrove in Northern Ireland, made an accidental but fortuitous landing at Prestwick aerodrome on this run in Nov 1940. As a result of this unexpected arrival, the virtues of Prestwick aerodrome for this operation became evident and it was quickly designated the principle terminal for all military aircraft flying from North America into Europe, navigating the hazardous North Atlantic route via Dorval (Canada), Goose Bay (Labrador), Bluie West 1 (Greenland), Reykjavik (Iceland).

Return ferry service aircraft parked outside Prestwick passenger Terminal, a BOAC Liberator, RCAF Lancastrian, and USAF C54

## 1941 — Prestwick becomes Northern Gateway to Europe

On the 3rd February a disastrous fire started in a waste paper basket in one of the offices in the administrative building and was not extinguished until the whole office was gutted.

View from the Airport terminal showing hundreds of military aircraft on their way through Prestwick en route to Allied forces in Europe. A typical wartime scene.

Among the losses in this fire were David McIntyre's flying log books for the period from May 1933 to that time. To provide temporary offices the Company rented a wing of the Orangefield Hotel before re-housing them in the "Palace" building once it had been suitably refurbished. David McIntyre reconstructed his log book as best he could for the period from 1936 to 1941 using flying school records, after this his log book entries returned to normal showing individual flights and serial numbers of the aircraft he had flown and he logged 31 Tiger Moth hours in this year with a couple of hours as second pilot in the Fokker and as a passenger in a test flight of a Liberator for the first time.

The Scottish Aviation flying school operations at Prestwick and Grangemouth, along with all the others in the country, closed in mid 1941 when the government moved all UK based flying training to safer quarters overseas in Canada and South Africa and this effectively closed the first chapter of the Scottish Aviation business. By the time the school closed in 1941, Scottish Aviation was training as many as 5 times more RAF personnel than any other company in the UK and turned out some 1,334 pilots. The Prestwick training school had also proved profitable and had established the Company with a very high reputation for efficiency, competence and safety.

The Ministry of Aircraft Production in July of 1941 appointed Scottish Aviation to their Civil Repair Organisation under the control of David McIntyre. In addition to the Spitfire repair work, Scottish Aviation modified Liberator (B24) bombers for the RAF at a rate of about 30 per month and also Fortress (B17) and Mitchell (B25) bombers. A special conver-

Dakota (C47) converted into VIP configuration for US general Maitland by Scottish Aviation c 1944.

sion programme was undertaken for the modification of Liberator and Fortress bombers into very long range anti submarine chasers to operate over the Atlantic. Later these aircraft were fitted with a Leigh Light invented by Robert Watson-Watt (father of Radar) to spot submarines at night. Some of the Liberator and Fortress work was conducted in the Anson Hanger in spite of its low doorway height.

Another type on which Scottish Aviation performed much conversion work was the

Liberator bomber converted into transatlantic ferry transport aircraft by SAL. Operated by BOAC crews seen parked at Prestwick in 1944.

Douglas DC3 Dakota (C47) and included among these were special VIP versions with an executive cabin layout. One in particular was for the American General Maitland Wilson. Some examples of the interior configuration and trim were quite elaborate.

By February 1941, Prestwick had become the scheduled destination for the inbound American and Canadian manufactured aircraft and the need to return aircrew to Canada to ferry across the next batch gave rise to the Return Ferry Service, which also operated from Prestwick. The aircraft first used for this return ferry service were Liberator bombers converted at Scottish Aviation with a wooden floor covering the bomb bay and an oxygen system supplying the 20 passenger seating arrangement. These 12 to 18 hour flights were

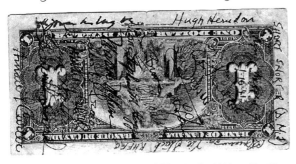

"Short Snorter" bank note initiated by DFM on 1st Oct 1941 marking his first crossing of the Atlantic during the war. Needed to avoid having to pay for a full round of drinks on arrival

cold and noisy and not without hazard, for one crashed into the hills close to Goat Fell on Arran shortly after taking off from Prestwick. Scottish Aviation was involved in the uncomfortable business of recovery of the crew and passengers from the accident site.

Amongst those making the return Atlantic crossing was David McIntyre who flew over to the USA in Oct 1941 and he had a 'Short Snorter' Canadian dollar note to record this travel in common with many WW2 aviators. It is possible to discern John Dobson's signature amongst the many on this banknote that also include the well-known pre-war aviators Hugh Herndon and Marion McKeen. Another signature is that of W.P Hildred who was one of Britain's signatories to the post war Bermuda agreement. Unfortunately no other reference to this journey has emerged to determine what its purpose was.

David McIntyre was instrumental in developing and installing the facilities at the airfield, which encouraged the use of Prestwick and made it viable for this Ferry service operation.

Wartime scene at Prestwick Airport as depicted by Tom Gilfillan in Airport Terminal lounge

One of the noteworthy achievements was the development of the Orangefield Hotel into an Airport terminal characterised by its control tower located on the roof. Scottish Aviation through the Air Ministry took over the Hotel in July 1941 after which many facilities were added as the traffic increased.

The development of the Orangefield Hotel and adjacent site created a major facility for Scottish Aviation and by the end of the war it had become arguably the best equipped and most active Airport terminal in Europe. Scottish Aviation added a 30 room annex to the hotel to accommodate RAF and RAFVR pupils with recreational and mess facilities pre-

SAL's Transatlantic dinner at Orangefield 29 Nov 1943. L-R, Sir Pat Dollan, David McIntyre, Tom Johnson, Duke of Hamilton, ?. Note blackout curtains.

war. The reception lounge walls were decorated with a series of colourful mural panels depicting aviation scenes across the world painted by a local artist, Tom Gilfillan. These panels will be remembered by many of the 500,000 who signed the visitor books during the war and who will also recall the dining room's Maitre D', Andrew Murdoch beloved of visitors and locals alike. The Orangefield passenger terminal was bulldozed to the ground in 1966 to make way for a taxi track to service the newly built Prestwick International Airport buildings.

The lasting importance of the ferry service to Prestwick in putting the Airport and Scotland on the international aviation map was recognised by David McIntyre through the introduction of the annual Transatlantic Dinners hosted by Scottish Aviation and held at the Orangefield Terminal Hotel on the Nov 29th anniversary of the first crossing to land at Prestwick. The dinners were held from 1941 to 1952, and were attended in the wartime

Control tower of Prestwick Airport located on top of the Orangefield Hotel looking northeast over the dispersal area in 1944.

period by the air attaches of several embassies such was the stature of the event. It was usually addressed by a major aviation personality and the then current Secretary of State for Scotland. David McIntyre also used these events to promote the position of Prestwick and reinforce his business objective of seeing Prestwick become established as a major International Airport.

Scottish Aviation managed most of the Airport services during the war under contract to the Air Ministry and thereby were able to maintain a significant influence in the developments, however not to the extent that David McIntyre and the Company would have liked, particularly in the wider reaching and longer term decisions. The rapid growth of aircraft

Prestwick Aerodrome looking northwest up the main runway shortly after the surfacing of the main and cross runways in 1942.

movements on the airfield quickly turned the grass landing ground into a quagmire in wet weather and a hard runway became imperative. David McIntyre was able, after considerable pressure and backing from the Director of the Atlantic Ferry Organisation, to get a 2,200 yard long main tarmac runway, 100 yds wide constructed by the Ministry at Prestwick, which came into use in September 1941. The second shorter 1,500 yard cross-runway was given a tarmac surface in 1942.

## 1942 — Manufacturing design capability established

With a view to expanding the Company's manufacturing capability David McIntyre in 1942, recruited a Chief Designer from Hawker Aircraft, Robert McIntyre (only latterly discovered to be related three generations past) to lead a new design team and establish an approved Aircraft Design office at Prestwick. One of the early designs to make an appearance was a twin fuselage six engined aircraft, which could operate either as a landplane or seaplane. It was designed to carry 160 passengers with a maximum take off weight of 300,000 lbs and was planned for the post war Scottish Airlines North Atlantic air route. The more immediate day to day work involved design modifications for the military aircraft undertaken for the Air Ministry at the factory at Prestwick and other sites.

David McIntyre made a second trip to the United States in 1942 to establish arrangements with the Consolidated Aircraft Co at San Diego, California to enable Scottish Aviation to conduct the maintenance and modification of Liberator aircraft at Prestwick. He was quite probably also taking in the long-

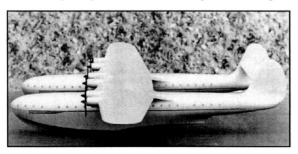

Early Scottish Aviation design for a long range passenger carrying seaplane for its post war transatlantic service.

term prospects for post war aviation activity and assessing the increasingly significant developments taking place in the USA.

The war severely curtailed David McIntyre's own flying activities and in 1942 his piloting hours for the year were down to 20. The company had acquired a 5 seater high wing monoplane communication aircraft with a retracting undercarriage called a Heston Phoenix X2891 in which he conducted several testing flights. He also logged four hours in a Miles Magister P2504, which was used as a trainer by the RAF, and on one occasion in November he took the co-pilots seat in a Catalina FP192 during a test flight being conducted at Greenock by Dick Ellison.

By 1942 David McIntyre's domestic life at the Cushats was becoming more and more hectic as the activities at the aerodrome and elsewhere expanded. Frequently he would

bring home some important visitor who had arrived at Prestwick unexpectedly whom he wished to entertain, particularly if there was a likelihood of influencing the future prospects of the business and the airport. Marjorie McIntyre ran a market garden in the walled garden with a land girl and a hen run was erected outside the backyard in which a dozen or more hens were kept for eggs. Later on some ducks were kept as well, which caused a number of problems not the least being a messy habit of laying eggs in the swimming pool. At one point there was a pig housed in an enclosure at the back of the garage, which was eventually sold for slaughter. This agricultural work was undertaken by his wife in addition to the maintenance of the household and looking after three young children, which became a considerable strain on her. It was probably due to this added burden that she was to suffer her second miscarriage, towards the end of 1942, not long after she had attended the wedding of David McIntyre's niece Louise Kilpatrick (one of their bridesmaids) on 18th November, an event at which he was unable to be present due the intense activity at the airport.

David McIntyre's mother died in the October of 1942 at the age of 81 and was buried alongside her husband in the family grave at Alloway. This left his parents home at the Durdans in Ayr to be run by his eldest sister Bunt who maintained the family home until her death in 1983 having outlived all her younger siblings.

## 1943 — Post War plans for Prestwick announced

In March of 1943 the Company obtained the use of an Airspeed Oxford ED190, a twin engined communications aircraft to replace the earlier Heston Phoenix. It was in the Oxford that David McIntyre conducted the major number of his flying trips around the country for some years to come. This aircraft was used for carrying personnel and equipment to various locations where Scottish Aviation were conducting work of one sort or another and in 1943 the most frequent destination in David McIntyre's log book is Aldergrove in Northern Ireland where Scottish Aviation had a repair and maintenance crew stationed. Other destinations he recorded visiting included Oban, Lyneham, Boscombe Down, Beaulieu, St Eval, and Manorbier. He logged a total of 34 hours in this year, 3 of which were in DH82 Tiger Moth BD171.

One of the visible signs of the importance with which David McIntyre's contribution to civil aviation through his management and development of the airport operations at Prestwick was recognised, is shown in his appointment by American Airlines to the status of 'Admiral of the Flagship Fleet' in Aug

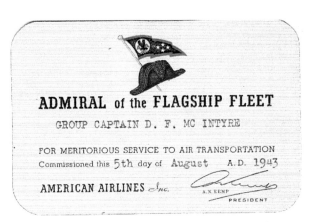

American Airlines membership card issued to DFM on becoming an Admiral.

Certificate awarded to DFM by American Airlines—in recognition for his work to enable the transatlantic air bridge at Prestwick and its impact on Airline development

1943, "For meritorious service to Air Transportation". He was presented with a certificate and a membership card, which represented an early version of an Executive club system, which American Airlines awarded free to important members of the Aviation Industry. David McIntyre noted in his 1944 trip report having enjoyed an excellent lunch at the Admirals Club at La Guardia airport terminal buildings New York, it being the first such use of his 'Admiral' status.

David McIntyre continually strove to establish a future post war role for Prestwick as

a major International Airport, having become convinced of the potential for air transport with the consequent expansion of international and intercontinental air routes. A Company Plan was published in 1943 and updated in 1944 to promote his vision for the future of Prestwick and he commissioned local artist Tom Gilfillan to illustrate the pamphlet. The classic art deco style images from the Plan show the 4-mile runway leading to a seaplane anchorage and landing jetty in Troon bay, which David McIn-

1943 SAL development Pamphlet

Cover for 1944 North Atlantic Survey proposal by Scottish Aviation for the development of the Airport at Prestwick as an International Hub for post war Airlines

tyre envisaged. Fortunately for the members of Old Troon and Old Prestwick golf courses, the pre-war dominance of seaplanes declined during the war as land based runways were built for military use throughout the world. Even so, the Company were still promoting this extended seaplane layout as late as 1947.

The Development Plan indicated the intention of Scottish Aviation to enter into the aircraft manufacturing business and to form a Scottish International Airline. This was seen by De Havillands' as a competitive venture and led to their amicable departure from the management and investment in the Company in 1943. By this time the fortunes of the Hamilton Trustees had improved sufficiently to allow them to buy out the existing shareholders. With the exception of McIntyre and Clydesdale (now the 14th Duke of Hamilton), the new plans were felt by all the remaining Directors to be financially unsound and led to their resignation. Stewart Kennedy, also unable to agree with the new plans, left at this time to make Hatfield his base, later becoming De Havilland's Financial Director. Stewart Kennedy's (ASK) biographical notes on this stage of the company development are revealing and read "While David McIntyre was a

wonderful enthusiast and leader with great imagination and the most likeable personality, he was not very money conscious and the programme he proposed was not considered economically feasible by the other members of the Board including ASK. ASK and R L Angus, a local Director, tried to get David McIntyre, on the airline proposition, to join up with Cunard who were willing but wished to have control. "No shipping greybeards" said David McIntyre".

In a letter accompanying these plans, which he sent to his father-in-law George William Potts on 6th Dec 1943, he recorded, "*I am afraid you will think that we are being very broad in our proposals, but I have been carefully preparing the ground for all of them for many years.*" He also commented, "*on my theory that transport is the most important factor in commerce and civilisation, I am sure there has never been a period in history which was so full of opportunities as the present*".

Certificate presented to DFM recording his crossing of the Equator during his South Atlantic outward route to the USA in 1944.

To support his theory and to promote the case for development at Prestwick he prepared a lecture in which he projected the growth in airline passenger transport at the expense of the shipping trade. His slides for this lecture still exist and it was reported on at least one occasion that his forecasts were challenged by the shipping industry as being unrealistic. In the event, history has shown that he was, if anything, too conservative in his predictions.

Sketch layout of proposed extension of the Prestwick Airport runways for post war international operations. It included an integral Railway station and freight terminal with associated seaplane facilities.

## 1944 — Groundwork for Scottish Airlines put in place

Another trip to the USA in Jan 1944 also took him to Ottawa, Canada having been invited by the Prime Minister of Ontario to deliver a speech to the Aviation Industry there. This trip was flown across the Southern Atlantic route in a DC4 of TWA crossing from Dakar in West Africa to Fortaleza, Brazil. During this flight he crossed the Equator, receiving a humorous certificate to record this celestial event. His visit to Consolidated on this trip involved flying across the States from New York to San Diego in a Dakota of TWA (Transcontinental and Western Air Inc).

The return trip was with United Airlines, and he recounted experiencing a number of hairy moments on both legs of the journey. He also negotiated with TWA to provide the handling and servicing facilities he expected to need for the transatlantic passenger airline service he planned that Scottish Airlines would run from Prestwick to New York when the war ended. He took the opportunity to examine the benefits, which were evident in the USA, of having a competitive and privatised airline industry, all the time looking for arguments and examples to counter the socialist thinking in the UK who imposed a single nationalised airline arrangement.

David McIntyre's 40 page trip report makes most interesting reading with comments on the social and political situation in USA and Canada as well as a detailed range of observations about the aviation operations and practices, which he had experienced during the three week visit. Interestingly he made little or no reference to the fact that the war was going on and all his thoughts were concentrated on the post war situation and its opportunities for the airport and airline business at Prestwick.

Under David McIntyre's encouragement the design team were looking for the most economic aircraft with which to launch their post war transatlantic passenger service.

The Liberator wing design was thought to be the most efficient available so a new fuselage was designed to go with it. This would be pressurised and the aircraft which he had named 'Concord', would be powered by

David McIntyre in wartime garb at Prestwick

Model of Scottish Aviation 'Concord' airliner design based on a liberator wing with a 30 seat pressurised passenger cabin for their Atlantic service.

advanced piston or gas turbine engines. Ministry support to help fund this project, proposed as early as 1943, was not forthcoming either for the airframe or engine work and although the Consolidated Aircraft Co gave manufacturing licence permission in Jan 1944, nothing came of it. Government reluctance to permit converted US aircraft to be used by British operators and the imminent introduction of the Lockheed Constellation with which the 'Concord' could not compete, although competitive with the DC4 (C54) transports of the day, brought the scheme to a halt in Oct 1945.

It would be fair to imagine that the activity levels for David McIntyre in this wartime period were very hectic. In particular, as the Airport operated round the clock, he could be called out at all hours of the night if a problem arose needing his attention or if an important

Early TWA Constellation at Prestwick c 1945 - wartime camouflage still visible on original watch tower opposite.

your ideas, but you go on satisfying my thoughts. The best of success go with you in 1945. I often wish we didn't need to put so many burdens on your shoulders, but thank heaven you seem to thrive under them."

His personal flying in 1944 showed his most frequent destination to be Silloth in Cumberland where Scottish Aviation had a dispersed repair unit for Dakotas and Liberators and where the USAF stored surplus Dakotas, but his total piloting hours for the year dropped to 16. In May of 1944 he recorded a return trip to Iceland in a Liberator as second pilot to Dick

visitor had arrived at short notice. There was not a Christmas day during the war when David McIntyre did not have to go into work for part or all of the day. In a letter to David McIntyre at the end of 1944, Carlyle Gifford one of Scottish Aviation's elder statesmen recorded, "as the year closes I feel I must send a line to express my admiration of the great work you have done and are doing at Prestwick! I often express my admiration of it to other people, but it is only an occasion like the closing of a year which gives the chance to do so to yourself. My feeling is very sincere. I don't think I am an uncritical person, and I do my best not to be carried away by sympathy for

USAF Liberator being prepared by a US crew during a stop over at Prestwick c 1944 (IWM–CH17464)

Ellison with an overnight stay at Reykjavik. This trip, taking about 4 hrs 50 mins each way, was to deliver spare parts to a Scottish Aviation maintenance work party at Meeks field in Iceland. He recorded a number of other trips in the Liberator as second pilot flown by John Dobson in 1944 including two which were noted as local gunnery tests and one wonders where around Prestwick these might have been carried out.

## 1945 — War in Europe ends

David McIntyre finished the war with the rank of Group Captain and this title was to be used by many of his colleagues and employees for a long time afterwards to refer to him although he was never to use it himself. His trips to Silloth continued in the early months of 1945 and were almost certainly involved with the provision of ex USAF Dakota aircraft for conversion at the Prestwick factory in preparation for the cessation of hostilities and the development of post war civil air transport operations.

David McIntyre returning to Prestwick from a wartime trip.

Fortress bomber in Anson hanger (almost) undergoing modifications for anti submarine duties over the Atlantic. (IWM-CH17438)

During the war there were some 15,000 military aircraft destined for the US Air Force in Europe, which passed through Prestwick, together with 5,800 bombers, which went into service with the RAF. These military movements when added to the return ferry and passenger traffic, reached an estimated total of 37,000 by September 1945 when the USAAF support operation closed down at Prestwick. At the peak periods it was not uncommon for 300 aircraft to pass through Prestwick in a single day and in the month of Aug 1944, the daily average was 260. Some 22,000 passengers made the uncomfortable crossing of the North Atlantic with the BOAC return ferry service which other airlines such as Trans Canada Airlines also took part. This undoubtedly put Prestwick firmly on the World Aviation map.

When the Civilian Repair Organisation activities, which Scottish Aviation undertook on behalf of the Ministry of Aircraft Production under David McIntyre's leadership, are looked at in summary, the list is impressive. As well as the local factories at Prestwick, Largs and Greeenock, there were units operating at Edzell, Silloth, Macmerry, Hendon, Doncaster, Melton Mowbray and working parties at Meeks Field in Iceland and in Northern Ireland. The list of aircraft types they worked

on is no less impressive being the Battle, Boston, Catalina, Dakota, Defiant, Hector, Hudson, Hurricane, Lerwick, Liberator, London, Lysander, Oxford, Proctor, Skua, Spitfire, Stranraer, Sunderland, and Tomahawk. By the end of the War the factory floor space at Prestwick had grown from 29,500 sq ft to 845,000 sq ft and at its peak the company had some 6,500 people working on their contracts at Prestwick, Renfrew, Greenock and Glasgow. Of the 48,000 aircraft returned to service throughout the Civilian Repair Organisation during the war, about one in fifty was contributed by Scottish Aviation. In spite of the considerable reputation, which the company had established through its war work however, the Air

David McIntyre and the Duke of Hamilton at Prestwick on receiving the Freedom of the town in 1945 in recognition of the community benefits brought about by the development of the Airport.

Certificate recording the Freedom of Prestwick bestowed upon David McIntyre in 1945

ministry advised the company in 1945 that they would not be receiving any post war contracts.

This brings to a close the World War 2 chapter, which saw the business at Prestwick, totally transformed and had given Scottish Aviation Ltd under the leadership of David McIntyre a major foothold in the British Aviation Industry, a position which the post-war British government seemed determined to deny and obstruct at every opportunity.

The Town Council of Prestwick recognised the importance to the local community of the developments at Prestwick Airport and saw fit to confer on the Duke of Hamilton and David McIntyre the Freedom of Prestwick at a ceremony held on the 27th of June 1945. However no other public recognition seems to have been considered appropriate by officialdom at the time for the achievement and contribution of the Company and its founders to the war effort.

Front side of David McIntyre's "Short Snorter" bank note carrying his own signature amongst many others.

# 7. Scottish Aviation—Post war ventures

In May 1945 the company chose to adopt a new Coat of Arms and a motto "The World O'er" proposed by its Director, Lord Nigel Douglas Hamilton, The Earl of Selkirk, to reflect the developing status and aspirations of the 10 year old company. This replaced, but still incorporated, the original winged Tiger motif, which had been established in the Flying Training School days.

Scottish Aviation Coat of arms design dated May 1945 but omitting the motto "The World O'er" normally seen below

By the end of 1945, the immediate post war situation was to half the Scottish Aviation work force, as military contracts were brought to an end and sub-contract work was hard to find since the whole industry was contracting and established aircraft companies brought all their outsourced work back to their home bases. David McIntyre was able to negotiate an agreement with the Douglas Aircraft Corporation for Scottish Aviation to become their authorised repair, conversion and maintenance centre for Britain, from which a lot of much needed work for the factory was obtained.

A logical extension of the Dakota conversion work was the overhaul of the Pratt & Whitney radial engines with which they were powered. David McIntyre arranged in December 1945 for Scottish Aviation to become an official distributor and repair centre for Pratt & Whitney in the UK. Engine repair work was later extended to the servicing and overhaul of Rolls Royce Merlin, Griffon and other types including gas turbines and this continued as a steady source of work for Scottish Aviation's Prestwick factory through into the 1980's.

David McIntyre amassed only 14 piloting hours in 1945, all in the Oxford ED190, which by the end of the year had been decommissioned and given the civil registration G-AHDZ in the Scottish Airlines fleet. His last recorded entry for the year on August 27th 1945, was a test flight in the Oxford with Noel Capper who had recently returned to the Company after his sojourn as a Training instructor with the RAF during the war.

Scottish Aviation's factory area at the end of WW2. Main runway finishes opposite the "Palace" main Hanger door

Oxford ED190 converted to passenger use after the end of the war.

## 1946 — Airline operations commence

David McIntyre had applied as early as May 1944 for the right to operate both Transatlantic and European passenger routes from Prestwick, however Scottish Airlines were not allowed to obtain and convert any aircraft for their own use until late in 1945. They were one of the first companies to commence airline operations after the war when on 28th Jan 1946, the Scottish Airlines, Prestwick - Belfast service commenced using their first Dakota G-AGWS. The Company was represented by The Earl of Selkirk and W. Oakely, the local Director of the Ministry of Aircraft

Lord Selkirk, Director of Scottish Aviation shaking hands with the Mayor of Belfast on arrival of inaugural flight of Scottish Airlines Prestwick to Belfast service 28 Jan 1946

Production who were greeted by the Mayor of Belfast on this inaugural flight. This service, at a fare of 30 shillings for the 35 minute journey, was initially routed to Sydenham Airfield but later transferred to Aldergrove Airport with Scottish Aviation also providing a bus link for passengers to the Belfast city centre. The early post-war operations were limited by government decree to 60 hrs flying per month per aircraft due to fuel shortages however Scottish Airlines also managed to operate a Prestwick -

London service for a short period at this time. Another early scheme proposed was to run a flying boat passenger service from Largs to Arran for which Scottish Aviation modified two Walrus amphibians to conduct the service. The company obtained a passenger carrying licence for one of these to operate but they never went into commercial service.

David McIntyre and the Duke of Hamilton made a visit to the USA in 1946 in one of the

Scottish Airlines Dakota parked outside the Orangefield passenger terminal at Prestwick in 1946. This aircraft was converted from military to civil passenger use by Scottish Aviation at the end of the war.

Scottish Aviation converted Liberators, which included a visit to Los Angeles to meet with Donald Douglas, with whom David McIntyre had become acquainted. The trip was scheduled as a "Survey Flight" and conducted in the first of the Liberator freighters due to be converted by Scottish Aviation into passenger use, which had been painted up with the mission statement emblazoned on the fuselage. The telegram authorising the trip from Prestwick to La Guardia (New York) was only received at the last minute on 15th March 1946 and David McIntyre's log book shows him as having been 2nd Pilot in the Liberator G-AGZH on the 3 hr

Walrus amphibian prepared by SAL for passenger use and intended for a service to Arran in 1947.

Scottish Airlines Liberator with David McIntyre, Sir Walter Elliot, and the Duke of Hamilton viewing logo prior to leaving on the Survey Flight in 1946.

55 min leg from Prestwick to Reykjavik on 16th March piloted by John Dobson. After their stop in New York, the route took them on to Washington and across the US continent to San Diego and Los Angeles (Santa Monica) with the purpose of visiting the factories of Consolidated, Douglas and Lockheed. Some embarrassment was caused when the Liberator, with John Dobson at the helm, overshot the end of the runway on landing at Los Angeles and the Scottish Aviation team, which included Sir Walter Elliot, had to disembark in a somewhat undignified manner some distance from the awaiting reception party. A photo of David McIntyre and the Duke of Hamilton taken in the Café Caliente restaurant in Los Angeles during this trip gives a little flavour of the transatlantic luxuries compared with the austerity back home.

The conversion work on Dakota and C54 Skymaster military transports into civil airliners was the factory lifeline immediately post war and there were at least 25 Airlines whose resurgent post war passenger routes were flown in aircraft converted by Scottish Aviation. The better known of these being KLM, Sabena, TAP, Aer Lingus, SAS, Cyprus, Olympic, and Scottish Airlines itself. In addition, Scottish Aviation provided Executive conversions for

Lord Beaverbrook and others such as the King of Belgium, the Maharajah of Baroda, Haille Selassie (Emperor of Abyssinia) and the first ever pressurised Dakota for the Prime Minister of India. Another of the Airlines which obtained 2 converted Dakotas from Scottish Aviation around this time was Westminster Airways. This was an outfit run by an ex 602 Squadron RAF adjutant named De Vere Harvey who had become an MP and with some other MP's had set up a charter operation from Blackbush near London.

The newly elected post-war Labour government lost little time introducing their Nationalisation policies and in Aug 1946 Scottish Airlines were barred from operating scheduled airline passenger services which were by then only legally permitted by the monopoly BEA and BOAC airline corporations. David McIntyre battled long and hard to enable the Scottish Airlines operations to continue however by October 1946 the Prestwick - Belfast contract was terminated.

David McIntyre's log book shows him taking three flights in the Dakota G-AGWS in January as second pilot to Dick Ellison flying to Aberdeen, Belfast and Turnhouse, possibly as proving flights prior to the start of the Belfast service. Two days before the Survey trip to the USA he flew as second pilot with John Dobson

David McIntyre and the Duke of Hamilton seen at the Cafe Caliente in Los Angeles in 1946 while visiting Donald Douglas of the Douglas Aircraft Corporation.

in the Liberator to Schipol and back also probably a proving flight prior to the USA trip. In May he took a similar trip with John Dobson in the Liberator G-AHDY to Reykjavik probably to conduct the negotiations with Icelandair for the forthcoming Iceland - Den-

Passengers boarding a Scottish Airlines Dakota at Prestwick in 1946.

mark service via Prestwick. Most of the rest of his flying for the year was in the Oxford G-AHDZ but he also included a couple of test flights in the Proctor G-AHMT. His total piloting hours for the year however only amounted to 14.

For a 3 month period from Sept to Dec 1946, Marjorie McIntyre was undergoing a rest cure to recover from the results of 6 years of wartime overwork which resulted in David McIntyre writing to her nearly every day. These letters have been preserved and give a small but magnified window into the almost daily life of David McIntyre recording his thoughts and difficulties which have allowed the events in this short but influential period to be amplified.

In his personal letters to Marjorie McIntyre at the time, he recorded his frustration at the attitude of a British European Airways Corporation bloke named Amherst with whom he had a number of frustrating meetings, after one on Oct 18th, he wrote, *"a hectic day and a little disappointing in that the Rat, Amherst is making our relationship unnecessarily difficult"* later he commented *"I shall try to get Whitney Straight or some sensible person in BEA, to have lunch with me and see if we can have someone, apart from Amherst to deal with."*.

The measure of his frustration can be judged by this comment in his next letter on Sunday 20th, *"I had intended to get through some work last night but I was so 'browned-off' with all the Amherst nonsense that I gave myself a complete holiday and finished with my hands instead, in making Dougal's glider."* A

week or so later he was becoming a little more relaxed and wrote, *"Amherst and his gang still get in my hair but I am becoming less sensitive about them since we seem likely to fix bigger things with Portugal"*. On 25th Oct he sent Marjorie McIntyre a leading article from the Glasgow Herald, which criticised the BEA decision to close the Prestwick - London service that they reported "merely resulted in the transfer of Scottish aircraft and crews to the employment of Air France." and brings "the Governments whole aviation policy under suspicion". (Scottish Airlines at this time engaged in assisting Air France with their Prestwick - Paris service).

After much lobbying and raising the visibility on the Prestwick issue during November, he recorded on Dec 5th, *"The menace Amherst shows signs of cracking slightly in the course of one or two heated telephone calls and I think will eventually come round to our ideas for the Belfast services"*, these were due to restart on 17th Dec. Latterly on 9th Dec he recorded *"Amherst is, if anything, being slightly less of a nuisance these days and shows signs of being easier to deal with."*

So with characteristic determination and no small personal effort, he had managed to wear down the opposition and re-establish domestic operations for the Scottish Airlines business which by this time had grown to a staff of over 70 for whose welfare he was showing considerable concerns. In his letters at this time he recorded the difficulty of getting suitable accommodation for the families of his new staff and for the need to arrange a Christmas party at the offices in the "Palace", the numbers now being too great to accommodate at the Cushats.

The reference to Portugal related to a deal he was trying to set up with the Portuguese Government to fly a service from Prestwick - London - Lisbon with potential future links to the Azores, South America and South Africa which he acknowledged would be in competition with 'Amherst's outfit'. He had 2 days of meetings with a Colonel Delgardo in London and with the Ministry of Civil Aviation during October and they finalised a deal which he described to Marjorie McIntyre as follows *"The present proposal is to start off with once weekly*

A Scottish Airlines Dakota airliner flying over Heathfield Aerodrome just after the end of WW2.

*return service Prestwick - London - Lisbon - Azores followed by an inter-island local service within the Azores and then extended from Lisbon to South America and South Africa. We will be in competition with Amherst's outfit between London and Lisbon but BEAC make a stop at Bordeaux taking seven hours whereas we will go direct in four and a half which is a selling point."*

He then wrote after a later meeting, *"I have the tail end of the Portuguese people to lunch and then most of the afternoon at MCA where I hope to get Henry Self down to spots. The intention is to persuade him that the Portuguese deal is so important to Britain that MCA should make it possible for us to buy Constellations or Skymasters for the service".*

Since passenger aircraft were in short supply at the time and these were U.S manufactured, he was playing a long shot here. At one point he made reference to a possible proving flight with The Earl of Selkirk and the Portuguese Government chaps to the Azores but there was no record that this took place. By the middle of November he recorded that President Salazar had turned down the proposal and although he noted an intention to pay Salazar a visit in December, it does not

appear to have taken place. There is no further reference to this venture, which bears out a comment he made in an earlier letter *"I imagine we will straighten it out again but these dictatorships are a chancy market".*

Another of David McIntyre's battles detailed in this period was with a Government parliamentary secretary appointed to the Ministry of Civil Aviation by the name of Lindgren whom he described before his first meeting thus, *"I am not expecting his visit to be more than one would expect from a railway porter. He only became an MP for the first time at the last election."*

The visit of Mr G.S.Lindgren to Prestwick was on 14th Nov, and heralded in the press with the comment "who cannot hope to examine even the local problems in detail, much less the effects of excessive centralisation of control on the national economy". David McIntyre made the comment of this article *"I hope Lindgren will read on arrival. He does not arrive until 6.30 (pm) so it sounds like another evening of solid shop, from which I do not expect any good will come."* However it was not quite as negative as he had feared, for after only a few hours sleep, he wrote to Marjorie McIntyre over breakfast the next day, *"Once Lindgren arrived we were hard at it until 1 am and I am writing this before the days work starts. We let our back hair down with Lindgren and I think it has made some sort of impression on him if that means anything. Like all the others, he arrived primed with false polices and prejudice, but I think we have scared some of this out of his mind. We shall know better by the time we have finished with him this afternoon.".*

At the end of this session he wrote that he was *"not cheerful after a bout with the Government machine in the form of Lindgren and his henchmen. I have no idea and little real confidence in the result of our battle with these Government people."*

So his early overnight optimism had been quickly dashed in the cold light of day. (PS. George Lindgren having lost his seat in the 1959 election, returned to the railway and worked as a clerk in the Eastern Region Chief Civil Engineer's Office at King's Cross;)

David McIntyre found a champion in the new Scottish Secretary, Tom Johnston who shared the belief that Prestwick and Scotland should be better served by the Government of which he was part. In a letter to Marjorie McIntyre on 3rd Nov he wrote:

*"I think I see signs of the worm turning up here. The press are once more full of Prestwick and its problems. Tom Johnston has now lost all patience with his Labour Government and is about ready to lead a rebellion so the sparks should fly on the 29th November when he is to propose a toast to 'Civil Aviation' at our* (Transatlantic) *dinner party and Lord Nathan is replying, followed by Walter Elliot, Plessman and the rest of us. Johnston has already told the Government that the Prestwick issue sums up everything that Scotland demands, and that unless they deal with it satisfactorily and quickly, it will be the issue on which they flounder as far as the North is concerned. Johnston now openly refers to Prestwick as the 20th Century Bannockburn. Isn't it fantastic that unity can be impaired for no other reason that Nathan, Winster and his predecessors have accepted advice from a few civil servants who happen to be incompetent and too small for the problems they tackle."*

The Transatlantic Dinner is the annual event David McIntyre launched in 1941 to celebrate the opening of the Atlantic Air Bridge for military aircraft coming in to Prestwick from North America and was one of the prestige Aviation events of the year at the time. He was clearly using this event to push the Prestwick and nationalisation issues, which are forefront in thwarting his plans for Aviation growth at Prestwick. On the evening before the dinner he wrote to Marjorie McIntyre regarding Lord Nathan thus: *"Nathan has just announced the names of the Scottish Advisory Council who are to advise the English Corporations on how to run Aviation for Scotland. It is as we expected - a great wad of Lord Provosts and other old women under the chairmanship of Pat Dollan, not a glimmer of aviation experience in any of them, in fact it is just laughable."*

Vision of passenger aviation post war, as depicted by Tom Gilfillan in the Orangefield passenger lounge.

When reporting the experience of the Transatlantic dinner to Marjorie McIntyre he recorded:

*"Dinner party really was a great success and I doubt there is anything to touch it in Scotland. Three Secretaries of State all fighting with each other, one Minister - and most of the guests from distance parts. Geordie had refused to join the Advisory Council but weakened in the course of Friday evening under pressure from Dollan and others. I am not sure whether he has done the right thing or not. I believe I shall be faced with a somewhat similar decision in the near future but there is a smell of Quisling about it all which I don't think will be easily dispelled, and self respect is the one thing to hold onto in these peculiar times."*

David McIntyre was using the Quisling reference to infer that he would not become involved with the Advisory Council as it represented all the things which he considered wrong with the Labour Government's policy in respect to the best interests of post-war aviation in Britain, and if he did so, it would be a traitorous act in his own eyes.

Lobbying through the House of Lords and the Commons was a regular method through which David McIntyre tried to get the message across to promote the cause of Prestwick in this oppressive period of Nationalisation, which threatened to unravel all the growth, and aspirations he has worked for in the previous 10 years. The Earl of Selkirk is one of their main spokesmen in addition to the local MP as he recorded in this letter to Marjorie McIntyre,

*"Sir T. Moore evidently asked in the house today for a comparison of profits shown on the 30/- Prestwick fare to Belfast and the 50/- fare from Renfrew and received the usual evasive and twisted reply from Lindgren who I shall have on my hands up here next week."*

The influence of this lobbying is recalled by David McIntyre in this letter on 7th Nov when he wrote:

*"Tom Johnston's theory this afternoon was that the more the Government Nationalise the quicker they - either fall - or pass a great deal back to local enterprise and Management. His estimate is not more than three months before we will have won our battle. He maintains that,*

Scottish Aviation Transatlantic Anniversary Dinner at Prestwick Airport Orangefield Hotel dining room. Tom Johnston Secretary of State for Scotland seated on DFM's right.

Scottish Airlines Liberator converted for passenger use at SAL in flight over Prestwick in 1946

*as a result of our Prestwick struggle and the widespread interest we have aroused, he has been able to keep such things as Electricity, Forestry, Finance and the Tourist industry under Scottish control and now he and many others are going to ensure that Scottish Aviation get fully repaid for the work we have done. He seemed very sincere and certain about it all but I shall believe it when I see it all happen."*

In the event he was right to be sceptical as the Airline was never allowed to compete on an even playing field and the Airport compensation argument raged on for another 7 years, however if his comment regarding the affect on Scottish affairs was correct, the post-war Scots have a lot to thank David McIntyre for.

During the 1946-1948 period, Scottish Airlines co-ordinated with their freight and travel agency subsidiary Scottish Air Express to ferry passengers to Lisbon to connect with an Anchor Line cruise ship. On one of these flights it also took David McIntyre and his wife with the Dobsons' to a golfing weekend at Estoril at a time when foreign currency was very hard to come by and the family folklore tells that David McIntyre, in order to find

sufficient funds to pay the hotel bill, had to resort to a risky but eventually successful stint at the roulette tables to make ends meet. Early in this period David McIntyre was planning to set up an Air Cruising holiday venture flying 24 passengers at £100 a time for a 2-week holiday in North Africa. He outlined his plans to Marjorie McIntyre thus:

*"Our ideas as regards Sunshine Cruises by Air are gradually taking shape and becoming simplified. I have more or less made up my mind to confine our attempt this winter to 14 days at Marrakech, leaving Prestwick twice weekly with 24 passengers on each cruise from the beginning of December to the end of February by which time we will have gained experience for more ambitious cruises.*

*I am afraid it is going to be expensive £100 but even so, I think a lot of people will like the idea of turning up at Prestwick for dinner at eight, leaving at ten and, after a comfortable night flight, getting out in a desert dawn at Marrakech to start 14 days solid sunshine in the native capital of Morocco, to live in luxury European type hotels with nice swimming pools and have winter sports on the Atlas mountains*

*40 miles away, with the absolute certainty of blue sky and hot sun all day and every day. We shall certainly test the market and I think we will find it a good one."* A month later he reported *" I think I have taken our Air Cruises a stage further today and I think we will open up to Lisbon (14 day cruise) on 20th Dec, and keep them running until the end of March, perhaps an Algeria or Tunis one as well."*

There was no record of this scheme having materialised but it shows the diversity of his thoughts in promoting further business.

In 1945 an unusual specification for a combined Army, Navy and Air Force front-line communications aircraft was formulated based

Prototype Pioneer I with gipsy Queen engine VL515 outside factory in 1947

on experience gained during WW2. The aircraft was to have a pilot and 4 passengers capable of being operated from rough surfaces and small landing grounds not exceeding 100 Yards. The specification called for steep angles of approach and climb-out in order that the aircraft could be operated in very confined spaces. It also had to be capable of withstanding long periods in the open and of being maintained by semi-skilled personnel in isolation from technical facilities and under severe climatic conditions.

Scottish Aviation, having established a manufacturing reputation during the war, was invited in 1946 by the Ministry to submit a design study for this new specification 'A.4/45', however they were given only 16 days notice before the tenders had to be delivered. It is to the credit of Robert McIntyre and his small team that they were successful over the rival bids from Miles, Folland, Cunliffe Owen and Heston. The Ministry were very slow however in placing the contract, which David McIntyre had estimated, could be for anything up to 400 aircraft. Scottish Aviation went ahead however

Prestwick Pioneer I painting by Tom Gilfillan c 1947

and built a prototype of this design which was a high wing cabin monoplane powered by a 240hp de Havilland Gipsy Queen 34 engine. Initially it was a 3 seater plus pilot and incorporated full span leading edge retractable slats and three quarter span Fowler flaps.

## 1947 — Airline operations widen - Prestwick Pioneer makes first flight

The prototype Prestwick Pioneer, VL515 - factory designation G.31.1, first flew in November 1947, designated Pioneer I and demonstrated a 33 mph stalling speed and a maxi-

Bell 47B helicopter at Prestwick being inspected shortly after arrival in 1946.

mum speed of 124 mph. Takeoff and landing distances were remarkably short, one well publicised photo in the snow recording a landing run of 26 yards. Testing and development work on the prototype continued throughout the rest of the year.

An aviation venture, which David McIntyre encouraged Scottish Aviation to pursue, was the formation in 1947, of a helicopter sales company in association with Bell, the helicopter makers and the Irvin parachute company, to sell the new lightweight Bell 47 helicopters in Europe. Noel Capper was sent off on a training course in the States with a couple of engineers, returning with the task of selling the machines into the European market. Business however was hard to come by due to the high price of the helicopter as compared with the cheap war surplus fixed wing aircraft available for crop spraying which was the main use to which they thought the helicopter was best suited. The venture continued through to 1949 when Cap was involved with training and crop dusting in France but there seems to have been nothing after this. Various photos of the Bell 47 are in the family collection and it was reputed to have landed at

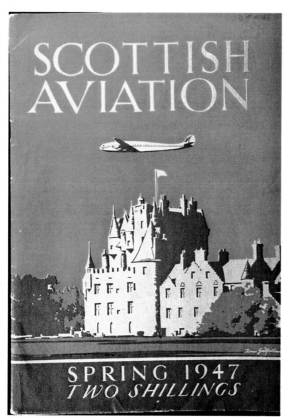

First issue of Scottish Aviation's magazine.

the Cushats on one occasion in the field to the south of the house. On examining Cap's log book this could have been an occasion on May 10th 1948 when he recorded piloting a Greek gentleman to the Cushats and this is confirmed by a similar entry in Marjorie McIntyre's diary.

By 1947 the factory was having difficulties making ends meet due to lack of aviation work and turned its attention to alternative schemes to create short term revenue and employment without the costly and lengthy investment commitments characteristic of aviation work. Various projects were embarked upon such as the manufacture of tractor cabs and bus bodies and other more hair brained schemes such as folding caravans, step ladders and fish boxes. None of these really made enough money to sustain the business and were eventually phased out in 1951 when contracts for more aviation work were achieved.

Early in 1947 David McIntyre decided to venture into the publishing field and introduced a magazine to promote and publicise aviation matters in Scotland, which was titled 'Scottish Aviation' and was mainly based around activities at Prestwick but also included articles of a more general nature. Two issues were published in the spring and autumn of 1947, at a time in the post-war austerity period, when raw materials were still in short supply and disposable income likewise. He referred to this enterprise in a letter to his wife, saying *"Early in November you should have the first issue of the monthly aviation magazine from Prestwick Press Ltd 'Scottish Aviation' which should be quite good although in miniature size due to paper restrictions. New publications have a thin time under present controls. There are also one or two money-making guidebooks on the way - of a superior type. That woman writer in 'Scottish Field', who was so good, is now on the staff of Prestwick Press."* This venture appeared to have been short lived and only two issues have been preserved in the family collection although there may have been others.

In spite of his incredibly busy and irregular working environment, David McIntyre made strenuous efforts to be involved in his children's upbringing and in providing activities and entertainment for them particularly at

DFM's early free flight model powered by an Ohllson 60 petrol engine.

Three children and dog pictured by DFM on Cushats lawn in 1947.

weekends after the war was over. The swimming pool at the Cushats provided the catalyst for buying and making a number of model boats over the period with which much fun was had.

David McIntyre was not unsurprisingly interested in model aeroplanes of which he built a number for the enjoyment of himself and his son Dougal. He recorded in one letter how he found the model building activity a therapeutic release from the politics and frustrations of his working life. In the early days these models were either rubber powered or free flight gliders and there was a good deal of clambering up and down the Brown Hill of Carrick retrieving a Frog glider that he had built. Later he acquired a free flight power model of a Colonel Bowden type design with an inverted Ohllson .60 petrol engine, which was test run at the Cushats, however David McIntyre did not attempt to fly it as far as is known.

David McIntyre was always very keen to get out and about either in the grounds at the Cushats for walks or clearing up the woodland and having bonfires, but also into the neighbouring hills. The Galloway region between Straiton and Glen Trool was the favourite area and the family had many excursions for walks and picnics over the years. David McIntyre was always an active individual, and rarely sat down to relax for its own sake. In keeping the children occupied he adopted a number of ploys, one of which was to play the piano, which he played only by ear but managed to keep up with most popular songs, and would also make up his own lyrics registering his disaffection with the political figures of the day particularly in the immediate post war period. As luck would have it, none of his children demonstrated any signifi-

cant musical talents to accompany him effectively in these interludes.

Golf, which had played such a major part in David McIntyre's courting days, continued to feature strongly in the family activities once the war ended. Living at the Cushats meant that Turnberry continued to be the main location although immediately after the war it

Bonfire on the banks of the Coyle prior to skating on the river in Jan 1947. MFM putting on Anne's skates while DFM wields the camera.

did not comprise a full 18 holes. All the children learned to play and the whole family would then take part in a weekend visit most years in the autumn to Gleneagles, another favourite golfing haunt of David and Marjorie McIntyre.

The January of 1947 saw one of the heaviest snowfalls in Ayrshire for many a long year and the Cushats was snowed in for over a week. David McIntyre was, after a couple of days, able to get to work by driving the Austin 7 over the fields between the snowdrifts to Sundrum and out onto the Coylton – Ayr road which by then had been cleared. It was also the time when the children learned to skate on the river Coyle which had frozen over to the extent that it was possible to walk across it on the ice with ease.

Latterly the Cushats became the venue for the Scottish Aviation Social Club sports day for a number of years and with Marjorie McIntyre's birthday being 5th November a fireworks event was always held on this date. One

Scottish Aviation Sports day at the Cushats sometime in the late 1940's

memorable occasion occurred when David McIntyre had managed to acquire a stock of surplus distress rocket flares from the shipyard at Troon some of which were of the parachute variety and others which exploded with such a noise that the animals in farmer Brown's piggery were sorely disturbed. He did not use them again.

Scottish Airlines were able to obtain a licence to operate the schedules of some of the Scottish services, which had been previously run by Railway Air Services under contract to BEA in Feb 1947. These included the Renfrew – Belfast route which was initially flown using the Fokker F22 G-AFZP, the ex KLM

Scottish Airlines Fokker F22 restored to Civil duties after wartime navigator training service. Used for a short time on the Renfrew - Belfast service by Scottish Airlines.

airliner which had been employed during the war on navigator training and then converted back for passenger use. In addition, during this short 6 month period, they operated the London to Aberdeen, Glasgow and Prestwick routes until these routes were also taken over by BEA themselves.

David McIntyre's low opinion of the way BEA operated in the early post-war period was such that he made a bid to take-over the BEA operations, presenting the Ministry of Civil Aviation with a business plan, which showed quite conclusively that Scottish Airlines could provide a cheaper and more efficient service. It comes as no surprise to find that the Government refused to take the proposition seriously.

The Company in 1947 recognised the efforts, which David McIntyre had been putting in on behalf of the organisation, and there is a letter dated 22 Dec 1947 from the Chairman, notifying him of a raise in salary to £3,500.

Scottish Airlines, in order to keep afloat, had to resort to operating Charter services which, in a number of situations, saw them opening up routes on behalf of a number of European Airlines such as Prestwick - Amsterdam for KLM with discussions on a winter

Scottish Airlines DH Dragon Rapide G-AKSF parked at Orangefield Terminal in 1948. One of SAL's Liberators is parked behind.

sports extension to Basel. Prestwick - Paris for Air France, and Prestwick - Brussels via Manchester for COBETA a newly formed Belgian Airline. Scottish Aviation also operated the Prestwick - Belfast and Prestwick - Isle of Man services on behalf of BEA for a time and also a service from Prestwick to Northolt in London. Occasionally these routes were operated with the Scottish Airlines DH Rapides and they also used the Oxford G-AHDZ for pleasure flights out of Prestwick for a time but mostly it was with the Dakota aircraft, which the factory had converted to civil passenger use. However as these early National Airlines became established with their own trained crews and aircraft, the Scottish Airlines involvement gradually wound down and finally ceased in 1948.

The converted 24 seat Liberator aircraft which Scottish Aviation had produced were used to provide another operation, a weekly service started in May 1946 for Icelandair from Prestwick to Iceland and a twice weekly Reykjavik – Prestwick – Copenhagen route.

Scottish Airlines Dakota at Vaago in the Faroe Islands in 1946.

This service in July 1947 was to provide the family with its first overseas holiday in Denmark when he flew with his wife and children for a 2-week rest in a fishing village at Dragör, near the capital. David McIntyre meanwhile conducted his business in Copenhagen but was unable to take any time off to stay at the seaside. Hardly a word of English was spoken in the village and rations were still very short, but it was sunny and the sea was warm enough to swim in. Activities included a boat trip to the offshore lighthouse and a ferry ride over to Malmö in Sweden and a day at the Tivoli gardens in Copenhagen amongst the rest of the seaside pursuits. Scottish Airlines continued operating this service till mid 1948 and had also operated a Dakota service to the

Strand Hotel overlooking Dragör harbour where family stayed in 1947. MFM, Dougal & Jane on harbour wall.

Faroe Islands for a while whose tricky airfield at Vaago at the end of a Fiord was usually fog bound for 300 days a year. There were also early discussions with Icelandic to convert the Consolidated PBY-5 Catalina for passenger use but these did not come to anything.

Charter work also included trips to Canada, the USA, India, South Africa and the Middle East with consequent hazards due to the ill-developed navigation aids at most airports at this time. Bad weather flying called for the highest levels of skill and experience, which Scottish Airlines had developed in their captains. The rapid growth of the airline had now created a fleet of 20 aircraft and 85 aircrew.

The partition of India and Pakistan in 1947 involved an airlift of refugees from Karachi to Delhi and a return traffic, during which Scottish Airlines operated five of its Dakotas over a two-month period and carried some 50,000 passengers, often in very crowded aircraft. One

Scottish Airlines Dakota at Quetta airfield during India/Pakistan air lift of refugees displaced by the 1947 partition.

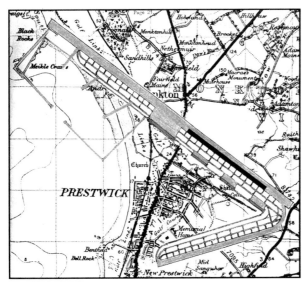

Scottish Aviation scheme for cross runway and main runway development at Prestwick in 1947. Existing 2,200yd runway shown in black

report quoted up to 50 people in a Dakota designed for 21, struggling to take off from these airfields.

Charter work often included freight trips; one of many entries in John Blair's log book records a sequence of five Liberator journeys, each load being 14,500lbs of apricots from Bergamo in Italy to Prestwick. Where they went after arrival is not known.

There was however during this period still a determination to wrest control of the Airport back from the Ministry and David McIntyre lobbied continuously for the interests of Prestwick as an airport and made submissions to review bodies, MP's and anyone who would listen and could influence government thinking. The Scottish Aviation development plan

Air Ministry proposal for the new cross runway development at Prestwick Airport in 1947—shown in red.

was revised in 1947 to provide guidance and direction on the need for additional runway services at the Airport and to counter proposals put forward by the Ministry which the Company felt were unsatisfactory and not in the best interests of the long term welfare of Prestwick. These primarily centred on the provision and location of a new cross runway which was needed due to the closure of the first cross runway which was now unsuitable due to the proximity of the town of Prestwick and the high ground approach from the north east already shown to be prone to incident. In one accident of a KLM Constellation in 1948, the

Luxembourg Airlines 1948 Time-Table of services

famous Dutch pilot Dirk Parmentier along with all 40 occupants of the aircraft were killed when it collided with power lines on a fog bound approach 3 miles from touchdown. Eight years later with some minor alignment changes the cross runway was eventually built in 1955. In the 12 years of his post war life while the airport at Prestwick was under nationalised ownership, he continued to do what he could to promote the Airport's development and was himself a frequent user of the airline services through the airport.

David McIntyre's personal piloting in 1947 continued at a low pitch and again only added up to 14 hours for the year. Mostly these were local test flights around Prestwick in the Oxford or the Proctor but also included trips to

Sydenham, Turnhouse and Dumfries. One unusual flight was a local one hour test on October 10th of a Fairchild Argus G-AJSV, which three weeks later crashed in France.

Scottish Airlines Dakota, transferred to Luxembourg Airlines in 1948

## 1948 — Greek and Luxembourg airline operations commence

The Pioneer series I was delivered to Boscombe Down in 1948 for a test and evaluation programme by the Ministry of Supply and RAF. This programme took them two years to complete and led to the primary conclusion that the Gipsy engine did not provide enough power and the Company undertook a modification to re-engine the airframe which had otherwise been successful. David McIntyre's log book shows him having flown in the prototype Pioneer I, G-31-1 on 27 Aug 1948 at Prestwick with Cap on a local test flight in the Gipsy engined machine.

Scottish Aviation, unable to operate their Airline subsidiary in the UK, sought other avenues to utilise their aircraft and crews. The Luxembourg Airlines deal was an arrangement with the Luxembourg government to set up a flag airline jointly run with Scottish Airlines who would provide the aircraft and the crews paid for by the Government and local businessmen with David McIntyre and one of his Captains, M.R Lacey amongst the Directors. It operated with Dakota and Rapide aircraft starting in February 1948 on routes from Luxembourg to Zurich, Paris, Frankfurt, and later including Athens, Brussels, London, Rome, Nice and Tel Aviv. The nature of this deal was that ultimately the Airline would be nationalised once it had reached the point of being self-supporting. In the event, in 1951, the airline Seaboard and Western took over from Scottish Airlines and the National air-

line, eventually called Luxair, did not form until 1960.

A similar flag airline arrangement was set up with the Greek Government in 1947 to form Hellenic Airlines, which became one of the forerunners of Olympic Airlines. David McIntyre seemed to be more closely involved with this operation, which commenced in Feb 1948 operating with Scottish Airlines converted Liberator and Dakota Aircraft. Initially Scottish Airlines crews manned these aircraft while the Greek employees undertook their training at Prestwick. As an example, John Blair of Scottish Airlines operated as a training captain for Hellenic airlines for an uninterrupted period from Oct 1949 to Sept 1951, flying the Liberators on the Athens - London route and Dakotas on the local routes to the likes of Rhodes.

John Dobson of Scottish Airlines emerging from the company's Liberator at Athens, 23.01.48. Hellenic Airlines director Zeppos and his wife on right.

The King and Queen of Greece at Athens during the inauguration of the Hellenic Airlines Athens–London service via Cairo and Rome in 1948.

Scottish Airlines also had a tie up with an organisation called Hotel Plan, the details of which have been difficult to determine, but

Hellenic Airlines Dakota at Athens Airport with ceremonial band c 1948. These aircraft were operated by Scottish Airlines crews while the Hellenic crews were being trained

which resulted in David McIntyre and his family spending two most enjoyable summer holidays in '48 and '49 in Switzerland at one of the Hotel Plan establishments.

The 1948 trip involved David McIntyre taking the family away in the school holidays at the end of July, staying on Lake Lucerne at the small village of Brunnen in the Grand Hotel having flown from Northolt to Zurich via Luxembourg with Luxembourg Airlines. Hiring an Austin 10 saloon, he took the family around the mountain passes to the Rhone glacier and Andermatt amongst the other local sights of Rigi and Pilatus. The family took their first ride in a cable car and chair lift up to the top of one of the local ski runs and several trips on the paddle steamers on the Lake with many walks along the shore. Swimming in lake Lucerne from the private strandbad attached to the Hotel and pedalo rides on the

DFM and family outside entrance to Rhone Glacier in Switzerland 1949

lake were favourite pastimes and ice cream soda's the luxury treat after the shortages of wartime. The return journey was by car via Zurich, Basel and through France to Luxembourg where the family stayed two nights and flew on to Northolt with Luxembourg Airlines.

In August of 1948, Scottish Airlines aircraft were again involved in charter airlift work, this time to relieve Berlin, which was being blockaded by the Russians. With a short break over the winter of 1948, five Scottish Aviation aircraft between them made around 994 sorties carrying freight, petrol and diesel fuel to the beleaguered citizens of Berlin through to July 1949. A point of interest was that the Liberator aircraft, which were used to carry the fuel, did so in their own wing mounted fuel tanks, while their four engines were fuelled with aviation spirit pumped from drums mounted in the fuselage. This was because the fuel from the wing tanks could be discharged far quicker into the underground storage bunkers, than man-handling drums out of the fuselage, and thus the turnaround of the aircraft was speeded up and more sorties per day could be executed. David McIntyre was keen to see how the operation was going and to give encouragement to the Scottish Aviation crews involved. He managed to arrange a visit on 27 May 1949, which he described in a letter to his wife in these words:

*"Everything went exactly to programme. Left (Prestwick in a Dakota) at 8am and arrived at our German base (Schleswigland) to the North of the Kiel canal at 11am in time to join one of our sorties to Berlin (Tadle in the French Zone) at 11.40. These take about 3 ½ hours and after return to base I had time to have a chat with our crews and engineers and arrived back at Prestwick at 9.30. I was very pleased to get over to Germany at last as our people there are doing a very hard and intricate job in a most efficient, professional manner and I have been feeling very guilty at not having been over there to see the conditions earlier. The Air Lift is a really beautiful example of perfect organisation on a very wide scale. Everything runs on split second timing and absolutely accurate navigation under almost all weather conditions. There is a steady stream of large aircraft in line astern - 9 miles apart - flowing night and day into three*

*Berlin airports and coming from bases which are anything from 200 to 300 miles away."*

Interspersed with the Berlin Airlift, Scottish Airlines were involved in a milk run (to overcome British milk shortages prevalent at the time) from Belfast's Nutts Corner Airport, to Blackpool and Liverpool. This operation began on August 31 1948, and continued until the middle of October 1948. The two Dakotas and one Liberator then returned to Prestwick (one of the Liberators being lost at Liverpool during the milk run). Charter and freight work continued throughout Europe and further a field, including 20 cargoes of cloth from Lille to London, a charter to Jamaica and a summer season route from the Isle of Man to Northolt and Zurich.

David McIntyre only managed seven piloting hours in 1948 again mostly local test flights in the Oxford or Proctor to keep his hand in and only venturing out for two trips in October to Nutts Corner in Northern Ireland in the Oxford with John Dobson. His only other log book entry was when he accompanied Dick Ellison as second pilot in the Dakota G-AGZG to Inverness in June while the airline operated a service during the week of the Highland Show.

## 1949 — Airline operations stagnate

Scottish Airlines was the only private British airline ever to operate the Liberator, and in an agreement signed on 1st April 1949, Scottish Aviation subsequently supplied B.O.A.C. with Liberator crews to fly the Corporation's Prestwick to Montreal passenger service. Through this agreement, B.O.A.C. was able to release ten of its own crews for training on newer types of aircraft. The schedule to Montreal was flown by Scottish Airlines crews three times weekly using six Liberators until they were withdrawn from service in Oct 1949. The Liberator airliners were maintained at Prestwick by Scottish Aviation.

The years 1949 and 1950 were lean years for the Airline with the only scheduled route being the Prestwick to Isle of Man service and a number of varied charters which included ships crews, athletes, boy scouts, with the bulk of the business coming from the shipment of

military personnel and families to a variety of overseas destinations.

Brunnen was the venue for the family holiday in 1949, this time flying Luxembourg Airlines direct from Northolt to Zurich. Similar activities were undertaken with one day devoted to David McIntyre driving the family over three passes, Grimsel, Furka and Susten in the one trip. Both these holidays coincided with the Swiss National Day when water displays were put on at the strandbad and a fireworks display in the evening. The activities included a moonlight motorboat ride on the lake on one evening.

Group of travel agents returning to Prestwick having been shown the delights offered by the Scottish Airlines service to the Isle of Man. - c 1950

David McIntyre had to leave a day or two early to go to Zurich on business and on this occasion the return flight was via Luxembourg. The Luxembourg Airlines flight from Zurich to Luxembourg was in a De Havilland Rapide biplane over the Alps in rough weather which proved quite exciting, before picking up their Dakota service back to London and on to Prestwick.

David McIntyre's personal flying in 1949 continued at a low pitch amounting to only 11 hours for the year. Apart from local tests in the Oxford and Proctor he recorded three trips to Turnhouse, and one to Manchester, Pwllheli and back. One of his Turnhouse trips was in the Scottish Airlines Rapide G-ALBH.

## 1950-1951 — Pioneer production commences - moves home to Troon

The Dakota conversion work continued on and off for a number of years and included a fleet of 38 Dakotas for BEA in 1950 upgraded

Fully loaded the Prestwick Pioneer II was rated with a 75 yard takeoff run and a 66 yard landing run and made its first flight on 5th May 1950, where its maximum airspeed was shown to have been increased to 145 mph. This prototype registered G-AKBF made its first demonstration at the Farnborough Air Show in Sept 1950 while still in the midst of its airworthiness trials at Boscombe Down.

Prestwick Pioneer II prototype G-AKBF landing at Prestwick

to a 32 seat configuration and called Pionairs, David McIntyre having insisted that BEA be dissuaded from using the name Pioneer which had been their first intention. An account of the history of BEA, records that Scottish Aviation were late in the delivery of some of these aircraft reportedly due to industrial relations problems.

In 1951 David McIntyre recruited a new General Manager, Mr TDM Robertson from Hawker Aircraft who was to invigorate the aviation work of the factory and remove the unprofitable ancillary projects. The new work included the construction of components for Canberra and Vampire airframes and conversion work on American aircraft coming into British military service such as Skyraiders, Corsairs, Avengers and Washingtons (RAF versions of the B29 bombers).

One of the companies for which Scottish Aviation did conversion and maintenance work was Ferranti who had a number of electronic radar carrying test bed aircraft. Scottish Aviation also did work on Meteor jet fighters in the early 1950's along with an overhaul contract for Royal Canadian Air Force Sabre jets based in Europe. This was conducted at their Renfrew plant where USAF Sabres had also been serviced. These varied airframe activities along with the engine work, sustained the factory at a low level until the Pioneer developments came into production.

The Pioneer series I, after its two year testing period at the Ministry of Supply was not awarded a production contract, however there was sufficient interest in the basic design for the Company to proceed with a series II version fitted with a more powerful Alvis Leonides 520 hp radial engine and larger fin and rudder.

While David McIntyre struggled with schemes to keep the factory and work force in jobs in the immediate post war period, the company slid into a precarious financial situation, with the Hamilton Trustee backers becoming very uneasy and looking to have their loans repaid. The major asset of the company, namely the airport itself, had been requisitioned by the Air Ministry in 1941, with the company carrying the station operating contract. At the end of the War the new Ministry of Civil Aviation (MCA) declared itself the new landlord and removed the station contract from Scottish Aviation.

However there had been no agreement on the rent to be paid to Scottish Aviation for its use during the war, nor was there an agreement on the value to be paid in compensation for its compulsory purchase. The Ministry offered in 1947 a paltry £87,000 against the Company's valuation of £300,000. The legal arguments waxed and waned through to 1950 when the Civil Aviation Act of 1946 was repealed and replaced in 1949 with another, giving more opportunity for legal argument. In 1951 the Ministry increased its offer to £176,000, which was again rejected by the Company in spite of its precarious financial position and they held out for further negotiations and arbitration.

By 1950, David McIntyre's business situation was calling for the nurturing of more and more business customers and visitors to Prestwick airport and as he preferred to entertain them at home whenever possible, the Cushats was really too small and for family reasons, too remote from the town of Ayr, the main school and shopping centre. There was a decision made to move house and a property at Troon known as Lochgreen House in the south woods was chosen. It is not known if any other properties were considered, and for lots of reasons it was a wrench to move from the idyllic spot, which in many ways characterised the Cushats.

Aerial view of Lochgreen House in 1950. DFM sketched the layout of the main reception rooms of the house on the back of this photo.

However considering other factors, mainly due to the isolation, maintenance cost of the extensive policies and a tendency to be rather damp, the move nearer the Airport and the centres of activity for the children, who would need less ferrying about, was a good one.

Lochgreen House was set in a 14-acre plot of woodland with a large undeveloped field on the seaward side with a blaze tennis court, and at the front a smaller formal garden with a walled garden backed by stables and a 4-car garage. The interior was well appointed with a large drawing room and panelled billiard room

Front view of Lochgreen House shortly after purchase in 1950. MFM seated on bench in front of billiard room and Wolsley CYN906 parked in drive.

at the south exiting onto a large panelled hall off which was the panelled dining room the front door and a door at the west leading through a loggia into the garden. The location proved ideal for David McIntyre's business and family requirements and his wife embarked on a series of garden and interior redevelopment to bring it up to the standard required. An added benefit being that its western boundary ran parallel with one of the holes on Lochgreen golf course and the gar-

den was in reach of a good sliced golf ball in the prevailing wind. Lochgreen was used extensively for the entertaining of business visitors and for a few years provided the location for the Scottish Aviation Social Club sports day, as had been the practice previously at the Cushats.

By 1951 a London service had been negotiated with BEA under an Associate agreement allowing Scottish Aviation to fly their Dakota's from Prestwick to London (Northolt) but with a stop at Burtonwood near Manchester, which was insisted on by BEA to prevent Scottish

Marjorie F McIntyre handing out the prizes at the Scottish Aviation Sports day held at Lochgreen House—early 1950's.

Airlines becoming a direct competitor on the Glasgow - London route. Even with the added burden of a stop at Manchester, Scottish Airlines were able to deliver passengers to a central London destination sooner than BEA could do via Heathrow, by dint of a fast car service in from Northolt. The London service ran until 1953 but never had a high enough load factor to become profitable. David McIntyre however still retained high hopes of break-

Scottish Airlines Dakota at Northolt  - c 1951

Convair XC-99 watercolour by Tom Gilfillan painted in the colours of Scottish Airlines commissioned by David McIntyre.

ing into the International Airline market when restrictions were eventually lifted and this was reflected in a painting he commissioned from Tom Gilfillan which showed a Convair XC-99, 400 seat passenger transport aircraft finished in Scottish Airlines livery.

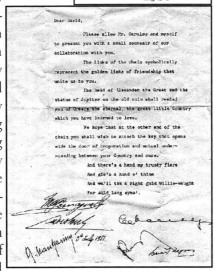

The Greek political situation made the commercial position for Scottish Airlines very difficult and by 1951 they were having trouble getting their money back while the Athens government were forcing a merger of Hellenic and Olympic, the two Greek airlines.

Greek coin key ring presented to DFM by his Hellenic Airlines Directors in 1951, with attached letter.

It was eventually resolved and it is clear that those whom David McIntyre had been mostly involved with, had established a great deal of mutual respect. Names such as Zeppos, Voyagis, Pesmasoglu, and Chris Corolu, whose wife was lady in waiting to the Queen of Greece, became well known to the family. His associates at the end of their venture presented David McIntyre with a key ring with a note describing their close association and friendship. However the business did not prove

very profitable, and in a far east trip letter in 1955, David McIntyre reflected on the visits he had made earlier to Athens on Hellenic Airlines business as follows:

*"This trip is worse than any of the Greek ones in so far as rushing around is concerned and always being at meetings or the guest of someone or other, but altogether different in that it is full of encouragement and results instead of Greek frustration and delay."*

His personal flying for these two years amount to only 6 hours each, Turnhouse and Speke featuring in 1950, with Burtonwood and Ronaldsway in 1952. The two Burtonwood flights were with Cap as second pilot and were probably in preparation for the scheduled London service they had been licensed to operate by BEA through Burtonwood.

## 1952-1953 — Airport sale agreement concluded - Airline operations retrench

Scottish Airlines sold all of their Liberator and most of their Dakota fleet as a result of the closure of the London service, replacing them in 1952 with three Avro York airliners (a development from the Lancaster bomber), which were used mostly on trooping and freight charters. The York's were ex-RAF aircraft converted for passenger use and fitted unusually with 50 rearward facing seats by the Scottish Aviation factory at Prestwick. A further five York's were added to the fleet in 1954. This charter enterprise proved reasonably profitable in the 1952 and 1953 period and proved a financial lifeline for the factory operations in the period.

The Airport compensation negotiation continued on until November 1953 when the Company finally achieved a settlement, which amounted to a total of £450,000 together with

Montreal 1953. Scottish Airlines York on a freight contract from Prestwick

David McIntyre in his office in 1953 beside the globe representing the Scottish Aviation "The World O'er" motto and with a photo of a Scottish Airlines Dakota flying in the background.

fortunes of the business were beginning to be turned around and put the Company in a stronger bargaining position by the time the settlement was finally reached.

David McIntyre over this period continued with his interest in model aircraft and in about 1953 spent some time building a radio controlled five-foot span ED Radio Queen cabin monoplane which was fitted out with the then latest ED soft valve receiver and ground based transmitter. This was usually flown from the 15th fairway on the Portland golf course on a number of occasions but there was never a flight, which could have been classed as radio controlled. Fortunately the model was well trimmed and flew on its own in free flight mode very successfully. It was however usually in the wrong direction, and on one occasion flew straight out to sea into Prestwick bay only to be washed in to the shore an hour or so later. David McIntyre had driven round to Prestwick beach in time to find a small boy dragging it out of the sea by its tail and a half crown coin was needed to persuade him to relinquish it. The radio was ruined but the airframe survived. Another similar flight by the same aircraft with a new receiver fitted, flew directly inland only this time to head straight for Lochgreen house and did itself considerable damage when it hit one of the pillars of the loggia. David McIntyre did not persevere with it thereafter.

Having soldiered on with a Wolsley 21 CYN906 for his personal and family transport for many years David McIntyre's one indulgence was the purchase in 1952 of a Sunbeam Talbot 90 tourer JSC789. This had a soft top which allowed him to drive in the open air

a 99-year lease of the factory site. The outcome was a great personal triumph for David McIntyre who at one time during the period had offered to raise the finance himself to buy out the Hamilton Trustees but had been unable to do so. It is likely that another factor in the success was that David McIntyre had engaged the services of Tom Overy from the London firm of Solicitors Allen & Overy who had served GWP so well in his business dealings over many years. There had been suggestions to bring the Douglas Aircraft Corp into partnership which had also failed and it appears that it was only through his great personal friendship with David McIntyre that the Duke of Hamilton was able to persuade the Hamilton Trustees to stay their wish to call in the receivers at one critical point in the period. It may have been a blessing that the settlements were not concluded at an early period, for by 1951, with the appointment of Mr TDM Robertson as General Manager, the

David McIntyre with family setting off for a picnic trip to the Galloway hills in mid 1950's

perhaps to remind him of his early days of flying. When travelling at any speed, the three children in the back seat however found the backdraught somewhat of a discomfort so in his inimitable way he found a solution by having constructed in the factory a Perspex wind shield extension which clipped on to the soft top mounting brackets.

His next flight in the Prestwick Pioneer was not until June 1952 in the Leonides engined MkII prototype while registered G-AKBF in civil livery when he conducted six local flights with Cap to make himself proficient on the type. After completing its airworthiness trials for the RAF the Pioneer II was ordered for production and the first aircraft was handed over to the RAF at a Ceremony outside the 'Palace' in Sept 1953.

David McIntyre's personal flying in 1952 was entirely conducted in the single Pioneer G-AKBF and in 1953 his only flights were in the Rapide G-ALBH on a couple of occasions giving a grand total for the two years of 2 hours.

## 1954-1955 — Twin Pioneer makes first flight and goes into production

One of the visions, which David McIntyre fostered, was that aviation could improve the lives of the populations in remote areas by providing speedy transport in and out of the territory. It was thus necessary to have an aircraft, which could handle passengers and freight from short rough airstrips and in mountainous terrain. David McIntyre expressed his thinking in a speech at a Scottish Aviation Anniversary Dinner in Feb 1955. Having first commented on his frustration of the slow rate of the Company's development, he went on to say, *"we have fashioned our minds and our own thoughts around an aircraft design which can meet a great and universal human need. That might not have resulted from an easier, faster upbringing. As it is I think we are on the edge of producing something quite unusual and something of real importance to civilisation. I can see it is very complicated and difficult and it could be very important to build pilotless missiles, atomic bomb carrying aircraft or super luxury*

Handover ceremony of first RAF Prestwick Pioneer II outside "Palace" in 1953. L-R Robert McIntyre, Sir Thomas Moore, M.P., David McIntyre, AM Sir Owen Jones, Duke of Hamilton, Provost F.M. Milligan, TDM Robertson, ?, Geoff Nelson, ,?,?,

The Twin was designed with virtually the same outer wing panels as the single Pioneer and the same high lift fowler flap and retractable wing leading edge slats. Two 520hp Alvis Leonides radial engines were mounted on a wide chord, centre section and a fixed undercarriage was mounted on legs descending from below the engine nacelles with a short faring connected to the lower fuselage giving a very robust landing gear system. The aircraft was designed for a stage length of 500 miles and employed a three-fin vertical stabiliser design to ensure sufficient rudder response for single engine emergency operation.

Twin Pioneer prototype G-ANTP on a test flight from Prestwick

airliners, but I think that our peculiar upbringing has led us into a much more satisfactory and satisfying field in which we design aircraft for the small man and the smaller and more isolated communities of this world. In other words aircraft that will land virtually anywhere without the appalling costs and complications of large airfields and without the even more appalling costs and risks of rotating wing helicopters.

We have designed towards sanity and simplicity and have developed long held principles to their maximum and applied them to the lifting of good commercial loads out of very small spaces. If you had seen as I did a week or two ago, our Pioneers operating from tiny little airstrips deep down in the Malayan jungle you would have seen that at last anywhere can have an airstrip and become quickly and cheaply get-at-able. That makes possible a very big expansion of civilisation."

The success of the single Pioneer provided the impetus to design and build the Twin Pioneer, which would carry 16 passengers and have the same short takeoff and landing ability. Planning for the Twin commenced in 1952 but the company were unable to fund the project from their own resources and looked for a Ministry involvement.

The Ministry, although interested technically in the Twin Pioneer, were reluctant to make an early commitment and would only support a third of the cost of developing a prototype. Having established that this avenue was impractical, the company eventually in 1954 were able to convince the Finance Corporation for Industry (FCI) under Lord Bruce to put up the capital for production. With this new impetus the work on the prototype aircraft started in earnest.

In July 1954 his log book showed him accompanying Cap on a month long sales tour across Europe with flight engineer Hugh McLaren in Pioneer G-ANRG. This trip took in Belgium, Holland, Germany, Austria, Switzerland, and Yugoslavia. In a letter home from Belgrade during this trip he reported:

"As a country it badly needs our type of aircraft but from all I hear it will probably have to obtain them through some military or economic aid policy of the United Nations. Meantime I hear from Robertson that the RAF has ordered another 6 Pioneers making 16 so far. This place is an education in itself. Entirely state operated including all hotels, shops and everything else. There is no private enterprise of any kind. It is very like Greece in many ways but it is definitely a Police state.

The weather is perfect and has been since we left Berne. In fact it cleared up in time to let us have a cloudless flight over the Alps, which was lucky, and it made our very complicated routing to Belgrade easier to navigate. So far the trip has been more useful than I expected and should show results in due course. Frank Beaumont is proving most helpful and Cap and McLaren are first class types to have with one."

With Troon providing a more varied choice of activities for the children, family holidays in the summer were given a miss until Easter 1954 when David McIntyre took his brood on a month long touring holiday in Europe driving through France, Italy, Spain, Andorra and back in the open Sunbeam Talbot 90. Marjorie McIntyre's diary for this holiday concludes "Lovely trip of 4,746 miles". David and Marjorie McIntyre managed a number of holidays on their own, favouring a touring formula through the Alps; visiting Clarens while their daughters were at School in Swit-

DFM and MFM en route from Switzerland to the South of France .

zerland and staying a week or so at La Napoule in the South of France near Cannes. Earlier when the Hellenic business was active they also took some time off during their trips to Greece to have a few days to themselves whenever possible in David's busy schedule.

DFM's photo of RAF Pioneer XE515 flying through the gap to the fort at Legap in Malayan jungle while on visit from Kuala Lumpur in Jan 1955

While his wife took the children off to Switzerland for their first skiing holiday, David McIntyre headed off on 27th Dec 1954 for Malaya. He paid a visit to the RAF's Pioneer operations in the Malayan jungle from Kuala Lumpur on 4th Jan 1955 which he described in a letter to his wife thus:

*"The highlight of the trip has been the jungle forts and the wonderful use which the RAF are making of the Pioneers. I still can't believe that what they are doing is possible but the fact is that they are operating into these impossible jungle strips day and daily and many times per day and carrying four fully equipped troops, or wounded or stores. At one fort we visited yesterday the end of the runway was a rock cliff and mountain rising almost vertically 1500 feet.*

*They had actually cut into the cliff to get another couple of yards landing run. To make it even more unbelievable the only approach from the other end started about 9 miles away and was like entering a steeply twisting and descending tunnel between mountains and under high trees and round a right angle bend at the end was the strip with the next mountain at the end of it. The climb out was equally unreal in the opposite direction.*

*I never thought that I would see anything new in this type of flying after all the years I have been in the game, but these RAF chaps we had at Prestwick are making aviation history and although only the Pioneer would have made it possible, I reckon 90% of it is due to the methods which they have developed over the past year and the extraordinary part is that they have made it safe and everyday.*

*Even apart from this wonderful experience I am glad I came out as it is obviously appreciated... They say that it is the first time they have seen anything more than an office boy from any of the aircraft manufacturers. The military operation 'Hand of friendship' is going well and the aborigines are gradually being won over as these Pioneer strips and forts are constructed in the deep jungle. One fort I visited yesterday afternoon already has 3,000 aborigines on its ration strength. There are now 13 Pioneer strips and more being built with 8 nearing completion."*

David McIntyre was so impressed with this experience that he had a promotional brochure prepared using the jungle operations in Malaya as the example of the capability of the Pioneer and later the Twin Pioneer.

DFM's annotation reads "Fort Shean, AVM Sinclair, Fl Lt Hickmatt, FO Hampton. The flight of two Pioneers had just landed at this Jungle Fort."

To support his sales team promoting the Prestwick Pioneer in India, he left on Boxing day 1955 and met up with Roy Smith and Hugh McLaren on Dec 28th who were conducting the sales tour across India. His log book records him piloting Pioneer G-AODZ on one leg from Jodhpur to Delhi, after which he returned home on Jan 4th. His last overseas flight in the single Pioneer was on 25th Feb 1956 when he recorded piloting G-AODZ during a demonstration flight in Delhi. He had continued on to India from Malta where he had to deal with an unfortunate accident involving one of the Scottish Airlines York troop carrying aircraft.

Prestwick Pioneer on sales tour of India at Gantok near Darjeeling. DFM accompanied this trip for a short period in Feb 1956. Hugh McLaren far left, Roy Smith left centre.

In 21 months, Scottish Aviation had the prototype Twin Pioneer G-ANTP conducting its maiden flight in June 1955. David McIntyre's log book shows him taking his first flight in the prototype Twin with Cap shortly after its maiden flight. On 12 Sept 1955 he flew again in the same aircraft from Hendon to Prestwick taking 3hrs 10mins, a good ½ hour or so longer than he was used to in the Hart some 20 years earlier. This was the return flight from the SBAC Farnborough Air Show where the Twin was first demonstrated in 1955 and for a number of years thereafter.

His piloting hours increased a little in this period due to his presence on the Pioneer sales trips, amassing 8 hours in 1954 and a couple of hours in 1955 in the single Pioneer.

## 1956-1957 — Twin Pioneer marketing intensifies - Aircraft crashes

Scottish Airlines had been formally incorporated as a separate company in 1954 with David McIntyre holding one share and being the sole Director. The North Atlantic trooping contracts and other military charters were operated out of Stanstead where the Company had set up a base under the control of W.M Cummings. The York's however proved to be a problem aircraft, five of which were written-off in accidents. One in Malta shortly after takeoff in Feb 1956 resulted in the loss of 45 servicemen and Captain Coker the Scottish Airlines pilot. David McIntyre wrote in a letter home after attending the funeral and handling arrangements in Malta, that it looked like a dual engine failure but was inclined to the view that they might never discover the true cause. One interesting comment he made was *"I had to start a round of visits at 9 am from the Governor downwards. I must say they were all very decent about it and this is where a reputation counts."* He also reflected *"I am more impressed than ever with our little airline team - they are essentially responsible and effective and so nice with all"*. The York's were eventually prohibited from carrying passengers.

The Airline persevered until by 1958 only one Dakota, G-AMPP was left, operating on the Isle of Man service and some flights to Belfast, which concluded finally in November 1960 when the one remaining Dakota and the business was sold to Dan-Air. David McIntyre who had championed the Airline business

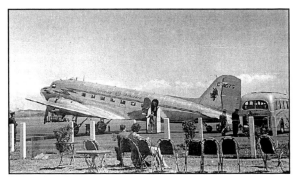

Scottish Airlines Dakota on Isle of Man service at Prestwick c 1951 (WW)

since its inception in 1946 did so often in the face of opposition from others of his board and investors but in spite of some lean times, the cash generating power of the Airline in the 1952 to 1954 period proved a lifeline for the factory operations at that time. At its peak the Airline had operated a fleet of over 20 aircraft and with 85 aircrew in active service carried between 30,000 and 40,000 passengers a year in the busy periods. During their 15 years of operation, they had maintained ground support and administrative personnel at four bases, Prestwick, Burtonwood, Northolt and Stanstead. Alan Robertson neatly concluded his chapter on Scottish Airlines by saying "while the scale of its operations may never have fully reached its founder's aspirations, the nature of its activities undoubtedly did. "The World O'er" had been turned from a statement of ambition into a statement of achievement".

The adventures of David McIntyre's Radio Queen model encouraged his son Dougal to build early radio control model aircraft for himself. His second project was the design of a scale model of the Scottish Airline Twin Pioneer G-AOEP, spurred on by having earlier built a successful free flight scale model of the single Pioneer and a first radio control model which showed some evidence of airborne guidance. By the summer of 1956 it was ready for it's first test flight, which David McIntyre assisted with, on the 15th fairway of the Portland golf course, which served as a convenient runway. A twin engined single channel radio controlled aircraft was a tricky subject but it took off perfectly, flying straight and level and climbed successfully to about 50 ft altitude. At this point the wing strut fixing failed on the outer starboard wing panel due to the increasing flight loads with the result that the wing fell off and the whole lot descended back to earth to finish as a pile of bits on the fairway. David McIntyre photographed this incident, which latterly proved a tragic coincidence, for it presaged almost a year earlier, a similar accident that ended his life.

Scottish Aviation delivered forty Pioneer II aircraft to the RAF between the first handover in Sept 1953 and 1957 when production ceased. The first aircraft saw valuable service

Dougal McIntyre holding crashed model Twin Pioneer on Portland golf course, photographed by DFM, summer 1956

in the Malayan jungle operation *Firedog*, a counter terrorist and internal security campaign through to 1960. Operating out of jungle forts in mountainous terrain from rudimentary airstrips, the Pioneers performed around 38,000 sorties carrying around 30,000 troops and an unknown tonnage of supplies to the widely dispersed forts in the territory. Other Pioneers were deployed to Aden, Libya and Cyprus in close co-operation support with ground forces. No 209 Squadron Pioneers were used extensively in the Borneo/Brunei campaign from 1962 to 1966 as well as operating in Singapore and Sarawak. The aircraft was an undoubted success and proved the ability of the Company to design and build reliable and durable products that did the job demanded of them. A total of 58 Pioneers were built only three of which went into civil use, one with the Austrian Air rescue service and two which went to the Iranian Customs service. The remainder going to the Royal Malayan Air Force and the Royal Ceylon Air Force. The Royal Malayan Air Force Pioneer acquisition came about through the encouragement of one of Scottish Aviation's early instructors Sandy Johnstone who in 1958 when an Air Commodore in the RAF was appointed the Deputy Chief of Staff (Air) in the Malayan Army and responsible for managing its army air force formation.

The single Pioneer was never specifically designed to have a civil role having too small a capacity for economic passenger carrying operation. There was however a thought that it might provide a role in the Western Isles and David McIntyre conducted a survey trip in August 1956 stopping at Mull, North Uist, Skye and other destinations to evaluate the opportunities.

Pioneer G-AODZ on Traigh Mhor beach strip on Barra in Aug 1956 during a Western Isles survey trip.

The Prestwick Pioneers in their military role were phased out of RAF service in 1969, their role being taken over by the military helicopters, which had developed technically and with a reliability, which enabled their greater versatility to be more effective in the continually evolving nature of warfare. The Prestwick Pioneer did have the capability of being configured to carry two stretcher cases and a medical attendant and on one occasion in Borneo was reported to have been used to rescue in one flight a mother, father and fourteen children trapped by rising floodwaters. It has the distinction however of being the first of only two aircraft to have been wholly designed and manufactured in Scotland in commercial numbers since Wm Beardmore conducted their Aviation business on the Clyde during WWI.

Design for a 9 seat version, the Pioneer IV named Pegasus had been drawn up which, if it had been introduced, would have made it a direct competitor of the De Havilland Canada Beaver. The Beaver ultimately became most successful and demonstrated the existence of a thriving market, but lack of Government backing for the Pegasus prevented Scottish

Aviation from taking advantage of this potential opportunity.

The prototype Twin Pioneer embarked on an extensive testing programme and over the next year and a half, the factory modified and tuned the aircraft to obtain the necessary Certificate of airworthiness for passenger carrying duties. During this period the factory was building an initial batch of aircraft which were to be used for trials and sales demonstrations. David McIntyre's log book records in May 1956 a couple of flights at Prestwick in the Twin G-AOEN with Tom Lyon Chief Aerodynamicist in the cockpit which he notes as "local climbs" during this performance

RAF version of the Twin Pioneer XM826 conducting flight tests over Arran

testing period. He also was involved in ARB test flights in the prototype earlier in March and Marjorie McIntyre's diary records a number of dinners at Lochgreen where various ARB officials were being entertained. This was clearly an anxious and frustratingly long period to bring the Twin to the market.

Significantly, the largest number of Twin Pioneer aircraft were sold to military customers, 39 of which went to the RAF, their first Twin completing its maiden flight in Aug 1957. They were used for troop transport, paratrooping, casualty evacuation, supply dropping and medium-level bombing. Needing only an area of 300 yds by 100 yds to operate, they saw active service in Aden, Kuwait, Keyna, Malaya and Borneo and made a notable contribution to 'Tana Flood' relief operation in Oct 1961. Known in the RAF as the 'Twin Pin', they were withdrawn from RAF service latterly in 1968 after 10 years useful service.

Prototype Twin Pioneer in the static display park prior to flight demonstrations at Farnborough 1956.

Twin Pioneer G-AOEO being demonstrated at Davos March 1957

G-AOEO, painted up in the livery of Swissair, where they visited ski resorts such as Zermatt and St Moritz as well as the major Swiss international airports to promote the suitability of the aircraft in this mountainous terrain. In the end however none were ever sold to this airline.

An indication of the rigours of the many sales demonstration tours undertaken can be given in the example from John Blair's log book of the 3 month trip he did to the far east and Australia from Jan to Apr 57 in G-AOEP. His trip recorded detail of 86 stages and over

The first commercial deliveries of the Twin were made in June 1957 by which time the capital loans for the development had reached £2.5 m and the Company was under severe pressure to obtain the substantial numbers of Customer orders needed. David McIntyre's hopes for an initial production rate of 8 aircraft per month had been reduced to 6 for the planned production of 200 aircraft. To stimulate demand strenuous efforts to market the aircraft through sales trips abroad were undertaken and David McIntyre accompanied

L-R, John Blair, Roy Smith, David McIntyre, Shah of Iran, and others at polo field in Teheran where the Twin Pioneer was being demonstrated, 15.1.57

Twin Pioneer G-AOEO comes in to land on 400 yd temporary strip on a snow covered field in the Zermatt valley, Switzerland on demonstration trip, 1957

35 locations where demonstration flights were conducted en route. David McIntyre left Prestwick for Amsterdam on 11th Jan and met up with the pilots Roy Smith and John Blair in Teheran where they demonstrated the Twin to the Shah of Persia and his ministers, after which he returned home on Jan 18th.

David McIntyre journeyed out again leaving on Feb 9th to join this trip in Malaya, flying in the Twin out to some of the Jungle strips he had previously visited in the Prestwick Pioneer

several of these to Europe, the Far East and South America.

One of the sales demonstration trips of the Twin G-AOEN in June of 1956 to Switzerland found David McIntyre taking part, where his log book shows him as pilot on the legs from Lausanne to Geneva and from Vienna to Munich. Another such trip, which he accompanied in March of 1957, was conducted in

Twin Pioneer landing at Harbour Island in the Bahamas on Demonstration tour May 1957

Twin Pioneer G-AOEN at a jungle strip in French Guiana May 1957

in 1955. He then continued out to the British territories of Sarawak, Brunei and North Borneo where he visited one of the native Long Houses. He returned home on 2$^{nd}$ March and the aircraft continued its tour to Australia and Tasmania, finishing there as the first Twin to be commercially sold to the Zinc Corporation of Australia.

Almost immediately he was off again to join the sales demonstration trip to the West Indies and South America during the month of April 1957. This time the chief pilot was Noel

David McIntyre with other spectators watch the Twin Pioneer taking off on a demonstration flight at Bogotá in Colombia. 9 April 1957

Capper who had in the preceding two months, flown the Twin from Canada down to Miami and from there along the whole arc of the Caribbean island chain down to Trinidad, stopping off to demonstrate the aircraft at numerous little landing strips on beaches and playing fields on the way. Trinidad was the base for trips to British and French Guiana, where the jungle terrain provided the opportunity to demonstrate the rough field performance of the Twin in conditions similar to that experienced in Malaya. Cap then traversed the northern coast of Venezuela to reach the

Colombian capital of Bogota at the beginning of April.

David McIntyre's letters back home from this trip describe that he flew in to New York from Prestwick on 5$^{th}$ April and immediately headed off for Jamaica by Avianco and managed to send off a post card from Montego Bay before arriving at Bogota in Colombia the following day where he met up with Cap and the Twin Pioneer G-AOEN. While in Bogota the Twin developed a problem with the port rudder hinge, which delayed them 4 days

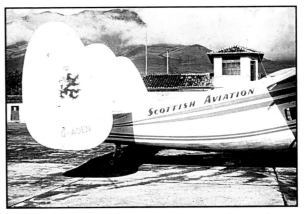
Quito airport at 9,400 ft altitude in Equador– where the Twin was demonstrated in April 1957

while a spare hinge was sent across. Here they were entertained to an outdoor barbecue/banquet by the Colombian President at his residence sited next to his own airstrip. Hugh McLaren, flight engineer on the trip, recalled that the meat was excessively tough to eat, that there were armed attendants standing behind the guests round the table, and that the President was playing his way around his snooker table all the while that the aircraft purchase negotiations were being discussed.

They then flew on to Lima via Quito over the next 10 days having conducted a number

Twin parked at Arequipa, Peru en route to La Paz from Lima 1 May 1957. A 20,000 ft Andean peak in the background.

Twin Pioneer flying past the Corcovado mountain with Rio de Janeiro in the background June 1957

of demonstration flights at stops on the way, arriving at Lima over Easter weekend. David McIntyre's log book shows him to be pilot on the leg from Chicklayo to Lima in Peru, but little was he to know that it would turn out to be the final entry in his log book. Here Cap and David McIntyre had a game of golf where he amusingly admitted to driving a ball into the hotel car park adjacent to the course, which his caddy described, according to his

Twin coming in to land at a remote air strip in Brazil to demonstrate its performance in outlying districts. June 1957

post card, as having "mucha hooka". It was here that his name McIntyre was misread as Mr Interior which made the paging of him in the hotel for a phone-call a long-winded process. His assessment of the progress of the trip lead him to decide that it was necessary for him to go ahead of Cap and the aircraft on the chosen route to prime the Embassy officials and agents in advance of their arrival and so make the time of the pilots and aircraft more effective when they arrived.

His route from Lima took him to Santiago, Buenos Aires, Rio de Janeiro, Caracas, Trini-dad, Nassau, Mexico City, Washington, New York and home to Prestwick with Pan Am on May 2nd. He commented on what he had found so far to his wife like this:

"Columbia will certainly buy six or more Twins although it is a tricky country politically. Ecuador is lovely at 9,000 ft and desperately needs our type of aircraft. I am confident that they will find the money somehow or other to purchase. Peru, or what little I have seen of it, is highly civilised, wealthy and has just the right mixture of mountains and jungles for us. The interest in the Twin is quite astounding and something like it should have been produced a long time ago. The development of these South American countries is 100% dependent on Air transport and for the majority of it, the Air is the only possible form."

He did not comment again until he reached Caracas where he got caught having to attend a Garden Party, something which he desperately tried to avoid back home, but this time it allowed him to make some useful business contacts. His next stop in Nassau was one which he did not relish for it brought him face to face with one of the Twins' strongest critics from the BOAC/ BWIA subsidiary who dismissed it for having a poor single engine climb performance. He described them as "Petty Empire Builders" and considered that they were being "very harmful to our chances in South America". His draft trip report notes on the West Indies section of the tour concluded "It looks as though we have wasted our time in the Caribbean - let it simmer for a year". Hugh McLaren has commented that the Twin used for this trip was suffering from a sub-standard engine performance which accounted for the lower than expected single engine climb rate,

Cap sitting on the running board of a local taxi at an airstrip somewhere in Brazil. The Twin can be seen behind this rather ancient and muddy vehicle.

David and Marjorie McIntyre on holiday in the South of France 8 July 1957 . The last holiday they had together.

and no doubt Scottish Aviation learned a lot regarding the high altitude characteristics of the aircraft during the course of this lengthy journey.

Cap's log book for this very arduous trip, shows that he started in Washington in the February, and returned for a well-earned break after the Brazil legs at the end of June having flown well over 100 stages in addition to local demonstrations across the continent. The Twin Pioneer's sales trip continued on up to Mexico, flown by another of the Scottish Aviation pilots where the intention was to sell the aircraft over there rather than have to bring it back to Prestwick.

In amongst this hectic schedule David McIntyre made time at the end of June and early July to take 2 ½ weeks off to motor with Marjorie McIntyre to their favourite spots, across to Le Touquet, on to Switzerland and down to the French Riviera for a break at La Napoule near Cannes. They returned via Le Touquet to Lydd probably on a Silver City car ferry and back up the great north road to Troon on 14th July.

Back home David McIntyre was busy moving up and down to London on Scottish

Aviation business matters and in June made a trip to Paris with Marjorie McIntyre for the Air Show. Here the Twin Pioneer was being used to demonstrate its inter city potential by providing a ferry service for Air Show visitors from the central Paris Heligare at Issy le Moulineaux, in sight of the Eiffel Tower, to the Air Show site at Le Bourget. This was in addition to the usual display flying during the show. The follow on to this was to be the development of plans in Oct 57 for a London-Paris service which was to fly from Issy to Wormwood Scrubs with a city centre journey time of 2 ½ hrs as compared with the BEA Viscount time of 4 hours and at a fare one third reduced.

Passengers boarding the Twin Pioneer shuttle service at Issy for transport to the Paris air show at Le Bourget in June 1957

Shortly after the early September Farnborough Air Show, where David McIntyre was accompanied by his wife and younger daughter Jane, he had to leave this event at its close and head off to the Far East instead of returning home as planned. This unexpected trip resulted from a crash of one of the 3 KLM subsidiary De Kroonduif NV Twin Pioneers operating in Dutch New Guinea, which David McIntyre went out to investigate. The aircraft had only been delivered a couple of months earlier and was one of the first three sold with only 250 flying hours to its credit. The initial assumption was that the accident had been the result of pilot error and David McIntyre wrote home en route Biak. Manila on 13th Sept to say: *"Briefly the position here was one of the most astounding lack of flying discipline I have met in 30 years. Young ex Naval pilots treating the Twin Pioneer with complete abandon and as a high-speed aerobatic type. Whether the structural failure can solely be attributed to this or not will only be discovered by long and detailed testing of materials and design features by Farnborough and other research establishments. However there is no lack of confidence in the aircraft and they should be in the air again by the end of next week using an earlier design of strut."*

The only eyewitness to the incident was a native fisherman who reported that he had seen a wing falling off as he was fishing off the Biak coast of New Guinea. David McIntyre in this same letter commented: *"Netherlands New Guinea is primitive, lovely and very interesting and I look forward to seeing something of it when the Twin Pioneers are in full operation."*

In his next postcard two days later, he clearly did not anticipate that the incident would have any long-term influence on the prospects for the aircraft and wrote: *"am satisfied that there can be no lasting harm from the Biak incident".*

In spite of the difficulty in recovering any of the underwater wreckage of the Dutch aircraft to determine the exact cause of the wing failure, as a precaution Scottish Aviation modified the suspect wing strut components on the existing aircraft to a different material specification. When David McIntyre left London for Tripoli on Dec 5th to join Roy

Twin Pioneer G-AOEO photographed by DFM in Libya Dec 57 while on demonstration trip for Standard Oil Co. Annotated by Cap as being between 5th and 7th Dec

Smith on the North African sales tour. This programme of modification had been completed on all the demonstration aircraft except one, G-AOEO. This trip had not been delayed to effect the modifications before it left due to the intense financial pressures on the company to improve its sales performance. The modifications were expected to be carried out on its return. This was the point in David McIntyre's life where his traditional 'luck' ran out, for while flying across the Libyan desert with representatives of a potential customer, the Standard Oil Group in Libya, the fatigue life of the wing strut connecting link ran out with

Crash site of Twin Pioneer G-AOEO in Libyan desert near Tripoli Dec 8th 1957.

catastrophic results.

David McIntyre and his companions died in the resulting crash and with him the long term prospects for the aircraft in which he had invested so much of his energy and reputation over the previous ten years.

There have been many eloquent testimonials to David McIntyre, speaking of his tremendous contribution to the development of aviation in Scotland and its value to long-term employment and prosperity in his local community in Ayrshire. They also make due refer-

Unveiling of memorial Plaque in Prestwick Airport to David McIntyre in 1965. Noel Capper is standing behind folding the Scottish Airlines flag which his widow Mrs Marjorie F McIntyre has just released to unveil the Plaque.

ence to the dedication and single-mindedness in pursuing this objective which characterised his business career. The other oft referred to characteristic was his concern for those who worked for him and the company and his charismatic charm and enthusiasm, which persuaded many to follow his direction, often in contradiction to their initial intentions.

Reading through the hundreds of letters of condolence received by his widow in the days following his tragic accident one is struck by the breadth of response, not just from home but also overseas. From Col Rothrock of the USAF who served on the "Arnold" line into Prestwick in 1941, from friends in KLM, from the high and the low whom he had charmed and inspired, to his close friends and contemporaries in the RAF, the Everest flight, Scottish Aviation and admirers in aviation such as Edmund Fresson, not to mention close family friends, officialdom, and many business contacts. The sense of loss expressed was universal with many reflecting on their memories of him such as Shep who wrote "someone of the greatest value with a sense of proportion and level-headedness remembered with respect and affection". Douglo Hamilton wrote "He always set a shining example, not the least in his private life". Irvine Watson described him as "a man in a million, with drive, foresight, guts and initiative". Geordy Hamilton said "an extraordinary number of people have come up to me in the Houses of Parliament and elsewhere to express the deep admiration which they had for David. Many disagreed with him,

but none failed to be impressed with his far seeing judgement, and dynamic personality. Viewed from the objective angle of the country as a whole, there are so few people who unite practical ability and vision.", he then added, "I could never repay all that David has given me and meant to me in friendship and inspiration.". One of the most telling comments was from his close friend Dennis McNab who wrote, "I probably knew him better than most of the chaps in the early days of the Squadron, and in those gay young days little did I realise that he would one day be one of Scotland's leading figures, although even then it was always very obvious to me that he was the real mainspring and drive behind that Squadron. It was his terrific personality and his light hearted way of trying anything new and making it work that attracted me so much. How proud you must be of his wonderful record and how tragic that the country, especially Scotland should be robbed of one of its most far seeing and able men."

What singles out this account is the insight gained from access to his inner thoughts as expressed in his personal correspondence and in this we see at the early stages of his career, someone who was both reserved and almost retiring but at the same time enthusiastic and full of fun. It is clear that his career was materially influenced for the better by the support, encouragement and advice of Marjorie Potts both while his fiancée and his wife and his devotion to her and his family is a striking example of his inner motivation. It is interesting to observe that he had virtually no interests outside his work and family, he exercised no activities which did not embrace one or other of these elements once he became engaged, and no examples have been found where he had become involved in personal pursuits, even his golf was either devoted to family or business associates.

During his career there were huge strides taken in the growth of aviation transport, which he had envisaged in his formative years but he was ultimately frustrated at not having played as great a part in this growth as he had aspired to. He demonstrated the energy and enthusiasm of one who can genuinely be credited with having a clear vision of the path he wished his enterprise to follow. However, the commercial and political jungle which he found his operation faced with in the immediate post war period defied his skills as an Aviator and frustrated the humanitarian conscience which he had consistently displayed. Timing was (and still is) one of the most important characteristics in determining business success and frequently David McIntyre was delayed in starting up his various ventures at the time he knew was necessary to assure progress, more often than not, by factors which he found unable to influence by his rational argument or charming persuasion. He also expressed the frustration of being geographically located too far from the seat of power at a time when frequent involvement was needed in Government circles to ensure that Prestwick's needs were fully understood and considered.

Alan Robertson wrote "He is buried, not amid the heat of the North African desert, nor in the frozen reaches of the Himalayas, but in the tranquil green of Alloway churchyard, in Scotland where his pioneering ultimately had most meaning. There is an appropriate memorial window in Alloway church, gifted by his family. Surrounded by Everest, by aircraft and by the dove of peace, which together represented McIntyre's fervent belief in aviation as a means of improving the human condition, the central figure is Moses, the visionary, the leader, the man whose commitment attracts fierce enemies and devoted followers, the man who persists through years in the wilderness in the pursuit of his goal."

On reflection the relationship that became established between David McIntyre and his 602 Squadron contemporary Douglas Douglas-Hamilton, the Marquis of Douglas and Clydesdale is an interesting one. They were men from widely differing backgrounds whose mutual love of flying brought them together at a formative time both for aviation and the growth of the Auxiliary Squadron movement. They formed a unique friendship and trust of each other's abilities in the air and forged an understanding of each other's capabilities, which blended without animosity.

It is clear that during the Everest expedition and in the activities associated with the Squadron, David McIntyre intuitively deferred to Clydesdale in his leadership role without question. However Clydesdale would always rely on David McIntyre's advice, which he knew, would be sound and thoughtful. However once they had come to the point of setting up the business at Scottish Aviation, Clydesdale would defer to McIntyre's leadership as the driving force behind the Business while he acted more as advocate and facilitator in his role as Chairman letting McIntyre get on with the running of the many facets of the organisation which grew from their early beginnings.

Their friendship was sufficiently close for them to become each other's Best Man at their respective weddings and Clydesdale was unhesitating in the loan of his newly acquired Leopard Moth to David McIntyre for his honeymoon trip. It was a friendship that was undemonstrative rather than cloying, built on mutual awareness and the shared values of trust, integrity and respect. This is not to say that they were unable to enjoy themselves, David McIntyre was not beyond the occasional practical joke or two and they both enjoyed the sporting challenges offered on the playing field and through participating in various sports and other social activities.

It has been asked what might have happened had David McIntyre's life not come to its untimely end and this question is never going to be easily answered. The business of Aviation has always been an unpredictable one, heavily influenced by the vagaries of National politics and global events. To second guess these and be able to profit from their movements has been as much a matter of luck as of foresight and knowledge.

David McIntyre was driven by a strong determination to position his native community at the forefront of the new industry which Aviation offered and at the time of his death Scottish Aviation had a number of development plans for the Single and Twin Pioneers to meet the future aircraft needs which he foresaw. These he would have been pursuing with vigour as well as the ongoing promotion of the Twin Pioneer passenger aircraft. The later success of aircraft such as the Beaver and Twin Otter which were both aircraft that Scottish Aviation had similar offerings on the drawing board suggests that it may have been possible for the Scottish Aviation designs to have succeeded with DFM still at the helm.

With the later relaxation in the Airline regulations which such entrepreneurs as Adam Thompson and Freddie Laker demonstrated were capable of being exploited, it is likely that DFM would have attempted to embark on a similar enterprise for he had already demonstrated his opinion that large wide body passenger aircraft held the way forward for passenger travel. The biggest problem with any venture would have been the raising of capital, which would have required confidence in the strength of the company management and its products. David McIntyre's reputation would certainly have assisted this process but it would have required the Twin to have made a reasonable inroad into the market, which at the time of his death was showing some promise, but not in the volumes, which had first been anticipated. DFM would have been faced with a continuing political battle to obtain support for the Twin in government circles capable of influencing foreign powers to assist the financing of the purchase of the aircraft in the territories to which it was most suited.

The parochial argument for the development of Abbotsinch as the replacement airport for Renfrew in the early 1960's in preference to Prestwick might have been more strongly challenged with DFM able to speak for the Prestwick case. It has been said however by a number of people that there would have been no question of a Prestwick decision, given the strength of local political and business opinion to keep the airport close to the Clyde, which even DFM would not have been able to sway. It is interesting to reflect however that once the management of Prestwick Airport was wrested from the dead hand of Nationalised ownership, its position was secured under Scottish Airports and later became privatised, David McIntyre's vision of a direct Rail link into the Airport was able to be implemented without hesitation.

In the event Scottish Aviation went on, with various ups and downs, to make much of the original inspirational investment which David McIntyre brought to the business. They achieved considerable success with the

Bulldog training aircraft and made a significant contribution to Lockheed's Hercules programme making over 700 fuselage panels over a number of years in the 1970's. In the 1980's they brought the Jetstream series of commuter airliners to a world wide market place thus keeping alive the reputation of Scotland's skilled engineering heritage now manifest at Prestwick. In the 1990's and through the second millennium a steady growth of aviation businesses have become established at Prestwick on the back of the local skills built up over the preceding years.

David McIntyre's Aviation career spanned

McIntyre family crest commissioned by David McIntyre

the period from Dec 1926 to Dec 1957, a total of 31 years during which he logged a total of 2,438 piloting hours (80% of which were in the first 10 years) and many more as a passenger on demonstration and commercial flights across the world. His major achievement was to bring an aviation industry to Scotland, which is still active after more than 65 years, and to have created a modern airfield which gave international status to Prestwick and its community and which performed an invaluable role in the conduct of WW2. The continued expansion of aviation industry at Prestwick is the lasting legacy of David McIntyre's vision and enterprise and fulfils his aspiration to provide jobs and welfare for the people of his native land.

Stained glass window in Alloway church in memory of David F. McIntyre (Ellen Howden)

# BIBLIOGRAPHY

| Author | Title |
|---|---|
| Smith, David J. | Action Stations 7. - PSL 1983 |
| Thetford, Owen | Aircraft of the Royal Air Force since 1918. – Putnam 1995 |
| Berry, Peter | Airfield Focus 42: Prestwick. – GMS 2000 |
| Cobham, Sir Alan, KBE | Australia & Back. – A &C Black 1927 |
| Gillis & Wood | Aviation in Scotland. –RAeS, Glasgow Branch 1966 |
| Johnston, Ian | Beardmore Built. – Clydebank DL&M 1993 |
| Lukins, A.H. | Book of Westland Aircraft. – Harborough Publishing 1944 |
| Penrose, Harald | British Aviation - Widening Horizons – HMSO 1980 |
| Bao, Phil Lo | British European Airways. – Browcom Group 1989 |
| Burge, C.G, OBE | Complete Book of Aviation. – Pitman 1935 |
| Taylor, H.A. | Fairey Aircraft since 1915. Putnam 1984 |
| McLean, Hector | Fighters in Defence. – Squadron Prints 1999 |
| Fellowes etc | First over Everest. Bodley Head 1933 |
| Cameron, Dugald | Glasgows Own. – Squadron Prints 1987 |
| Cameron, Dugald | Glasgow's Airport. -  Holmes McDougall  1990 |
| Neill, William T. OBE | Just one of the Pioneers, - Cirrus 2002 |
| Robertson, Alan | Lion Rampant & Winged, - Robertson 1985 |
| McRoberts, Douglas | Lions Rampant. – William Kimber 1985 |
| McIntyre & Clydesdale | Pilots Book of Everest. – Hodge 1936 |
| Ewart, Jim | Prestwick Airport Golden Jubilee. - Scottish Airports 1985 |
| Douglas-Hamilton, James | Roof of the World. – Mainstream 1983 |
| Jordanoff, Assen | Through the Overcast. – Funk & Wagnalls 1939 |
| James, Derek N. | Westland Aircraft since 1915. – Putnam 1991 |
| Johnstone, AVM. Sandy | Where no Angels Dwell, - Jarrolds 1969 |
| Allan, James | Wings over Scotland. – Tervor 2002 |
| Douglas Aircraft Co | Year's pictorial history of Flight. - YEAR 1953. (50th Anniversary) |

# INDEX